HEALING
TRAUMATIZED
CHILDREN

HEALING
TRAUMATIZED
CHILDREN

NAVIGATING RECOVERY
FOR CHILDREN
WITH TURBULENT PASTS

Faye L. Hall, Jeff L. Merkert and
John A. Biever, MD, DFAPA

New Horizon Press
Far Hills, New Jersey

Requests for permission should be addressed to:
New Horizon Press
P. O. Box 669
Far Hills, NJ 07931

Faye L. Hall, Jeff L. Merkert and John A. Biever, MD, DFAPA
    Healing Traumatized Children:
    Navigating Recovery for Children with Turbulent Pasts

Cover design: Charley Nasta
Interior design: Scribe Inc.

Library of Congress Control Number: 2014950534

ISBN-13 (paperback): 978-0-88282-495-6
ISBN-13 (eBook): 978-0-88282-496-3

New Horizon Press

Manufactured in the U.S.A.

19   18   17   16   15   1   2   3   4   5

AUTHORS' NOTE

This book is based on the authors' research, personal experiences, interviews and real life experiences. In order to protect privacy, names have been changed and identifying characteristics have been altered except for contributing experts.

For purposes of simplifying usage, the pronouns his/her and s/he are sometimes used interchangeably. The information contained herein is not meant to be a substitute for professional evaluation and therapy with mental health professionals.

TABLE OF CONTENTS

FOREWORD

Often, much too often, families are challenged in the most complex and pervasive manner by relational trauma and attachment disturbances or disruptions that leave all family members mistrustful of each other and of the professionals who attempt to guide, support and help them to heal. Often, much too often, professionals focus on the behaviors of the parent or child that need to change, without understanding the roots of these behaviors, which often are the reasons that these behaviors are so resistant to change. Too often these behavioral strategies are not utilized by professionals who are trained in trauma and attachment or who are using strategies that are not congruent with this training. When relational trauma and insecure attachments prevent any semblance of safety for family members, there is little likelihood that they will have sufficient motivation and ability to try something new that is resting on a foundation of fear, isolation and shame.

All families exposed to significant trauma and attachment problems must first heal if they are to then begin the difficult but very rewarding process of developing the relational and developmental competencies needed if the family is to survive and even thrive. *Healing Traumatized Children*, by Faye Hall, Jeff Merkert and Dr. John Biever, presents a model of parenting and intensive family interventions that is based on central theories and research involving trauma and attachment. These interventions require a complex understanding of each unique parent, child and relationship along with sensitive, multidimensional responses to the current environment and its roots in the past.

The authors have developed an Emotional Cognitive Trauma Model of intervention that integrates the theories that are critical in family disorganization and mistrust and provides a guide for a practice that may lead to healing and restorative change, while being detailed and comprehensive.

This model was developed as a wraparound program for very challenged families which were at risk for having the children placed outside their homes. It also has great relevance for the outpatient treatment of families whose challenges are less severe.

The authors do not pretend that helping families with pervasive problems will be easy. They ask a great deal of parents, but they ask this with empathy for how hard it is and with an attitude of compassion that avoids shaming and blaming. They provide guidance, with many practical ideas and resources along with a great degree of support. They help parents to feel safe by communicating an attitude that conveys confidence and hope, assuming that the parents have good intentions and appropriate goals for their children. Initially, they focus with parents on helping them to understand and develop their relationships with each other and their children. They then assist parents to develop their emotional and cognitive skills in a manner that will strengthen and heal rather than cause divisiveness and despair.

Hall, Merkert and Biever also help us all to see the importance of adopting a *trauma lens* to hold our perceptions of the behavior of both children and their parents. They give many examples of how our behavior interventions will change when we acknowledge the role of trauma in the development of troublesome behaviors. They equally show us how crucial it is to understand the negative internal working model of self and other held by many children who have experienced trauma and who have insecure attachments.

Often, we, as adults, forget that the deep safety that comes from a committed relationship with our partner is based on having confidence that the relationship is "for better or worse." This frequently-heard phrase indicates that the relationship is bigger, stronger, and will outlast any particular conflict, disagreement or separation. The safety that comes from this conviction enables parents to address their relational problems rather than deny them and then to face them with the goal of improving the relationship rather than "winning" the conflict or hurting their partners.

Many traumatized children with significant attachment insecurities do not assume that their relationships with their parents are "for better or worse." Lacking safety that the relationship is strong enough to handle a conflict, they react with deceit, rage, withdrawal or fear, avoiding the engagement needed to address and resolve a family problem. First and foremost, it is the task of the parents to convey that the relationship is "for better or worse" and "We'll get through this together." At the same time, the first task of the professional is to help parents develop their own sense of safety so that they can acknowledge their challenges and develop their competencies.

Because these children have experienced relational trauma, the authors stress the need to use "nurturing actions which far exceed the norm. Love, care, intimacy, touch and affection must occur every day and not be dependent on good behavior." This core concept might well evoke a sense of "Of course that is the case if these children are going to learn to trust." Regretfully, such guidance is often not stressed or even acknowledged in many intensive family treatment and support programs. Too often the primary emphasis is on behavioral consequences, without addressing the core sense of isolation, fear and shame that the children often experience, and have for years, prior to the development of their "problems."

In short, this is a challenging book, full of important and creative understandings and interventions, needed to work with highly challenged, and challenging, families. There is no quick fix here, but there is a strong, comprehensive and integrated model for family interventions. Hope lies within this book but we need to see the importance of giving careful thought and sensitive engagement to each unique family that has lost its way in providing its members with the experiences of safety, comfort and joy.

If we keep our perception on creating the healing home, we may enable the family to embrace this goal and develop the necessary skills to attain it.

—*Daniel Hughes, PhD*

When child psychologists Faye Hall and Jeff Merkert invited me to co-author a book based on their team approach to helping children with attachment disorders and their families, I knew I had to participate. Hall and Merkert became certified to provide clinical services for families with dysfunctional "dynamics" via a category of treatment offered within Pennsylvania's Behavioral Health Rehabilitative Services system, referred to as Family Based Mental Health Services. They became known throughout the central Pennsylvania area for their remarkable clinical success in applying the principles of Dr. Daniel Hughes' Dyadic Developmental Psychotherapy (DDP) in the treatment of children with Reactive Attachment Disorder and other mental health diagnoses complicated by insecure attachments.

Since Dr. Hughes relocated from Maine to my outpatient campus in Annville, Pennsylvania, several years ago, Hall and Merkert have taken advantage of their opportunity for in-person monthly supervision with him. DDP involves a set of principles and techniques developed by Dr. Hughes to specifically address the emotional and relational difficulties that are typically present in children and adults with insecure attachment histories.

In this book, we reach beyond parents and clinicians as our target audience and into the extended community. This book is about children who, for various reasons, survive through their first several years of life without having developed the ability to securely attach to caregivers. It is about those caregivers—parents, adoptive parents, foster parents, daycare workers, teachers and others—who struggle to make a meaningful connection with them. But just as importantly, it is about the *village* in which the struggle to connect takes place: friends, relatives, neighbors, policemen, coaches, social servants, legal and political office holders, legislators and so on. This book illustrates how we all have a crucial role to play. But beyond that, it is filled with practical suggestions as to how we can fulfill that role.

The first part of the book focuses on the special parenting challenges presented by children with disordered attachment styles and ways to meet those challenges. Then, in the second part, the focus shifts to the assembled team of professionals who join together with caregivers and the child to address the attachment difficulties. We also discuss special environmental considerations necessary to meet the unique needs of the attachment-disordered child. The village dimension will be an important topic in this section in particular.

The next part of the book will discuss what the authors have called *Trauma-Disrupted Competencies* (TDCs). That is, it will address the ways in which the early childhood trauma that leads to attachment disorders causes the child to have serious difficulty with specific areas of function that we take for granted in children. Aware of these TDCs, we can then be on the lookout for them and utilize suggested means for helping the child to overcome them. The final parts of the book will focus on practical interventions and handouts that parents and "villagers" can utilize to help their traumatized children.

Faye Hall has experienced both the joy and anguish of working with children with an impaired attachment style from the inside out, as well as from the outside in. She raised an adopted son who had Reactive Attachment Disorder. We agreed that key parts of her narrative as a parent would help explain the content to the reader. Therefore, many chapters either begin with or contain a relevant passage from her narrative.

—*Dr. John Biever*

PART 1

The Team Approach to Treating Attachment Disorders

CHAPTER 1

Trauma in Adopted Children: Meet the Families

We were quite a typical rural central Pennsylvania family—my husband David and I and our teenaged son and two younger daughters. Traditional roles were working well for us. David was an engineer by profession. He maintained our Christmas tree farm and rental properties, while I was trained as an educator and homeschooled our daughters.

This changed when my sister and her husband were in the midst of adopting an infant; a relative of my brother-in-law asked them whether they would be interested in adopting his nephew. He was a little boy being shuffled through the foster care system and in need of adoption. My sister thought that a second boy would create perfect gender symmetry in my family and volunteered us as foster parents!

That little boy eventually became our adoptive son Allan. By the time David and I made the commitment to bring Allan into our family, he was in a shelter with other hard-to-place children. We had to complete foster care training and go through the clearance process. In the six hours of foster care classes we covered such topics as necessary paperwork, possible behavior problems, ways to deal with birth parent visits, legal responsibility of the agency and family and not relying on the foster care subsidy to pay bills.

Learning of our intention to foster a child, friends were extremely enthusiastic. One woman, herself a former foster child, told us how very grateful to us any foster child would be. We heard, "The child will benefit from the pleasures your family could offer," and "The child will thank you for rescuing him." Such comments strengthened our resolve to become foster parents.

—Faye Hall

Now that Faye has introduced you to her "real life" story, let's meet four other families. We have created each of them to represent a composite of the common struggles parents have faced in enabling an attachment-disordered child to become part of a family. We will refer back to them throughout the book in order to illuminate points we are making.

Introducing Amy's Family, the Smiths

James and Lori Smith adopted two-year-old Amy later in life. James was a research scientist and Lori a teacher. Lori was able to stay at home with Amy. They were happy to finally be parents; they indulged her with all her desires. Amy never had to ask for anything. Lori was in heaven, having a little girl to dote on all day. Lori bought Amy fancy dresses like she had wanted as a child but that her parents could not afford.

Lori grew concerned when Amy began to destroy things. She ripped many of the fancy dresses, broke most of her toys and "accidently" damaged the furniture. It seemed as if her defiance was increasing daily. Lori tried to explain her fears to James. He attributed the behavior to Amy's age.

Lori planned fun things every day for Amy. Lori had missed having fun when she was growing up, because her mom had to work and never seemed to have time for her. Amy refused to play with Lori but demanded that Lori entertain her. By bedtime, Lori had no energy left for James. Some nights, Amy demanded that Lori sleep with her. James began to resent Amy for taking his wife's energy and he wanted to find a babysitter. Lori refused, thinking that Amy would be too scared to be away from her. James and Lori were drifting apart.

As Lori and James despaired over how far they were from their imagined ideal family, they decided to seek help. During the initial stages of finding answers, it was difficult and embarrassing for them to describe their parenting styles and Amy's behaviors. Yet their shame decreased as they found professionals trained in trauma and attachment.

Introducing Corey's Family, the Joneses

Rebecca and Danny Jones began fostering children soon after they were married. Danny worked second shift, leaving the house at noon every day and often working overtime to supplement their income, as Rebecca did not work outside the home. Rebecca was a good "case manager" for the foster children, arranging meetings and transporting the children to a multitude of appointments. Their home seemed like it was open to caseworkers at all hours of the day. Fortunately, their three birth children were self-sufficient and needed less "mom time."

Upon placement of a new foster child, they gave him or her a toiletries basket, four sets of clothing and housing rules with a time chart. Their style was to set firm rules for all the children. The family routine included scheduled times for bathing, eating, homework, chores and free time. Weekend schedules did not include homework.

The family adopted foster child Corey, four years old, who had a history of six previous foster placements. Birth children Sara, Andy and Lane were happy to have another brother in the family. Rebecca and Danny did not change their parenting style after the adoption and Corey was expected to maintain the established foster child routine.

Over time, Corey's behavior problems increased. He did not regulate his eating, always asking for more food. Rebecca found moldy food under his bed and food wrappers in his closet. She discovered that he went to the kitchen during the night for more food. Rebecca began hiding food and locking cabinets. Their birth children constantly complained about Corey "stealing all the food." Rebecca and Danny could feel the hurt and loss of the children on top of their own frustration at not being able to provide for their children. The inaccessibility of food may be a trigger for a child with early trauma. Rebecca and Danny added more rules to try to stop Corey's inappropriate behaviors, yet he routinely broke those rules.

Rebecca and Danny debated whether they should arrange for Corey to be placed back in foster care. Maybe he was just not a good fit for their family. The tipping point occurred when Rebecca attended training on attachment and trauma. She was given resources that challenged her way of seeing Corey's behaviors. Thus began a new parenting strategy.

Introducing Sally's Family, the Browns

Jane Brown, a successful businesswoman, placed very little importance on dating or relationships. As she grew older and listened to her co-workers talk about their children, her desire to be a mom seemed to awaken. She considered adoption her best option since she could adopt an older child and not take time off from work. She thought that an older child would be more self-sufficient, as well as a good companion. Jane would help society by giving an orphan a home. She envisioned this child thanking her for all the good things she provided. Jane chose Sally from a website. Sally was removed from her birth family at five years of age and began the first of three foster placements. One family declared that they would be her "forever" family, until she hurt their dog. Sally did not like that dog. He was like her mom's boyfriend's dog, the one tied to her doorknob to keep her in her bedroom and told to eat her if she tried to leave.

Jane was happy to have Sally. Weekends were for fun, with Saturday activities and Sunday church—their special times together. During the week, Sally stayed home alone, with a neighbor available for touching base if needed. Sally's routine was simple: She ate a prepackaged meal for dinner, completed her homework and bathed. Because her work commute was long, Jane arrived home just in time to tuck Sally in every night. After a few months, Sally was less fun to be with, complained about weekend activities, refused to go to church, wanted to shop more often and would not finish her morning chores. Jane no longer planned Saturday activities, working instead. She figured Sally could just occupy herself if she wasn't going to be fun. Sally was given chores and books to read and told to stay home. In retaliation, Sally began sneaking out as soon as Jane left for work. Sunday was Jane's time to see her friends at church, but she could only get Sally to go to see a boy she'd met there.

Jane had no support system as a parent. She did not want to stress her elderly parents and her sister refused to help because she thought Jane was wrong to adopt in the first place, so Jane asked her secretary to find answers for her. Things began to improve between her and Sally when both began to participate in specialized trauma services.

Introducing Brandon's Family, the Lewises

Bob and Deena Lewis were first-time parents of newly-placed six-year-old Brandon. Bob and Deena attended all the classes their agency offered, read many books and watched DVDs. They were ready. They knew this child would love them, because they were such loving people. Brandon seemed like a perfect fit for them, since six-year-olds can follow rules, maybe even read a little and do a few chores. They would have a ready-made family! Deena could continue working at the hospital while Brandon was in school. Bob, a teacher, would be home with Brandon during the summer. Bob knew how to manage children—he had created some of the best behavior management programs at his school.

Both parents believed that children comply when rules are explained. Besides, they knew Brandon would be thankful for his new home. They explained to him how he was expected to behave, their family rules and his boundaries. The first week went well, although Brandon seemed to forget the rules. Bob used one of his favorite behavioral charts featuring a reward system. He knew Brandon would enjoy earning rewards! Brandon worked for a week before protesting that the rewards were too hard to earn. However, when Bob made the system easier, Brandon still did not comply.

In the second month, Brandon tore up the chart and stated he didn't care about Bob and Deena's stupid rules. By the third month Brandon began breaking valuable figurines and rummaging through their belongings. Bob and Deena did not know how to make him respect their property. Deena dreaded coming home to a discouraged Bob and an out-of-control Brandon. She inquired at the hospital behavioral health department and was given the phone number for an attachment and trauma center. She and Bob changed their parenting style after a few helpful sessions with trauma professionals.

Look in my eyes can you see
Life filled with complete misery?
Look in my eyes can you say
Tomorrow will be a better day?
Well, tomorrow is now and things are the same.
I am still nothing to most but a faceless name.
Hurt more now than ever before
With each day bringing more and more
Unpleasant thoughts to keep me down,
Things to turn my smile to a frown.
Why am I cursed with a life like this?
A faceless name that nobody will miss
A life filled with so much pain
A faceless name with nothing to gain.

—*Allan Hall, 2004*

SEEING THE WORLD FROM THE CHILD'S POINT OF VIEW

Good mental health is essential for healthy child development and success-ful adult living. Not all children have sufficiently positive life experiences during the first critical months and years of life. Children become part of the foster and adoptive community, because their birth parents cannot or will not care for them in healthy ways. Many of these children are maltreated and have repeated traumatic experiences. Dr. Alexandra Cook, Associate Director and the Director of Development at the Trauma Center at Justice Resource Institute in Massachusetts, and her colleagues note: "Emotional abuse and neglect, sexual abuse and physical abuse, as well as witnessing domestic violence, ethnic cleansing or war, can interfere with the develop-ment of a secure attachment within the caregiving system."[1]

In the United States, 20 percent of children and adolescents are di-agnosed with mental disorders.[2] Foster and adoptive children often have an alphabet soup of psychiatric diagnoses, including Oppositional Defiant Disorder (ODD), Attention Deficit Hyperactivity Disorder (ADHD), Conduct Disorder (CD), Reactive Attachment Disorder (RAD) and others. According to Dr. Cook and her colleagues, "Each of these diagnoses cap-tures a limited aspect of the traumatized child's complex self-regulatory and relational impairments."[3] During 2006, approximately 129,000 children were in public foster care in the United States and 51,000 were adopted from that group.[4] These children may have been abused or ne-glected, causing a devastating break in the relationship with their primary caregiver, usually the mother.[5]

Pre-verbal experiential learning creates the internal definition of self, others and the world, forming an "Internal Working Model" (IWM). The IWM helps to interpret experiences, generate emotions and make decisions, mostly below the child's conscious awareness. Successful or unsuccessful early emotional "co-regulation" of fear by caregivers in the child's pre-verbal months is instrumental in the formation of the IWM. Will the child's IWM become one of basic trust in a reliable world or one of mistrust and fright?

EARLY TRAUMA AND RELATIONSHIPS

During removal from the birth family and during subsequent investigations, social workers, police, judges, teachers and new foster parents ask hard questions. Children may feel like they are betraying their birth family by answering. They may have seen their parents being arrested. They may have become separated from birth siblings when placed in different foster homes. Foster children are often overwhelmed with worry, fear and anger. From their perspective, controlling adults are perhaps the reason for their problems. They may feel that silence about their family's troubles is preferable to this horror. With their world seemingly going from bad to worse, these children erect defensive walls for survival, walls that may be invisible and masked by a charming and engaging façade.

Not understanding this, parents of traumatized children may rely on familiar parenting methods that are destined to fail. They are confused by their child's maladaptive behaviors and wonder why their parenting skills are being questioned. They may not understand why school concerns, poor peer interactions, developmental delays, sensory issues and even personal hygiene do not improve via consistently applied rewards and consequences. Gently delivered explanations with little expressed emotion never seem to work for these children. Even if they understand the wrongness of a behavior, they will continue to repeat it. Parents become disheartened and ultimately worn out by trying to connect with a child who uses disruptive behaviors to avoid intimacy and maintain a sense of control.

Foster and adoptive parents need help in dissolving the child's defensive walls that thwart loving outreach. By the time parents seek help, they have often built their own walls that also must be dissolved. David J. Wallin, a clinical psychologist who specializes in attachment theory, notes in his book, *Attachment in Psychotherapy*, "Parents discover themselves as parents through the impact that they are having on their child."[6] Without successful treatment of their child, parents perceive themselves as inadequate and may become depressed and isolated. Their other relationships often suffer. The children may be removed from the home, may develop emotional disorders and may become physically dangerous. Families deserve relief from the impact of trauma.

In-home family treatment is ideal for many families. This environmental approach is systemic, not focusing on "fixing" the child, but rather on creating healing relationships with a supportive environment. Research supports active parent involvement in treatment. Working with a child in the isolation of a therapist's office creates a treatment that may become "compartmentalized" without improving the home environment or the parent/child relationship.[7] Child psychologist Nicole Cox suggested that family therapy is preferred to individual therapy, because the child is part of the family system. Success or failure is dependent on the health of the system. If the parents are minimally involved, treatment may not generalize back to the family.[8] Given that children with traumatic histories may demonstrate a range of maladaptive behaviors that warrant therapy, therapists working exclusively with the child only address that child in an isolated context.[9]

If the child is focused on the therapist relationship apart from the home environment, problems generated by the original family and those faced by the current family are not adequately addressed. The therapist must consider the unique past and current experiences of each foster/adoptive child.

IMPACT OF EARLY TRAUMA: RECREATING OLD PATTERNS

When foster or adoptive parents bring a child into their home, they desire and expect a reciprocal relationship. A child with early trauma and attachment disruptions will have a different "map of the world" from the new parents' (remember the IWM). Their views, priorities, values and perceptions are different and this new home with loving, capable adults is unfamiliar. Early interpersonal experiences forced the child to try desperately to be in control of the environment, to be hyper-vigilant in order to maintain safety and meet basic needs. The child may strive to regain a sense of safety and control by creating an environment similar to one from his or her trauma history. Parents will interpret the child's "normal" as disruptive, unhealthy, dangerous, illegal and dysfunctional. The child may feel comfort and safety, but parents may be frightened and overwhelmed. Some families with sibling groups may consciously or unconsciously divide their home into "theirs and ours." The adopted children may have different schedules, sleep in separate quarters and even eat in other locations or at different times. Healthy attachment is unlikely under these conditions.

Unrealistic or uninformed parental expectations may get in the way. Some parents become focused on the child's fitting into the family and on abiding by family rules, instead of inviting this new child to join the family. If disruptive behaviors become more frequent, some parents make more rules in hopes that the child will finally "shape up." If the parents respond to the child's behavior with anger and disappointment, they will reinforce the child's negative belief system (*I am bad, The world is evil*, etc.). The only way for this child to heal is by forming a healthy relationship with the primary caregiver—thus, the importance of overcoming unrealistic initial expectations and instead empathically meeting with the child on his or her current level.

Families naturally become distressed by a child's disruptive behavior. Dr. Carl J. Sheperis, chair of Counseling and Special Populations at Lamar University, et al listed behaviors that frequently interfere with family functioning, including tantrums, aggression, interrupting, inability to play independently, whining and crying.[10] Here are other common disruptive behaviors:

1. Child is sweet and charming to strangers: "I could go home with you!"
2. Child is bashful and coy with strangers.
3. Child is destructive to property—his own and others'.
4. Child engages in multiple control battles.
5. Child "triangulates" (divides or splits up) adults to maintain control.
6. Child is oppositional to authority and those with whom he has a relationship.
7. Child steals from family and strangers, sometimes useless objects of no practical value.
8. Child is reactionary to parental affection.
9. Child lacks trust in adults.
10. Child's problem/target seems to be the mother.
11. Child implies false claims of abuse.
12. Child projects that he is not lovable.
13. Child lacks healthy interpersonal boundaries.
14. Child has poor personal hygiene.
15. Child has abnormal eating habits.
16. Child has unusual bathroom behavior.
17. Child has abnormal sleeping patterns.

18. Child uses poor communication skills.
19. Child may dissociate.
20. Child appears hyper-vigilant.
21. Child is aggressive toward anyone with whom he has a relationship.
22. Child displays emotional, physical and cognitive development delays.
23. Child has poor peer relationships.

Our intentional, constant and unrelenting determination to see the traumatized, attachment-disordered child's world through his or her lens is aided by putting ours aside to understand the disruptive and sometimes outright bizarre behavior of the child. Then we have a chance to replace despair with hope—hope that will take form in myriad "trauma-informed" interactions with the child that over time will heal his or her damaged Internal Working Model. In the following two chapters, we will look more specifically at how the traditional lens creates a foggy, distorted understanding and approach to these children and then focus on what we call "the trauma lens paradigm shift."

CHAPTER 2

The Lens We Are Accustomed to Using

*Days of excitement followed the introduction of Allan into the family.
He seemed to fit in! We were competent parents. We "got" parenting.
Our birth children were responsible and fairly compliant. We treated
Allan just like the other children. He had a few chores and was given
consequences when he did not obey. The children had freedom to roam
our twenty acres of trees and woods. The front ten acres were filled
with long rows of sheared pines, firs and spruce waiting for holiday
tree customers. The rear property was more adventurous, with steep
terrain, large pines and a slow, shallow stream. Allan enjoyed the out-
doors, running through the fields, exploring the woods and playing in
the stream. He and his younger sister shared toys, games and activities.*

*The family referred to Allan as "the Energizer Bunny," because
his batteries never ran down. He shared a bedroom with his new
older brother and he was homeschooled along with his sisters. I felt
that he could learn how to be in this family if he spent more time
with its members. I was pleased that I was allowed to homeschool
Allan. Typically, foster children had to attend school. I challenged the
caseworkers to make this decision in Allan's best interest. His previous
school experiences were problematic. All seemed well.*

Until it wasn't.

*David and I assigned daily chores. The girls and Allan were asked
to clean their rooms, help with kitchen clean-up and complete their
schoolwork. I stayed close to Allan to supervise him cleaning his room.
I broke the tasks into small chunks, just like I learned in my education
classes. Allan was to pick up his clothes and put them in the laundry,
put away his toys and make his bed. He would not pick up his clothes.
He played instead. The longer he played, the madder I became. I was
wasting my time. "Why don't you get your work done?" I asked. He
answered with sincerity that he just wanted to play. I pointed out that*

he was getting behind in his schoolwork, hoping that he would hurry. This never helped.

As I watched Allan, I began to compare his play with my other children's—something was different. He moved from toy to toy, pulling more out but not really playing with them—just scattering them around the room. I felt powerless to make him comply. No reward was good enough and no consequence severe enough to make him obey.

These long days of supervising him left little time to be with the girls or to complete my work. Every day I felt we were getting further and further behind in life. Giving directives and trying to make Allan comply consumed my time. The girls suffered because Mom was so focused on Allan's lack of compliance that she had little time for them. My patience was replaced by fear—fear of getting behind, fear of failing, fear of not being competent enough to parent Allan.

—Faye Hall

In the traditional foster and adoptive process, parents must attend classes, be assessed for suitability as parents and be found competent to parent a foster or adoptive child. They ask friends to provide references and their homes are inspected. Parents then anxiously await the new child. Everyone is convinced that lots of love and structure will enable the child to grow and flourish. They are taught that when a child understands the rules, he or she will behave. Parents envision that this new child will proudly identify with and represent the new family. Parents are primed to make sure the child eats healthy meals, is obedient, is successful at home and school and has a bright future. In *this* family, he or she will *always* have his or her needs (and many, if not all, "wants") met! Good behavior will be rewarded and poor behavior will be given "consequences."

LOOKING THROUGH A TRAUMATIZED CHILD'S LENS

Imagine having your first, most important relationship with your mom disrupted while an infant or toddler. There may not have been a loving caregiver to tuck you in at night, to smile at your first steps or to send you off to school. The most important person, your mom, may have been emotionally unavailable. Even worse, she may have been the source of (or tolerated) your neglect or abuse. Through your lens, you began to see yourself as worthless, your mom as untrustworthy and the world as unsafe.

Now imagine confident foster or adoptive parents who vow, "I've got this!" when beginning the foster or adoptive process. They attended all the parenting classes, completed the interviewing process and finished the home study. These parents are positive their skills are adequate for any child entering their home. They will use their ideal model in parenting: good structure, lots of love and many opportunities for success.

Then imagine the first few days or weeks as being uneventful. Sometimes, the child does not want to complete chores. Then hygiene problems begin—refusing to shower or brush teeth. During a quick search of the child's bedroom, the parents find food packages and stolen items. Sometimes the child roams through the house at night, destroying property, eating strange items and going to the bathroom in odd places. The following morning the parents find remains of the night roaming and begin the day with an elevated stress level. The child, sensing Mom's stress and "knowing" from early on how best to survive with a stressed caregiver, becomes oppositional to Mom's directives; he may even become aggressive toward her and battle for control. The child goes to school and describes Mom's "mean and controlling" attitude. Now "triangulation" between adults begins when caregivers outside the home intervene on the child's behalf. The child may lie about not having breakfast or not being provided a lunch. Feeling sorry for the child, school staff may offer the child a snack, school supplies or a hot lunch. They may even notify Child Protective Services if fearful the child's needs are not being met. If this spiral continues downward, the child may be removed from the home and placed with another family!

Imagine the impact on the mother. She anticipated the adoption of a child who would respond reciprocally to her love, not react to her in fear and anger. She feels the pain of the child's past but has no usable tools to help the child to heal. Her absolute best efforts at "normal parenting" are failing. She may lie about her child's academic and sports successes to fit in with "normal" families. One by one, everyone begins to view her as the problem. If she would only be more loving, be more kind, be more firm, say "yes" more often, say "no" more often or just relax. This mother may lose her sense of self, as she does not have time for activities she once enjoyed. Her ability to relax diminishes. To relieve her distress, her partner may offer to take the child to the park or out to eat. Since the child is happy to go to the park with Dad, it looks and feels to Mom like he's rewarding the child for misbehavior. Misinterpreting Dad's motives, she may feel that her partner has become aligned with the child against her. Losing her partner may be the end of the family.

Imagine the impact on this family if mental health services begin and the therapist lacks training in early trauma, child development and attachment. Interventions may be purely behavioral, based on rewards and consequences. The therapist is confident in a behavioral approach. Everyone knows that you want to reward positive behaviors and "consequence" (punish) negative behaviors. The child is given a chart for the parents to monitor. "Catch your child being good and reward with a great amount of praise" is the directive. During the next therapy session, the child blames Mom for the lack of praise. He proclaims, "She did not notice all the good things I did this week!" Mom is admonished to be more observant next time. Mom feels that something is wrong but cannot identify the problem. She knows she does not feel good about the session. Throughout the treatment process the child vacillates between compliance to the therapist and refusal to comply with parental directives. The therapist is further convinced the parents are inadequate, overly critical and unloving. After all, what's so difficult about following the therapist's skillfully crafted behavior modification chart?

Over time, if the therapist remains involved, some children will become less amenable to the rewards. The therapist may give up or the parents may become angry about being blamed. Treatment is discontinued. Each will blame the other for the failure. This process is the migration of the child's belief system ("I am bad") into the treatment. Some refer to this process technically as "the parallel process" or "isomorphism" with the child's original family. As the child's belief system of "I am bad" transfers to others, the therapist views the parents as "bad" and may also feel personally inadequate to correct the family's problems. Parents and therapists encounter failure.

Under these circumstances, the child will not heal and the family could be destroyed. Families on the Downward Spiral (see figure 1) may have the child removed from the home. Some children are moved to another foster or adoptive home. Others are housed in shelters, children's homes, residential treatment facilities or juvenile detention centers. The process is emotionally and financially costly to the child, family and society.

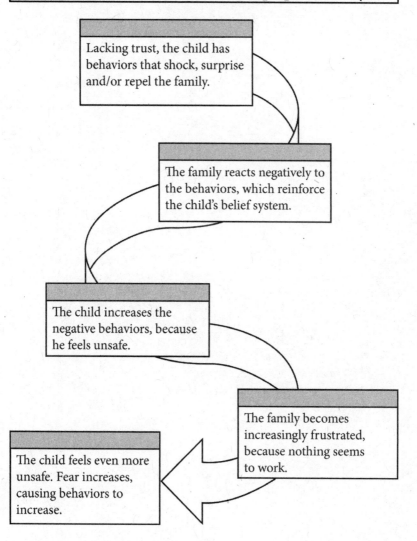

DOWNWARD SPIRAL

Implications of behaviors on an **unprepared** family

Lacking trust, the child has behaviors that shock, surprise and/or repel the family.

The family reacts negatively to the behaviors, which reinforce the child's belief system.

The child increases the negative behaviors, because he feels unsafe.

The family becomes increasingly frustrated, because nothing seems to work.

The child feels even more unsafe. Fear increases, causing behaviors to increase.

Figure 1: A spiral that results from families reacting to a child's behavior.

CHAPTER 3

The Trauma Lens Paradigm Shift

I tried to keep Allan close by so that I could keep him safe. But he would slip away. One day he came into the house after playing outside. My sister and I were visiting together in the living room. Allan could not stand still while talking to us. He kept shaking his leg. My sister, a nurse, was always concerned about Allan's health. As she investigated his ailment, a live bird fell out of his pants. He gathered up the bird and freed it outside. His grandfather witnessed a similar incident wherein Allan hid baby rabbits he'd captured in the field.

My quest for answers continued. I searched through training documents given to us when applying for the foster care license. With six hours of training, they should have covered noncompliant behaviors. I found nothing. I searched through stacks of files the agencies provided about Allan's early years: court documents, foster care placement reports, psychological evaluations and school reports. Hours of reading provided detailed information about Allan's abuse, neglect, abandonment and his multiple diagnoses. A new world emerged for me with unfamiliar mental health terms and diagnoses.

As I read more, Allan's behaviors started making sense. His trapping skills were learned from a dad who earned extra money from trapping alligators to sell and trade. He learned to hide from the police when the authorities were attempting to arrest his father for his drug use and dealing. His chaotic lifestyle did not lend itself to good hygiene or healthy meals. He learned to scavenge through the neighborhood for food. He did not live with his mother, making "mom" experiences unfamiliar.

I could now make more sense of Allan's strange behavior—why he was responding to me so differently from my biological children. But my search for new parenting skills was futile. The problem was that this was 1994 and no resources existed. I was determined nevertheless to find answers on how to parent this child.

The following year, while searching through the vast number of books at the largest library in the area, I found a new book, The Discipline Book, *by William Sears, MD, and Martha Sears, RN. It differentiated the "connected" from the "unconnected" child. Their description of the unconnected child sounded like Allan. I then called the director of the volunteer agency and asked whether they were teaching new parents to attach to their infants. How would you teach a parent to attach to a nine-year-old child? The director had no answers. Some may think that the answer is obvious—it should be just like the myriad of ways you attach to your birth children.*

But my experience was different. The things I could do for my birth children seemed to make Allan's behavior worse. Days flowed into weeks, weeks into months and nothing improved. The Downward Spiral continued. Allan began to sneak out of his bedroom at night and raid the kitchen for the foods he was allowed in limited quantity during the day. He would eat ice cream straight from the carton. I began to lose sleep, worried about his safety overnight. When we installed a motion detector at his bedroom door, he began to entertain himself by setting it off "by accident."

Finally, while Christmas shopping in December of 1996, I found the greatest present I could have received. On a rack of sale books outside a store I found a book entitled Adopting the Hurt Child *by Gregory Keck and Regina Kupecky. The authors gave a description of Reactive Attachment Disorder. There in the cold of December, I couldn't stop reading the book. Our life started to make sense. The authors clearly understood children like Allan—here were some answers to my quest. I had no illusions that the road ahead would be easy. But now my despair was assuaged with hope.*

—*Faye Hall*

Predicting treatment success begins by assessing two factors: the family's engagement in treatment and their faith in the treatment professionals. Our new model offers a third factor: Treatment success for children with a history of early trauma and attachment disruptions rests on the parent's *paradigm shift* of viewing the child and his or her disruptive behaviors through the "trauma lens" and accepting and using a different parenting model.

Imagine the impact of parents and professionals educated in trauma, child development and attachment before the child is placed in the home. Parental expectations will be aligned with the child's capacity for healthy relationships. The parents and professionals will be equipped with effective interventions to support restructuring internal belief systems, emotional maturation and opportunities for attachment. Parents will have support and encouragement from trained professionals. The child will be encompassed by treatment consistency while developing relationships that heal. Treatment will be difficult but energized with new hope.

Even after a child is placed in the home and the family is coping with disruptive behaviors, hope is not lost. An educated treatment team can help the family repair damaged relationships and spur new connections through trauma psychoeducation and healing interventions. It may take more time, but these parents will truly understand that trauma impairs a child's development, decision-making skills and the ability to form healthy and reciprocal relationships. Underlying parental issues, attitudes and personal characteristics may prevent the paradigm shift, thus hindering success. When these barriers are identified and addressed, they can be diminished, if not fully removed, by the parents and the treatment team.

FLAWED ELEMENTS OF FAMILIAR PARENTING STYLES

1. All Human Beings with Problems Respond to Behavioral Interventions.

The current therapeutic culture strongly emphasizes behaviorism and assumes that human beings can universally learn via rewards and consequences. If one rewards good behavior, good behavior will ensue and continue. If one "consequences" poor behavior, the poor behavior will stop. If the modification plan fails, then one assumes the reward was not good enough or the consequence not severe enough. An underlying principle is that all behavior is a choice. Behavioral approaches foster the delusion that parents can address every problematic behavior effectively. They also assume that early trauma does not impede the child's ability to choose good behavior. Finally, behavioral environments are often overly structured, with little time and energy for nurturing relationships.

Brandon's Family

Bob decided to start summer vacation with a new behavior chart he had created for the emotional support classroom in which students could earn token rewards for each good behavior. Brandon liked playing with building toys, so Bob thought he would be motivated to earn a new set each week for completed chores. Bob proudly hung the chart on the refrigerator. Brandon was excited to earn the fireman set and the first week went well: Brandon got the set. Yet he struggled completing his chores the following week. He was very disappointed that he did not earn another set, but promised he would try harder. By Tuesday of the third week, Brandon was angry and defiant. He declared that Bob gave too many chores. He stopped playing with the building sets and became more interested in physical activities.

Brandon had developed a *negative internal working model* (N-IWM) from his early trauma. He could transfer his belief system to the external world through the "miracle" of disobedience and have this belief system reinforced through consequences administered as part of the treatment plan. Poor behavior would be identified as "bad," "evil" and "mean." A N-IWM causes an inability to effectively make decisions in a positive environment. The child feels a sense of "wrongness" when behaving in the expected way, as it runs counter to the N-IWM. Therefore, this inability to make positive decisions is essentially a "hurt part," an injury that needs to heal like a broken leg would need to heal before a child can run again. Behavioral approaches assume that the child does not have this "hurt part," but is instead capable of making good decisions (that is, that the child has a positive internal working model [P-IWM]).

Even after Brandon lost the reward, he preferred to believe, as Bob did, that he had "made the choice" to lose. Instead, the trauma-informed understanding is that Brandon is currently too weak for now to tolerate the fear that comes with success and the challenging of his N-IWM. Most children with early trauma damage will feel more comfortable with the interpretation that they chose the behavior ("I am bad," instead of "I am too weak to do right.") The negative consequence feels better to the child (accurately aligns with the child's belief about self and adults) than the assumption that he or she is weak. But in reality, this child is no more able to make positive choices than a child with a broken leg is able to walk. By trying to implement a strictly behavioral approach, parents fail to account for the trauma damage—namely, the resulting negative internal working model (N-IWM) that will inevitably sabotage the behavior modification plan.

2. Parents Are Capable.

To begin the foster and adoptive process, parents must attend classes, be assessed and be found competent to parent a child. Responding to reference requests, friends and colleagues vouch for their moral integrity and social competence. Their home is inspected and other children in the home are questioned. Successful completion of the evaluation process and granting of the adoption or foster care license convinces parents that they are capable of parenting any child brought their way. Their flourishing birth children further persuade them that "We can do this!"

Corey's Family

Rebecca felt so confident when Corey arrived. He took his toiletries basket to his room and politely asked about dinner time: "I want to make sure I wash up before we eat," he said. Rebecca was sure that he was a good fit for their family. He reminded her of her son Andy. A few weeks went by before she noticed food missing from the kitchen. Rebecca searched Corey's room while he was outside playing. To her dismay she found food and wrappers hidden all over his room. That evening, Danny and Rebecca explained to Corey that he was not allowed to take food without asking. He promised he would never do that again. Unfortunately, the next night Andy's friend was coming for dinner and Rebecca could not find the dessert she'd made. Rebecca began to question their decision to adopt.

During the integration process, most parents use their familiar parenting skills. It is not until problem behaviors escalate that parents begin to question why their child's behavior is not improving. Rebecca calmly and clearly outlined for Corey why the behaviors were wrong or not needed. She checked his understanding by having him repeat her explanation, just as parenting classes advise. She provided him with suggestions for alternate behaviors and obtained from him a commitment to do things differently. After all, the parenting manual they had received provided the same techniques that they'd been applying successfully to their birth children. Their intuition told them that Corey really did understand and was contrite about the "oversights."

But Corey continued to steal and stash food. Rebecca and Danny were faced with either needing to modify their perception of themselves or of Corey: either "I guess we are wrong. We are *not* good parents, just lucky that our birth children are all right," or "We are good parents, but Corey is just bad." And there it was, Corey's N-IWM invading the here-and-now and infecting the parent-child relationship.

The parents' belief of themselves as capable and good directly clashes with the child's belief of the parents as incompetent and hurtful. Successful, capable parents like Danny and Rebecca can be comfortable (or at least less afraid) by interpreting the dilemma as "this child is bad." They now must grieve the loss of their conviction that their parenting of their adoptive child would require not much more effort than that of their birth children and accept that they will have to put in long, hard work requiring constant attention and active learning.

Danny and Rebecca gained access to a new in-home service. They told the team about their flourishing birth children and how difficult it was to parent Corey. They said with a combination of sadness and frustration that unless this new service could "work magic," other placement options might become necessary.

3. My Child's Problems Are a Reflection on My Parenting Skills.

Once parents feel they are competent and have a "We can do this" attitude, the child's persistent poor behavior may eventually begin to feel like a flaw in their basic parenting skills rather than the persisting aftermath of early trauma. Parents then routinely perceive others as judging them when their child misbehaves. Well-meaning friends, family and sometimes strangers just as routinely suggest that the parents should be more loving or more strict. Schools often reinforce this belief when the child is problematic. Eventually the parents begin to worry that the child's misbehavior is reflecting badly on the extended family—grandparents, aunts and uncles.

Sally's Family

Jane needed to have someone to talk to about Sally's behaviors: someone to listen, have empathy for the problems she was experiencing, brainstorm solutions and validate her experience of the difficulty. Yet every time she called her sister, she regretted the call. Her sister would begin a tirade about how Jane had had no parenting experience and should never have adopted Sally. Her sister clearly interpreted Sally's poor behavior as proof positive of Jane's lack of parenting acumen. Jane could not turn to her parents for moral support—her mother considered worrying a virtuous badge of honor! Jane felt alone. Her sister, like so many others with no understanding of early trauma in children, fell back on the simplistic notion that good parents don't have poorly behaving children.

Sally's school staff eventually called Child Protective Services after Jane continued to insist that Sally complete her homework even if it took four or more hours per evening. This intervention instilled even deeper in Jane's heart that she was an incompetent parent.

Parents see and hear blame from many sources. They feel directly accountable for the child's misbehavior. They are the ones who must pay damages for property destroyed by their children. They are the ones who must pay truancy fines. So once again, the child's N-IWM is reinforced rather than confronted and challenged. Eventually, more and more of the parents' energy is dissipated in the service of defending against the perception that they are bad, that they are the problem. Almost inevitably and ironically, their constant efforts to "look good" are seen by others as proof of their inadequacy as parents. Jane had never imagined the scenario of forcing her daughter to sit at the table for over four hours in an evening to finish homework, but only inadequate parents have children who do not complete their homework!

4. All the Child Needs Is Love.

Parents desire to love a child and perceive that the child will respond to their love. They are convinced that enough love will enable the child to grow and flourish. After all, "All you need is love" and "Love conquers all" ooze abundantly out of our daily diet of songs, books and movies. Often agency workers convey that the child's core problem is not having been loved enough in his birth home or in prior placements. This further bolsters the parents' conviction that their bottomless spring of love will make the difference. Parents inflicted with unrelenting fertility problems and desperately wanting a child may be even more susceptible to this fallacy.

Amy's Family

Lori was so happy to be a mom. She could not have loved Amy any more than she did. She was pleased to start her workday early so that she could transport her daughter to soccer practice in the evening. She worked overtime on Saturdays to pay for the expensive bike Amy wanted. If Amy needed a little "extra picking up after" from time to time, it was all worth it. After all, doing things for others demonstrates love via sacrifice. Surely, Amy will feel loved and will reciprocate. But then, why did Amy tantrum nightly and destroy property and threaten to hurt her mom? Eventually Lori had to halt all her outside interests. She spent all of her time and energy "filling Amy's love tank." She became exhausted, lonely and resentful. Lori began to feel like a failure. Her love was not healing Amy. Maybe Lori's love was even making Amy worse! But thinking it not enough, Lori was determined to try to show more love to Amy every day.

Because there are books upon books written on ways to express our love, the belief that all our child needs is love will result in a burnt out, exhausted, emotionally bankrupt parent. With each new expression of love the parent strives to provide, the parent experiences rejection, failure and condemnation when the child's behavior does not change. The impact of early trauma is present but unrecognized, rendering the child incapable of accurately understanding and feeling the loving actions. As parents repeatedly experience rejection, exhaustion and condemnation, the relationship begins the Downward Spiral, the end of which is that nobody is experiencing love in the relationship. Again, the child's N-IWM is mirrored and reinforced.

5. The Child Will Be Filled with Gratitude.

It seems so logical that a child from a deprived environment will be thankful for a new home and family. We evaluate ourselves as parents and can realistically list all the positive opportunities and items that we can provide for a child. We naturally believe that the child will experience them as positive and be grateful to us for them.

Human communication and interaction undergird the principle of reciprocity. We give and receive. We expect to receive based on what we give. When we work hard, we should be paid well. When we provide good gifts, we should receive gratitude. But consider this analogy: Can you express gratitude to a serial killer who offers to take you to dinner? The N-IWM of traumatized children forces them to view their parents as scary and hurtful. Therefore, even when parents give them good things—like the serial killer springing for dinner—the children experience discomfort. Their N-IWM actually produces a fear reaction to the good things the parents are providing, seeing the kind gesture though a lens of suspicion and mistrust, resulting in some sort of wary, guarded response, if not an outright hostile one.

Amy's Family

James and Lori knew that Amy had suffered years of deprivation. Their hearts ached when thinking about Amy's missed experiences. They decided to "make up" for those years. At first it was a delight to be able to buy her all the most hip styles and brand-name clothes for which Amy expressed interest. Who could blame her for wanting so much after having so little? But Lori noticed over time that Amy's "thank you's" became fewer and more perfunctory. She did not take care of the clothing, tearing or staining items or giving them away on a whim. Lori became angry and reduced her spending on Amy. Amy resented this "deprivation" and, in screaming fits, also blamed Lori for her not fitting in at school.

James brought home a new toy for Amy every Friday. It would be a family thing, something they would remember later in life. Amy usually played with the toy briefly and then relegated it to the cavernous box of ignored toys. That is, if the toy were put away at all. Usually it was just left wherever it dropped. Lori always reminded Amy to thank her dad for the toy. Finally one evening Amy griped that she did not ask for the toys and they were not even the ones she wanted. She said she was just being nice by playing with them, so that Dad would not be angry with her.

The child driven by a N-IWM will commonly declare that his new bicycle is not the best bike on the market and find fatal flaws in it—"It's not good enough to do the jumps. What a piece of crap!" The child will "fulfill the prophesy" by "accidentally" stripping bolts with excessive tightening and then complaining when the wheel falls off. Children from deprived environments may experience excessive stress at the effort it takes to manage possessions: cleaning, storing, organizing, choosing and matching. These children may express dissatisfaction or even condemnation of the parent's purchases for them. Thus, parents experience an emotional slap when expecting a "thank you." Constant repetition of this theme leaves parents fearful and avoidant of giving. So, once again the child's N-IWM is reinforced in the current environment. Amy's teacher complained to the therapy team that the parents did not have the proper school supplies. Lori and James responded, "We don't feel like buying her anything. What's the point? She doesn't appreciate it anyway!"

6. The Family Assumes Negative Motivations and Intentions.

If parents are unsuccessful in changing the child's behavior, they are vulnerable to assuming that the child has negative intentions or is incapable of doing right: "He does not like me. He is a totally bad kid. He just did that to get under my skin. He is just trying to make me mad." Once parents assume negative motivations behind their children's behaviors, all parental interactions will eventually be tainted by these beliefs. Children with a N-IWM naturally assume negative parenting motivations. And negative parenting motivations do not correspond with parents giving good things. Children become fearful when their external world does not match their internal world. So they act as if their parents are bad in order to match the N-IWM and harmonize their external and internal worlds.

Corey's Family

Rebecca liked cooking for her family. She took pride in the quality of the food. Corey yelled at her for "trying to kill him with this slop" and spat out his first bites. Food was not an issue for him at school or at friends' houses. Rebecca could never please him. He consistently disliked her cooking. She expressed her hurt and offered to cook any meal he wanted. Rebecca reported, "I cannot make this child happy. He doesn't like me." One day, Rebecca set food in front of Fred, her biological child, with a smile and pat on the back. When she gave Corey his food, she avoided eye contact and made no attempt to engage him. She was protecting herself from the anticipated rejection and thereby once again inadvertently reinforcing Corey's N-IWM.

WHAT IS THE TRAUMA LENS PARADIGM SHIFT?

Shifting from the Familiar to the New Model,
How the Elements Change

Now, let's make the shift to a new paradigm, where the child and maladaptive behaviors are viewed through the trauma lens. We will adjust traditional elements of the parenting paradigm in making this shift. If we fail to make this shift, the traditional style will remain a barrier to effective parenting as well as to effective therapeutic interventions.

> **Old:** All human problems respond to behavioral interventions.
> **New:** Trauma damage must be healed before consistent behavior change can be expected.

Much behavior is driven by a perceived need to feel safe. Humans are more fundamentally motivated to be less afraid than to be happy. As we have seen, children with a N-IWM will behave in such fashion as to bring their belief system into their world. Strict behavioral approaches bring out the N-IWM in bold relief. They do not bring about favorable change, but they do clearly identify those behaviors in need of change.

Parents cannot always address every problematic behavior. Sometimes we as parents are powerless to promote positive behavior change in our children. It requires great emotional strength and support from others in order to simply be sad about our children's misbehaviors—instead of becoming angry or demoralized—while waiting for the slow process of positive change to unfold.

Brandon's Family

When Bob created the behavior chart, he understood how to "structure" Brandon toward greater success. He felt good about his ability to address each behavior to shape and mold his son into the man he could become. Brandon's past was just something to be overcome. The problem was how to motivate him to make better choices.

Brandon knew he was different from other kids. They seemed to get more fun stuff and did not argue with adults like he did. He constantly had a feeling that something bad was about to happen. He was excited about the behavior modification chart and promptly earned the first reward. But something vague inside told him that bad things were coming. Bob kept talking about how successful Brandon could be as he grew up and kept accomplishing bigger and bigger tasks.

Brandon began to feel weak and scared of failing, sometimes becoming hopeless. He did not recognize that this feeling was identical to the fear he used to feel years ago as a tiny boy who could not keep himself safe. With each "success" Brandon then became more fearful. Accordingly, the fear would diminish substantially if Brandon stopped trying to meet expectations. Bob raised his voice when asking Brandon why he gave up on working for his next reward. Brandon could not recognize within himself nor articulate to Bob that he was fearful of being controlled with prizes and that he felt like a slave having to knuckle under in order to get scraps. Losing a reward comes easily to someone who already feels like a failure.

Brandon did not like feeling weak or like a slave. So he used his anger to be strong and in control again. So what if he didn't earn the stupid reward that his untrustworthy dad might not give him anyway? It's better to feel strong and in control without the reward, than weak and vulnerable while trying for success.

Unrestrained behaviorism, when applied to a child with a N-IWM, often leads to "consequences after consequences." By midsummer the family was sacrificing game nights and outings, because Brandon needed consequences for raiding the freezer and eating all the ice cream. Bob saw this as Brandon choosing bad behavior. The family responded to him with blame and resentment. But Brandon already knew he was a "bad kid" and he knew how to handle shaming. Family life became organized around providing negative reinforcement (ignoring) or punishment for Brandon's problematic behaviors. There was little time or energy left for nurturing relationships. But nurture needs to occur independently of poor behaviors. When the goal is healing the trauma damage, nurturing activities and connections remain the high priority even during episodes of poor behavior. The hurt must be healed before the child can effectively make good choices. The parental relationship is the "tool" for healing the trauma.

Training in trauma-informed parenting helped Bob and Deena to use the trauma lens to reframe Brandon's behaviors. They could see that he had different "parts"—a healthy part that wanted to love his parents and a hurt part that was always afraid. They used some new tools that helped them to be sad rather than angry about his behaviors and reframe them as attempts to feel less afraid. They did not feel "perfect" as parents then, but felt great relief at discovering new ways to understand and engage Brandon.

As the parents changed in their approach, Brandon initially grew angry more easily than ever. He redoubled his efforts to provoke anger in Bob and Deena. Their expression of sadness for his hurt infuriated him. He insisted that he had no such part and was choosing to get the consequence, which—by the way—didn't faze him at all. But his parents persisted in expressing sadness and their hope that he would "feel" the weakness. Each time he made a healthy choice, they celebrated the choice as evidence of his healing and predicted that good choices would become progressively easier for him. To Bob's great surprise, one day Brandon commented that a consequence "sucked" and expressed pleasure that his hurt "baby part" was healing.

By highlighting the N-IWM with empathy and sadness for the child's early trauma, parents can provide an alternate experience of self. Poor behavior previously understood by Brandon and his parents as "I am bad but strong" is viewed through the trauma lens as "I am a good kid with a hurt part." While this paradigm is initially irritating to the child, it provides a framework for long-term growth. As stated before, it's as though behavioral interventions expect the child with a broken leg to "choose" to run. With this paradigm shift, a child may initially fear acknowledging that he has a "broken leg." But ultimately, with the focus on trauma damage and recovery from it, running eventually becomes possible.

> **Old:** Parents are sufficiently capable to parent this child.
> **New:** Even capable parents require additional training that addresses the child's early trauma.

Parents can be perfectly capable of successfully parenting birth children and meeting adoptive or foster agencies' parenting requirements. They can have advanced academic credentials. But raising a traumatized child necessitates additional training and skills. This fact does not diminish the qualifications of the parent, but instead it underscores the reality that parenting a traumatized child is so very different from ordinary parenting.

When a child with early trauma enters into a family system, the system changes. This system will absorb and react to the child's N-IWM. The natural reaction is to begin a Downward Spiral. The Trauma Lens Paradigm Shift offers techniques and interventions that will reverse the spiral and promote healing. These techniques will feel counterintuitive and may be viewed negatively by others. Parents using the old, familiar parenting model would "consequence" a child for a tantrum. The new model explains why the child needs "time in" with the parent rather than being sent for a time out. *Being with* a sad or scared child—instead of fixing the behavior—requires training and practice in co-experiencing the child's emotions and co-regulating them with the child.

Corey's Family

In most cases it is neither easy nor inexpensive to return a child to "the system" after adoption. Rebecca and Danny were willing to try something new to preserve Corey's placement even when it seemed hopeless. With time and trauma-specific treatment they were able to grieve their lost parenting expectations and accept the new paradigm. They recognized that their parenting failures stemmed from their old parenting methods. The shift did not require so much additional effort as it did adapted strategies.

At first they were incredulous at the idea that they did not need to change Corey, just themselves. They were being asked to embark on a parenting effort seemingly more complicated and time-consuming than the crisp behavior modification principles they used so successfully with their birth children.

Rebecca and Danny were annoyed and taken off guard when Corey told them he should not have consequences for making decisions from his "baby part." But they recovered and with sadness informed him that he needed to learn to recognize how much that hurt part was costing him. "Don't worry—you're getting this. I can remember when you didn't even believe you had a baby part!" they assured. Success is energizing.

Old: My child's problems are a reflection of my parenting skills.
New: My child's problems are a reflection of his/her early trauma.

We cannot be ashamed or afraid of our children's problematic behaviors while at the same time expecting them to acknowledge ownership and endure the fear of recovery. When we say, "No child of mine behaves like this," we disown the child. Other common damaging statements include: "I cannot handle these behaviors," meaning "Your behaviors are too big for me." "I cannot stand it when you behave this way" means, "I cannot stand you." By learning to see the child's behaviors as a reflection of his early trauma, we preserve our self-image. We free ourselves to be sad with the child and for the child instead of fearful for ourselves. By increasing our ability to feel the child's sadness and fear ourselves, we are able to assist him in experiencing his own emotional world. Our reduction of defensiveness makes forming alliances easier, as we no longer frame the problem as one of our defective parenting skills.

Families need to instill in the child a feeling of having been "claimed" by them and "belonging" to and with them, in order for healing to proceed. Statements like "No one in our family does that" or "You cannot behave like that because Granddad is the mayor" send the message that the child will never be a member of our family. The new paradigm allows for the recognition that this family and these parents are working to help the child heal from the early trauma. It transforms and properly elevates the parenting effort as heroic in joining with the child to overcome problems caused by someone else.

Sally's Family

Jane's new in-home staff was quick to reframe Sally's behaviors through the trauma lens. They identified Sally's attempts to deflect emotional closeness, disrupt adult communications and relationships and recreate the chaos from her past. Jane was reluctant to allow the staff to talk to the school, because of the protective services report with its inferences of her being too harsh with Sally. She had noticed the looks between teachers and heard from them in muted form the same derogatory remarks inflicted by her sister. Nevertheless, she decided to give the staff a chance to meet with the school personnel along with herself. She was surprised at how credible the information sounded coming from knowledgeable professionals. One teacher even admitted that a family member was showing similar behaviors and asked for resources. Buoyed by this experience, Jane scheduled the in-home staff for a meeting with her parents and sister in order to explain to them how early trauma damages a child, the impact on the new family and how to help. The support system thus created allowed Jane to begin to effectively parent a child hurt by someone else.

Old: All the child needs is love.
New: Love is expressed differently to children with early trauma.

Unconditional love is a requirement for healing. Expressing that love to a child of early trauma becomes highly complicated. Parents must understand that the actions that typically express unconditional love actually become fear-inducing due to the child's N-IWM. Early traumatic experiences predispose the child to assuming that parents are untrustworthy and dangerous. Once that "knowledge" is pre-verbally acquired, the child will experience *any* parental interaction with suspicion and fear. Parents must understand this, label the child's behavior as emanating from the early trauma and become able to predict resulting behaviors. That is, we must be able to read the child's internal state before we can successfully demonstrate unconditional love, assist in recovery and accurately express our emotions to the child.

Otherwise, parents can only offer conditional love and are unable to help their child navigate fear, sadness and anger. Before recovery, most children cannot achieve "average" levels of emotional intensity or regulation. Parents are handicapped in expressing their own full range of emotions due to the constant background of the child's projected fear. Before the child can accept our love, she must know why it's so scary to do so. Children absolutely need love. The traumatized child needs to learn how to experience love before she can receive love and interpret the experience. The early trauma damage leaves children without the ability to receive the very thing they need.

Amy's Family

It was clear to both James and Lori that "just loving Amy more" was not working. They began a new in-home service that was to help Amy learn to love them. Amy stated that she did not feel loved by her parents: "They are just trying to please Child Protective Services. They don't like me, 'cause I'm too bad." James loudly protested, "If anyone else treated my wife the way Amy did, I would have kicked them to the curb long ago!" As treatment progressed, the family learned why Amy constantly feared good things. Lori was taught to help her daughter notice the fear in her body and see how it affected her behavior. Amy enjoyed the activities with her mom and was able to voice when she had "too much good." James and Lori learned to reduce the number of gifts to special occasions and infrequent surprises. They expressed sorrow and reframed destruction of property as Amy saying that she had "too much."

Amy was scared of her parents' deeper understanding, but her fear slowly decreased, as they consistently did not regress to angry reactions toward her behavior. She felt for the first time that her parents understood and accepted her. Working together, the family recognized the early trauma damage, found ways to connect with Amy despite the damage and eventually developed ways to express love that facilitated Amy's healing.

Old: The child will be filled with gratitude.
New: Because of early trauma, even the good things that I provide will be experienced fearfully.

When the child's internal world does not match his external world, he will experience fear. A child with a N-IWM will experience a situation as ominous despite others not seeing bad intentions in either themselves or their parents. It's like the fear you or I would feel while swinging from a trapeze as novices; the performer who slowly learned the skills growing up in the circus would not feel any fear at all.

Parents need to recognize their child's fear and label it ahead of time. Until the hurt part of the child is healed or begins to heal, they will be scared by, rather than grateful for, any attempts to provide good things.

The new paradigm helps parents to be more reflective and forgiving about the child's behaviors. Parents are encouraged to find alternative ways to feel good about themselves without expecting reciprocity from their child. Parents can be freed from the need for gratitude and from feelings of rejection, making them more emotionally available to co-regulate with their children.

Amy's Family

James and Lori assumed that Amy would reciprocate their kind actions. None of the caseworkers explained why this would not occur. Consequently, they interpreted Amy's actions as rejection and negatively reacted to her in turn. When the family began the new in-home service, Amy could not explain why she felt uncomfortable when receiving gifts. As the team explored Amy's emotional world, they noticed that she would not talk about being sad or scared. But they recognized and interpreted her nonverbal behavior as "talking."

For example, Amy deliberately tore a hole in her new jeans. She quickly responded that she did not want these jeans. But what was she really "saying?" In this way, she could avoid feelings of fear or looking good and having good parents. The tearing reduced any feelings of loss to zero and ripping the jeans evoked anger in her, an emotion with which she felt more secure.

But without the paradigm shift, James and Lori interpreted Amy's behavior as: She'll destroy things just to get more; she doesn't appreciate what we do for her; we'll go broke trying to make her happy; she thinks she's entitled to anything she wants and we don't supply good enough things. All of these inferences caused fear in James and Lori. Without the paradigm shift, families succumb to the Downward Spiral. With training and practice, James and Lori were able to stop asking Amy why she did the things she did. Instead they would define the experience through the trauma lens and label her fear.

At first, Amy was angry in response. "That's not what I'm feeling!" But with constant repetition she began to recognize and tolerate more vulnerable emotions. She went from "I know what you're thinking" to "it makes sense but I don't like it" to "when will I stop feeling this way?" It was calming to be able to anticipate feelings and behaviors. The family members felt better about themselves and were able to enjoy their relationships.

Old: The child has negative motivations and intentions.
New: My child's problematic behaviors are motivated by the need to feel less afraid.

Until parents believe that all of their children's problematic behaviors are motivated by want of safety, the healing cannot begin. With the new paradigm, "Why can't he earn a contract reward?" is answered with, "He doesn't trust the person who created the contract" or "He does not feel he is competent enough to complete the contract." "Why does he say things like that about me?" is answered with "He doesn't trust me." By recognizing the damage of early trauma, parents will have an alternative explanation for the child's misbehavior. "Parts" theory can help the parents to understand that the "hurt part" of the child is behind poor behavior, while they look to foster development of the "healthy part." The concept of "parts" also helps the child to become reflective about self and parents and thereby able to ponder whether they may in fact have benevolent motivations, too.

Corey's Family

Corey had an answer for everything. If someone brushed up against him or he fell, he claimed "abuse." He complained that his parents overheated his food and caused him to burn his mouth. Some bruises from a recent fall led to a Child Protective Services investigation. When he accused Danny and Rebecca of inflicting the injuries, they could not understand why he lied. What did he have to gain? He must really hate them. The parents fell victim to Corey's N-IWM, as caused by traumatic experiences at the hands of his birth parents and possibly also by prior foster parents: He was bad and adults were dangerous.

The new in-home service's staff answered the "why" questions. Corey's early life experiences taught him that he was not valuable, that adults were dangerous and that the world was unsafe. He needed to keep himself safe in every situation. His internal monitoring system was always set on "red alert."

Treatment focused on psychoeducation regarding trauma, attachment and development and on helping the parents notice signs of anxiety in Corey. Their "homework" was to share personal emotional experiences. The family became more aware of fear and sadness. The other children understood how their behaviors spread fear throughout the family when they were reacting to Corey's fear. Corey was uncomfortable when others seemed to recognize his emotions before he did. The family began to enjoy sharing their daily experiences at dinner. Instead of attacking Corey for his lies, they gave him space and told him his unhealthy part was making decisions. As the family completed their homework in helping Corey notice his emotions and talk about theirs, he relaxed. Gradually the family learned to handle fear better and accept comfort when sad.

HOW IS THIS PARADIGM SHIFT ACHIEVED?

In the previous section we detailed six traditional foster and adoptive parenting tenets. Each family will adhere to the tenets in varying degrees. But a change to the new paradigm is necessary for successful parenting of a traumatized child. How can the Trauma Lens Paradigm Shift be achieved?

Shifting paradigms is hard work and requires education, resources, support and guidance. Parents must have a team of friends and professionals with whom to share responsibilities and from whom to get stress relief. We will address development of the treatment team in the next chapter. We will proceed here as though the family has a treatment team.

Psychoeducation for the Family, Friends and Professionals

The Emotional Cognitive Trauma Model (ECTM) begins with the *Two Babies Narrative*, a description of how two babies develop opposite internal working models. One baby has an attuned primary caregiver with "good enough" parenting.[11] The second infant's caregiver lacks attunement and responsiveness. This caregiver may hurt the child or allow others to do so. The narrative identifies how the IWM affects relationships, decisions and behaviors and increases understanding of where emotions come from and how the trauma damages were done. It enables the reader to feel empathy for the birth mother and sets the stage for future "reframes."

The ECTM: *Two Babies Narrative* leads to the parent's ability to make the following paradigm shifts:

1. A reframing of current events and behaviors through the Trauma Lens, by linking current behavior to the early abuse or neglect.

2. Thinking of the trauma damage as a "hurt part." The hurt part is not the whole child. If it's only a part, the part can be healed.

3. Understanding "parts" as thinking, feeling and acting components. We all have parts, the strength of which varies given different events and triggers.

4. The ability to demonstrate how anger avoids feeling fear and sadness. Anger gives power, while fear and sadness are difficult to manage for a child who lacked an attuned caregiver.

5. The understanding of these children as either more or less angry, but rarely happy.

6. Better parental skill at regulating their own emotions, along with an expanded range of emotional awareness.

Two additional skills parents are encouraged to use are "narration" and "affect matching." The *Two Babies Narrative* highlights the role of parental narration of everyday life and of definition of experience. This is an automatic process for healthy parents and children. But children who come from stressful, abusive and neglectful environments most likely have not had this interactive experience. In the new paradigm, parents use the ECTM to narrate their children's emotional worlds and to define their experiences.

Parents narrate the world for their infants, if you notice. The baby's every interaction with the environment is described and defined in great detail; what a good sleep the baby had, how comfortable the crib is, the smell of the diaper, the taste of the milk, the empty feeling and the full feeling. Dozens of times a day, parents show baby the world.

So often the parents of traumatized children find themselves asking them questions like, "Why did you do that?" and "When will you stop doing that?" The ECTM encourages parents to stop asking and use the model to provide answers. This greatly reduces defaulting to the N-IWM of "I am bad" and "You are bad." Now, "Why did you do that?" can be reframed as "You did not trust me, so you took the candy." Parents will understand that the answer to "When will you stop?" will come with healing.

Corey's Family

Over the years, Corey continued to steal food from Danny and Rebecca. Danny stated that he did not understand why Corey did not trust them to take care of his needs. Each time he stole food, he had the feeling of meeting his own needs, of being in control, thereby demonstrating that he didn't need parents. Danny and Rebecca began to narrate their actions as they provided for Corey. Rebecca pointed out times when Danny played with Corey. Danny voiced his appreciation of Rebecca as she took care of each meal. Both Danny and Rebecca described the other parent as being trustworthy. Each reframe of the parent's trustworthy behavior added meaning to the experience.

Another skill parents are encouraged to use is affect matching. Parents of infants match their affect with the child's to calm them. This natural process is essential for infant co-regulation. Children with early trauma missed this vital developmental interactive experience. Parents of traumatized children must be taught the importance of affect matching, be provided with examples and encouraged to practice it. The foundation of affect matching is adult emotional self-regulation, followed by intentional co-regulation of the child. Parents use the skills of narrative and affect matching as they shift their paradigm.

The paradigm shift continues with understanding of what we refer to as *Trauma-Disrupted Competencies* (TDCs). Infant and child development is incremental and builds on each previous skill. If a skill is not learned, the incremental process is disrupted. Parenting a traumatized child becomes easier as the parent looks for TDCs in their child; misbehaviors can then be understood as missing skills instead of behaviors that need consequences.

- **Negative Internal Working Model** (N-IWM or "maladaptive schema"): A schema is an internal working model of oneself, one's caregivers and the world. If a child endures trauma from child abuse, neglect and/or loss of the primary caregiver, the result may be distorted and maladaptive schemas. Maladaptive schemas may be linked to adult personality disorders that are very difficult to treat. Consequently, early recognition and attention to maladaptive schemas in children can be preventive. Typical behaviors consistent with a maladaptive schema include not trying (fearing failure) and stealing and lying (not trusting parents to provide).

- **Developmental delays:** Disrupted relationships are emotionally and developmentally costly. Severely disrupted attachment often engenders lifelong risk of physical disease and psychosocial dysfunction.[12] These children may have atypical development of their ability to play or to occupy themselves, may regress under stress to behaviors typical of a younger child, be hyper-vigilant with an inability to focus or use controlling behaviors. Typical behaviors include being bored (an inability to occupy oneself) and not finishing games and projects (lacking in developmentally-appropriate skills).

- **Inappropriate emotional response:** Children may become frightened if they sense danger or feel that they are losing control of their environment. The child may have an exaggerated physiological response to stimuli, activating the autonomic nervous system with changes in heart rate, blood flow, respiration and stress hormone secretions. Otherwise stated, their "fight, flight, freeze" reflex is unnecessarily activated. Cognitive processing is then reduced, resulting in an inability to answer questions or make logical decisions. The brain processes information from the autonomic nervous system more rapidly than rational thoughts, as the former call for activation of automatic reflexes to keep the person alive. Typical behaviors include fighting, running away and being unable to answer.

- **Object relations problems:** Many children have a history of impermanence. Adults appeared and disappeared, caregivers changed, homes changed, people were not constant or permanent. For healthy development, children need consistent, constant and permanent caregivers and environments. Typical behaviors include reliance on smells for comfort (smells provided clues to the environment) and inability to sleep (fear of what happens at night).

- **Self-regulation problems:** Research reveals that complex trauma leads to "impairment in attachment, biological functions, affect regulation, dissociation, behavioral regulation, cognition and self-concept."[13] Many of the children with whom we have worked are dysregulated in eating, sleeping, temperature regulation, elimination, energy and emotion. Typical behaviors include not knowing when to stop eating (inability to recognize "full") and wearing a coat in summer (inability to recognize "hot").

- **Sensory processing problems:** These often have their roots in early deprivation and abuse. The children may be sensory defensive and hyper-sensitive. Touch tends to be uncomfortable or scary. Food choices may be limited due to previous deprivation. Hearing may be on hyper-alert for dangerous sounds. The children may appear hyper-vigilant to environmental stimuli. Typical behaviors include rejecting mom's touch (inability to differentiate good touch from bad touch or suspicion about the other's motives) and only eating macaroni and cheese (comfort with familiar food and little past exposure to a variety of foods).

AN OPPORTUNITY FOR ATTACHMENT

Child Development and the Secure Base/Safe Haven

The Trauma Lens Paradigm Shift encourages changes in the parent's perception of the child and the child's behaviors. Parental actions and interactions must support the new paradigm. Parents must form a relationship with their children as they are now, not based on a preconceived notion of who the children should be. New positive interpersonal experiences and interactions build healthy relationships. Attachment research has found that children need a secure and dependable relationship with attuned caregivers before they can explore the unknown. Renowned developmental psychologist Mary Ainsworth depicts the attachment figure as a secure base that allows the infant or child to venture away and return to the parent.[14] Gillian Schofield and Mary Beek studied children with early trauma and found that these children have a "profound lack of trust" in the caregiver that prohibits the child from perceiving a secure base. Such children are "highly resistant to accepting or learning from new experiences of responsive and secure care giving."[15] Sheri Pickover, Clinical Director at University of Detroit Mercy Counseling Clinic, notes, "Attachment patterns become a self-fulfilling prophecy, trapping the child in a circle of despair."[16]

Intentional therapeutic parenting revolves around emotional and physical security. The child's perception of that security will ebb and flow over time. Some days the child will be more open to the security than other days. Figuratively, this secure base must be like a concrete foundation without cracks and swept clean of dust and debris. The family will not be perfect, but must be conscious of personal shortcomings and openly share their life struggles. They must "sweep" their foundation daily by discussing life's difficulties, how they resolved problems and how they managed distress. These experiences become the child's building blocks for how to handle distress, accept others' and their own imperfections and learn problem-solving skills.

The secure base includes the child experiencing the parents' taking care of all physiological, safety and relational needs. At times when the child "perceives" the parent not meeting one of these, their secure base is threatened. Trust is the first relational skill babies learn. When a baby can trust his caregivers to keep him safe, the baby is free to explore. Without this safety, a baby's exploration is restricted. Early trauma and attachment disruptions prevent healthy growth. Children with early trauma do not always know how to play or even occupy themselves without making poor behavior choices.

Amy's Family

Lori felt like she was a one-woman entertainment program. All day long, Amy demanded to be played with or occupied. When Lori ran out of ideas, she and Amy went shopping for new toys or clothing. Lori was afraid to ask Amy to play by herself, because she always got into trouble—mostly rummaging through her parents' belongings or breaking things. Amy was not developing independence or a healthy curiosity about how the world works. Evaluating Amy from a secure base/safe haven model, one would say that she did not have a secure base from which to explore.

Each new independent action supports the child's belief that "I can do it myself." Through years of exploration and returning to the secure base/safe haven, children will move through stages with mastery. In a secure base, parents are emotionally regulated and available. Emotionally-attuned parents of infants *co-regulate* with their children. Co-regulation is a corrective interpersonal and emotional experience that occurs when an infant expresses fear to the parent (cries), the parent feels the same emotion (fear), the parent calms him or herself (understands the infant's need) and then connects (soothes baby) and conveys that same calmness to the baby via words and actions (meets need). This series of events calms the infant. Healthy babies and caregivers interact similarly dozens of times a day.

Emotionally-dysregulated parents equal insecurity and fear. A dysregulated parent may not be safe or able to meet the child's needs. Parents will have emotions. As they demonstrate ways to handle their emotions, their child will learn new skills. These skills will be addressed in a later section. Treatment professionals frequently ask that children be taught to regulate their emotions. Emotional regulation cannot be cognitively taught, as cognitive information is stored in the thinking part of the brain. We all lose our ability to think when emotionally dysregulated. We all have emotional responses. Children benefit by watching their parents regulate their own emotions and thereby experiencing co-regulation.

CHAPTER 4

Creating the Healing Home with Parenting Goals and Skills

Allan excitedly opened his mail, a letter from his maternal grandmother. She rarely contacted him, but she did remember his birthday. When Allan gazed down at the card, he exclaimed, "Doesn't she know I am not a little kid?" Throwing down the card, he walked away. I tried approaching the topic throughout the day, but he always changed the subject. It felt like he was punishing us for the card. All day long I was settling fights and handing out consequences. I knew I should talk to him about his fears and sadness, but I could not force him.

Nothing provokes him enough to express his deep feelings. Even letters from his birth family don't seem to interest him. He did like the dog drawing his birth father sent. Shouldn't he want to talk about everything that has happened to him? When I told him that he can talk to me about anything, he said, "Why is it that everyone says that to me?" I have no answers.

—Faye Hall

EMOTIONAL COGNITIVE TRAUMA MODEL

Fourteen years of hard work, research, training and experimentation gave birth to the Emotional Cognitive Trauma Model (ECTM). It has changed and morphed since co-author Jeff Merkert began using storytelling to illustrate the impact of trauma on developing infant brains and internal beliefs working with client families. Over the years, Jeff has perfected the presentation and provides it to families and their support systems. We struggled with naming it. Faye gravitates to emotional work and Jeff to cognitive work; thus the name. The story links neurology, the impact of trauma on the brain and the damage created with attachment disruptions.

41

Throughout this book, parents are encouraged to see themselves as the ones who will help their child heal. The task can be overwhelming, especially for families with more than one foster or adoptive child in the home. The parents are on duty 24/7.

In this chapter, keys to success and goals are clearly defined and parents are instructed in interactive skills with their children. These are the foundations to navigate healing, without which treatment will not be successful. Please remember this is relational and emotional work, not behavioral.

Keys to Success

1. **Parents explore their own emotional and cognitive world.** Some of our most successful families are those who have explored their own history. They've done or, even better, are still doing, the hard work of examining their own fears and changing their response to them. These parents have empathy for their child and can be an encouragement as the child is challenged to do the same. Parents with a trauma history that is not explored or integrated into their narrative tend to be punitive and demeaning. Some have stated that "I got over it, why can't they?" This lack of empathy prevents co-regulation between parent and child.

2. **Parents increase or improve their self-regulation skills.** Self-regulation is needed for co-regulation and the ability to remain calm when the child has disruptive behaviors. Our own histories and upbringings leave some parents with a "short fuse" or a feeling of being easily overwhelmed. Parents need to be on their "A" game in self-regulation when interacting with traumatized children. This leaves most of us with room to grow. Fortunately, this growth actually facilitates the same growth in our children. Children with a history of abuse and neglect likely have not learned to co-regulate with their birth parent. This will be one of the first interventions that occurs with treatment. Parents will be handicapped if they cannot regulate their own emotions. Without regulation, parents can overreact to the child's behaviors and reinforce the child's N-IWM. Sadly, parents are often counseled to over-regulate their own emotions. The professional may state, "Keep yourself calm; don't communicate sadness or fear to avoid triggering your child, which causes an escalation cycle." The problem with this strategy is that observation is the primary tool for learning personal emotional regulation. Can we really expect children to learn from lecture alone without observation of our own emotional responses?

Being emotionally regulated does not mean being unemotional or flat in our expression of emotion.

3. **Parents model for their children ways to explore their emotional and cognitive world.** Parents know that their children follow the parents' model much more than their words. Children with early trauma are always watching their parents to maintain a sense of safety. This hyper-vigilance drives the child to learn from the parent's behavior, on a deep, experiential level, much more than the many lectures parents tend to give.

4. **Parents use interactive repair.** Parents are the adults in the relationship. They should model appropriate behaviors for their children. Interactive repair demonstrates how to repair relationships. Parents have to demonstrate for their children the skills they want them to use. These skills are not gained by lectures or demands. Sometimes, parents state their child was wrong and the relationship cannot be healed until the child "takes responsibility and apologizes." This stance assumes the child is reflective, evaluates the behavior as wrong and desires to repair the relationship, all of which are higher-level thinking skills and require a healthier internal working model.

5. **Parents build the environment to support the child's development of healthier affect regulation and healthier views of self, others and the world.** The environment will either support or hinder healing. The essence of parenting is simply the agreement to supply the growing environment for our children. Chapter 16 has suggestions for environment interventions.

6. **Parents recognize and label their child's fear level.** Parents learn to read their infants' internal states. Now, the task is reading a child's internal state that has grown to avoid even the perception of fear. Hurt children often take great care in keeping others from knowing their thoughts and emotions. For healing to begin, parents must recognize their child's fears and label the emotions for the child. These skills will be new to the child and may initially create more fear.

7. **Parents address the child's stress but not necessarily always the circumstance.** In some ways, addressing a healthy child's stress is easier than changing the circumstance that created the stress. Parents may go to great lengths to eliminate stressors to keep the child more regulated instead of helping the child develop new self-regulatory skills. When a parent knows the child is stressed, they can help with the stress. Not all circumstances have resolutions. Further, it is not unusual for the

child's emotions to not match the circumstances. Identify the disparity.

8. **Parents reduce the use of cognitive interventions during emotional responses.** As parents use the ECTM, they will understand the neurological impact of trauma and the brain's response to triggers. When a child has an emotional response, the brain has less ability to process or respond to cognitions.

9. **Parents label emotional states and notice the increased cognition.** As parents read and label their child's emotions and offer comfort, the child's brain may become less emotionally flooded and be freed up to have increased cognition. The goal is for the child to notice how his or her body changes with/without stress. Complex early trauma causes children to avoid feelings of fear and sadness. In the early stages of life, the baby's brain was dependent upon the caregiver's brain to facilitate moving out of "fear." If the relationship with the caregiver did not prompt this change of state, children will lack a dependable means of regulating emotions. They feel as if any small fear could wind up being overwhelming! Since they have no experience with modulating and changing emotions, they default to avoidance. Consequently, such children grow to have just two "emotions," mad and more mad! We as parents must demonstrate that first we and then they can feel fear and sadness and then stop feeling it. We all have a wide variety of tools we use to accomplish this for ourselves. It is very hard to teach these skills to little brains that have already learned to avoid those feelings as a survival skill.

10. **Parents explain what their child experiences without shame or blame.** Parent self-regulation is important with this intervention. The parent's task is to relay what is going on with the child, separate from their frustration about the problematic behaviors that may have occurred. They can use storytelling or just describe the events as if they were talking to a younger child.

11. **Parents use "helpful statements" to assist their child in internalizing a healthier sense of self.** Interventions are provided in chapters 16 and 17.

12. **Parents provide a wide range of developmental activities for their child.** Due to Trauma-Disrupted Competencies, most children with early trauma experience developmental delays. To help children mature, they must be exposed to multiple age activities. Children who have not fully mastered skills at one developmental

level will experience "gaps" in their ability to function at the next developmental level. When healing begins and the child feels security, he or she will often automatically gravitate toward activities that are not necessarily age-appropriate. These activities will become the building blocks for more "mature" activities. They should not be seen as primarily pathological.

13. **Parents accept, enjoy and parent their child at his or her developmental level.** These children need unconditional love, not relationships based on academic success, appearance or skills. Their egocentric nature causes them to blame themselves for removal from their birth family and changes in placements. Even when children deny it, there is no motivational substitute for parental attention. They will always grow in the direction of our attention. It can be extremely difficult to find and enjoy the small, fearfully hidden positive elements of traumatized children. Our attention that nurtures their growth may require a very strange skill set to enjoy playing with building blocks with a nineteen-year-old or a twelve-year-old sitting with mom reading a picture book. But these activities are often just what the child needs to facilitate acquisition of previously un-mastered skills. The new skills in turn allow for eventual mastery of chronological age skills.

TREATMENT GOALS

As with any model, success is dependent on the participants. We have established goals that can be measured (useful in treatment planning) and explain what needs to be accomplished during the process. Goals are dependent upon the number of times the parent uses components of the ECTM.

1. To explain confusing emotional reactions. This reduces a child's feelings of shame.
2. To explain the source of the emotions driving a child's behavior.
3. To reorganize and redirect the familial system's efforts at recovery from an external focus (to change others) toward an internal focus (how I can change).
4. To illustrate that the child is not "sick" or "bad," but has a hurt part, a part that learned not to trust others, that the child is unlovable and the world is dangerous.
5. To increase internal reflection for parents and children by the application of an alternate and more accurate assessment of their own emotional world as the motivational source for their actions.

6. To interpret present emotions and behaviors and link them to past events.
7. To predict emotional responses to future events.
8. To base personal responsibility and accomplishment on something other than immediate change in the child's behavior.
9. To reduce parental interpretations of malice as the origin of children's behaviors.
10. To increase parents' healthy trauma-informed behavioral expectations for their children, the verbal and non-verbal expressions of which will build the child's self-image.

PARENT SKILLS

Now, let's get to work and define skills that parents will use every day, many times a day, to connect with their children. Parents of infants "help keep arousal within manageable bounds but also help infants develop their own ability to regulate arousal."[17] These children are lacking in such experiences and in the relationships that create the experiences. They may now be relationship avoidant and extra skills must be learned and used to form trusting relationships and manage stimulation. We will give examples and encourage parents to follow the examples. These skills are not limited to the parents. Anyone in the village who supports the family or treatment will find them valuable. As with all interventions, no one will be perfect, but rest assured the child will repeat the behaviors that allow you to try again and again, until you perfect the interaction.

Parenting is time consuming and exhausting. Slow down and be more mindful. One must be intentional and mindful of emotional reactions to the child's disruptive behaviors. Being intentional will help parents prioritize the values and beliefs they want to reinforce. This allows parents to pay attention to their internal experiences, sooth their own anxiety and inhibit negative responses. The resulting increased cognition allows the parents to control their emotions and stop trying to control the child. When parents are more mindful and calm, they are open to reading the child's cues and expressing empathy. As we will cover in the following section, empathy helps the child feel heard and builds the parent/child relationship.

Corey's Family

Corey stomped into the therapist's office with a scowl on his face. His anger was obvious. The therapist asked Corey to find the emotion he was feeling on the emotional chart hanging on the wall. Corey glared at the thirty different emotional faces staring back at him. He mumbled, stammered and declared, "frustrated, no frightened, no irritated." The therapist inquired about his irritation. After ten minutes of traveling down a dead-end therapy road, the therapist asked him to try again. Mom watched impatiently. Time was ticking away, again. Like always, session time was being wasted.

Due to children's inability to identify and express their emotions and become vulnerable with parents and treatment staff, our model builds on the foundation of four emotions: happy, mad (angry), sad and scared (fear). The limited number allows parents to remain focused on using specific emotions and reduces the children's avoidance of acknowledging their internal distress. Anger is viewed as a secondary emotion, spurred by sadness or fear. Therefore, when one declares he or she is angry, they are challenged to find the underlying emotion of sadness or fear. A sort of "micro-focus" occurs then, linking the trigger to the underlying emotion more quickly.

KEYS TO CO-REGULATION

According to Bessel Van der Kolk, a clinician, researcher and teacher in the area of posttraumatic stress, "When a baby is in sync with his caregiver, his sense of joy and connection is reflected in his steady heartbeat and breathing and a low level of stress hormones."[18]

This is co-regulation at the infant level and occurs infinite times during infancy and toddlerhood. Unfortunately, most traumatized children missed these vital interactions, which equip the child with the knowledge that "intense sensations with safety, comfort and mastery are the foundation of self-regulation, self-soothing and self-nurture."[19] We have devoted this section to teaching similar skills that will reproduce this connection. We will explore and learn **affect matching, emotional regulation, empathy** and **narration.**

AFFECT MATCHING

According to parenting and relationship authorities Marion Solomon and Daniel Siegel, "Within episodes of **affect synchrony** parents engage in intuitive, nonconscious, facial, vocal and gestural preverbal communications."[20]

- Attunes to child's emotions, matches affect with empathy and co-regulates
- Identifies and labels child's emotions
- Narrates the environment for the child
- Remains in close proximity to the child, especially when the child is dysregulated
- Provides comfort if needed[21]

During parent/infant interactions, parents respond frequently to their child's bids for connection through sounds, facial movements and gestures. These interactions are reciprocal and predictable, creating multiple pleasurable experiences for both parent and child. Babies learn to turn away when over-stimulated. Each learns to read each other's signals. Just like Goldilocks and the three bears, parents learn how much interaction is "just right."

Children with histories of early trauma and attachment disruptions may lack pleasurable and reciprocal interactions with their previous caregivers. Even worse, the child may have experienced maladaptive or traumatizing responses from previous attempts to connect to primary caregivers. These children become neurologically wired to avoid parent/child interactions. Parents of foster and adoptive children are challenged to provide new experiences that replicate and/or correct parent/infant interactions via matching affect and co-regulation.

A parent's face mirrors the child's experience: "Then her face is an 'accurate enough' mirror of the baby's state" and "not being mirrored reduces the felt experience of the world-making sense of the infant's inner states."[22] Parents of foster and adoptive children have the opportunity to provide new experiences that replicate the parent/infant interactions via matching affect. When matching the child's affect, the attuned parent allows the child to "feel heard."

Let's pause and examine "feeling heard." It's common for parents to report that their children state that no one listens to them and they "do not have a voice." Some parents blame therapists for giving them these words, because the parents do listen to their children. By examining the child's history you will find clues about why the child does not feel heard. Most likely, the child was abused and neglected without any way to make adults stop, removed from the birth family without being asked, forced to change placements when case workers or foster families requested it and even asked "do you want to be adopted by this family?" knowing he or she may never have another chance for a family. Yes, these children experience "not having a voice." Matching affect will help the child overcome not being heard.

Examples of Matching Affect

1. If your child is happy when arriving home, parents express happiness.

   •   "I am really happy that you are home safely."

2. If your child is mad when arriving home from school, because of not having his homework completed, causing him to miss recess, parents match the emotion of missing recess.

   "I know what missing recess is like and it's no fun!"

3. If your child is sad because her friend will not talk to her, parents should match and act as if a friend would not speak to them.

    "I hate it when good friends don't talk to me too."

4. If your child is bored with nothing to do on a summer day, parents should match and speak about their own memories of being frightened of having nothing to do.

    "I wouldn't like being bored at any time,
    much less on a nice summer day."

CO-REGULATION

1. Humans share emotions! This is unavoidable. The emotional parts of the brain (like the deep limbic system and the prefrontal cortex) are designed to communicate together.
2. Dysregulated brains demand support whether calm or when escalated. A dysregulated brain cannot remain at the peak of dysregulation indefinitely.
3. Children emotionally co-regulate with an adult before learning to self-regulate. Emotional co-regulation is the responsibility of the adult brain. Emotional co-regulation is habitual, often accomplished without cognition.
4. Parents match their child's affect to begin the co-regulating process, then calm themselves and calm the child via the parent's own self-regulating efforts.
5. Children crave to be understood via sharing emotions with their primary caregivers.
6. Anger is an emotional coping strategy for fear and sadness.
7. Parents narrate the world for their children to help them make sense of the world, thereby enabling them to manage greater emotional regulation.

EMOTIONAL SELF-REGULATION

The parent...

1. Identifies and labels own emotions
2. Regulates own emotions
3. Models and communicates modulation skills
4. Models range of emotions

Examples of Co-Regulation

1. **Parents model expressing emotional distress and how they handled it**, referring to "parts" of themselves ("Part of me felt..."), identifying their fear and/or sadness beneath their anger:
   a. "I was driving home tonight and a truck pulled out in front of me. Boy, was I scared! I honked my horn. Then I calmed down, because everything was okay."
   b. "When your dad came in and yelled for me to get him a sandwich, I got really irritated. Then I remembered he forgot his lunch today. He apologized for yelling after he ate."
   c. "I was very angry with your dad when he yelled at me. Looking back, I was afraid he didn't like me. I guess I was so afraid, I couldn't handle it, so I got mad instead. Good thing that didn't last forever!"

2. **Parents notice and label in child's emotion the relationship between fear, sadness, anger and the parts of the child.** Parents provide as much information as child is able to emotionally maintain:
   a. "I noticed that you seem tense, your arms are crossed and you have lines on your forehead. I am wondering if you are angry that you cannot go outside?"
   b. "Your eyes are so stormy. I was wondering if your 'mad' is really 'sad,' because you have to go to bed early tonight?"
   c. "There is a part of you that is really afraid of adult rules. I bet it's getting pretty mad right now!"

3. **Parents encourage their child to begin talking about their emotions by expressing curiosity about how the child feels:**
   a. "I was wondering about you not talking at dinner tonight. Anything happening?"
   b. "You were yelling so loud tonight, I couldn't understand what was going on. Any ideas?"
   c. "You are stomping again. Does that mean you are mad?"

4. **Parents link behaviors to child's history and emotional state:**
   a. "I am guessing that you learned to yell at your birth mom to get you food when she was drinking and that is why you yell at me when you get hungry. Maybe, even, you may be scared that you won't get food."
   b. "There is a part of you that learned it's better to be mad than scared. I bet it helped you in the past. But is there really anything to be afraid of here? I'm on your side."

c. "It's really tough doing a job with that old part feeling so scared and turning it into anger! It probably tells you stuff like 'It's too hard' or 'She'll just add more jobs when this one's done.' But I know you can help that part heal. Give it a new experience…one of getting what you want by working with me."

EMPATHY

Empathy stimulates the "thinking" part of the child's brain and conveys:

1. You sincerely care about this child.
2. You understand this child's struggles.
3. You are this child's emotional coach.
4. You are on this child's side.
5. You want the best for this child.
6. You have confidence in this child's choices.
7. You know that this child will learn from his/her choice.
8. This child's behavior is his/her problem.

Examples of empathic statements while matching your child's affect

1. If your child is happy when arriving home from school, a parent's similar emotion would be happy to have your child safely home. Offer to share tales of your day during snack time.
2. If your child is mad when coming home from school, because of not having homework completed and missing recess, you can match the emotion with empathy by saying, "Oh, no! Missing recess is no fun! You need a hug!"
3. If your child is sad, because her friend would not talk to her, you can match the emotion with empathy by saying; "Oh, dear! She was such a good friend. Come let me cuddle you."
4. If your child is bored with nothing to do on a summer day, you can match them with empathy by saying; "Wow, nothing to do! Such a luxury. I know how you feel; I can only stand so much of that myself!" Then you can transition to, "What are you going to do about it? How can I help?"

NARRATION

When babies are born, parents talk to them about everything. After the delivery, Mom and Dad describe all the things the baby experienced and how happy they are to finally meet their new son or daughter. They tell the infant about the grandparents who will visit shortly. They tell the baby they like the baby's hair, smile, fingers and toes. They tell the baby that he or she is hungry or needs a nap after the long birthing process. As the infant becomes a toddler, the parents continue describing life for the child. They tell the child that lunch will be soon, that naptime is over, that it's bath time and the child enjoys baths. They tell the child when he or she is cold and how they will take care of the cold. It's a never-ending process of helping children understand how the world works and their place in the world.

Now imagine an infant left in a crib for hours with no one or nothing to do. Imagine a toddler, sitting in a high chair or crawling around in a play-pen while adults are using drugs. What words are these children hearing that will help them understand the world and their place in it? These are the children with early trauma. Foster and adoptive parents are given a great responsibility to help these children learn about the world. By narrating the world, parents use word pictures to develop insight and understanding in children.

Examples of narrating the environment

1. **Categorize:** Parents can categorize the world by putting persons, places and things into "boxes" to make sense of the past, present and future:

   a. "Over the years, people have let you down and disappointed you. Are you thinking I will be one of those since I didn't make breakfast this morning?"

   b. "People just frustrate me. Sometimes, you cannot predict what they are going to do or say or even if they will follow through with projects. You may have noticed I am having problems with the people at work lately. I get short tempered when I am scared."

   c. "I doubt people, because of the bad things that happened to me in the past. Sometimes it's hard for me to trust anyone."

   d. "Here we go again; it seems like I just finished this chore and I have to do it again. I know there was a whole day in between, but it feels like all I do is chores."

2. **Link emotions, behaviors and thoughts to other events.**

   a. "I noticed that you got angry today at lunch. Was it because you thought you would not get a soda? I was wondering if you were scared that I would not let you have things you like?"

b. "I dread calling the repairman. Last time when they fixed the car, it broke again after a few days. I never know what to expect anymore. Now I'm avoiding the call. Your dad will be disappointed if I end up avoiding it all day."

3. **Imagine: "Painting" pictures of events, with sensory descriptions**
   a. "Just think, the park has so many slides, wonder if you will go down the little yellow one before the long green one? Or will you swing first? You really like to go high on those swings."
   b. "Homework! Reading and writing, when you would rather be playing outside in the sun."

4. **Steps: sequential ordering of events**
   a. "We will have three stops today: two errands for dad and then lunch."
   b. "You will need to do four things to get ready."

5. **Emotions: projecting onto self and others emotions that have or may occur**
   a. "You may be saying 'I don't want to go' because errands are not fun, but then the other part says, 'Yeah, lunch at my favorite burger place!' So many things happening in your head."
   b. "I was thinking that you might want a snack before helping with the chores. I always liked it when mom and I had a snack before cleaning."

6. **Choices: descriptions of choices the child had during the events (offering opportunities for reflectivity)**
   a. "Did you notice? At the park, you were able to choose what you played on first. I noticed you slid down all the slides before swinging. At lunch, you picked apples instead of fries. You worked hard today!"
   b. "Yesterday, when we had a snack, you did not know if you wanted popcorn or an apple. What do you think you want today?"

MODELING

Learning is experiential and modeled. Most likely early trauma was experienced by the child and perpetrated by caregivers during their earliest developmental stages. These children may have experienced horrific abuse, severe physical neglect and the absence of vital, caring relationships. Their caregivers may have modeled drug use, domestic violence, fleeing from authorities, indiscriminate relationships, poor financial management and lack of proper hygiene.

These behaviors may have been necessary in the child's past to survive or provide comforting sensory input. The smell of urine may be reassuring when sitting in a dirty crib for hours. The sight of a policeman may incite children to flee, because of their dad's need to run from the police. The feel of a toothbrush against their teeth may cause pain because they did not brush their teeth while with their birth family. Wearing socks may irritate their feet. Hearing dad's car in the driveway may spur them to hide, because their dad was so dangerous. Their world *is* different from ours. Their emotions and memories are connected to emotionally-charged stimuli.

Parents and professionals desire to change these behaviors as soon as possible. The first thing some parents ask the child is, "Why do you do these things?" The child may not have the cognitive abilities to explain "why" or trust the adults enough to communicate his distress. To change these behaviors, parents can model appropriate behaviors while adding the narrative. Because the child is only slowly adaptive, the change will probably not be as quick as desired. Keep in mind your child's emotional age. Model what you want your child to learn. If you want your child to wear a coat, you must wear a coat.

Example of Modeling

The narrative for modeling is "I wear a coat to keep warm when the temperature is cold." Other narratives are: "You look cold. I wear a coat when I am cold" and "You are shivering; I wonder if you are cold." Be careful: The child will probably deny being cold. Do not get caught in a control battle over the issue.

Each desired behavior change begins with parental modeling. The parents want their children to be respectful, have appropriate responses, care for possessions, display a loving attitude, etc. The responsibility falls on the parents to model each of these behaviors; i.e., respect for mom is modeled by dad. The children are always watching. Parents must model all skills they want their children to learn including: how to play, how to eat, what clothing to wear, how to sit quietly to read a book or listen to music, how to care for oneself and how to participate in a hobby. Even though your child may be twelve (or eighteen or eight), the emotional age may be much younger. Interactions must project patience and care as one would if the child was a toddler.

In chapter 17 you will find a detailed presentation of key principles for affect matching, empathy, modeling and narration. We have included useful exercises for developing these skills.

PART 2

The Team and the Environment

CHAPTER 5

Assembling the Team

During my frequent Internet searches I located a group of therapists in an adjacent county who offered treatment for Reactive Attachment Disorder. Maybe there was help! I quickly contacted the practice and scheduled an intake session. I was flooded with incomprehensible relief. I imagined that this is what it must feel like to have a rare disease for which treatment is finally discovered and offered. Looking back, I believe my greatest source of relief, though, was in feeling that we were no longer in this alone. A team was being organized!

—Faye Hall

In addressing the needs of the traumatized child and his or her parents, the team greatly enhances the probability of success by providing a cohesive, intentionally therapeutic environment. This affords more physical and emotional safety for everyone. Intentional therapeutic parenting is very hard work. Parents of children with attachment disorders do not get a pass on their other responsibilities, as wives, husbands, daughters, sons, employees or employers, neighbors or church or synagogue members. They need plenty of support and encouragement through words and actions. Sometimes they will need a hand to hold or a shoulder to cry on. Sometimes they will need someone with whom to celebrate successes. Sometimes they will just need someone to listen.

They will need professional respite providers, case managers, therapists and special educational staff. Parents must surround themselves with a team of family, friends and professionals. The team must be properly educated regarding the effects of early trauma, must have open and frequent communication, must coordinate interventions and must use common language and strategies.

As parents begin the Trauma Lens Paradigm Shift, the team is vital. Some families already have a team in place, because their children are or were in foster care. Others may be isolated with no support, out of a need to avoid being judged or viewed as incapable.

The team will challenge the child's old beliefs, stop the child's triangulation of others and consistently identify the child's problems as his or her own without blaming the child. The team can assist in locating services (including respite), arrange for meetings, assist in collaboration and provide educational resources. Team members can be very helpful in attending meetings with the parents. They provide professional and moral support and identify problems and strategies. Parents are less likely to feel intimidated when accompanied by trusted helpers.

Corey's Family

Corey stole his teacher's cell phone. Standard punishment was detention in a room near the office with secretarial staff observing him from a distance. Rebecca tried to get the school staff to understand that Corey should not be isolated for punishment. She arranged a meeting between Corey's foster care caseworker and the school staff. The caseworker was good at explaining the impact of trauma on Corey and how scared he was when he was alone. The school staff needed to be educated to see that fear would not motivate Corey to change his behavior, but instead reinforce his belief that adults were cruel and scary.

If the family is open to the idea, a team member may participate in or observe therapy sessions. Another person present at the session may remember the points discussed, help in reinterpreting the child and parents' behaviors and help to design and apply interventions to reinforce the therapy. In the team approach, there is no time or place for a secret keeper. In the past the child may have hidden from the truth because it was too painful. Now, the truth is shared with discretion and love. The integrity of the child must be maintained to build a healthy sense of self. Disrespect and criticism must be eliminated.

A unified team provides the family and child with the environment, energy and opportunities to heal. The team members' trauma education must take place before interacting with the child, so that they are able to make the paradigm shift necessary to effectively engage the child and family. Without this shift more harm could be perpetrated, exacerbating rather than removing barriers to healing. By the way, team composition is limited only by the imagination: teachers, lunchroom assistants, scout leaders, neighbors, grandparents and/or other extended family members, friends, coaches, school bus drivers, respite workers, mental health professionals and pediatricians can all be team members.

QUALITIES OF AN EFFECTIVE TEAM

Sometimes teams are assembled quickly. A successful team will be able to identify the strengths and accept the limitations of the various members for the common good of the child and family. Healthy attitudes, enthusiasm for problem solving and liberal brainstorming for creative ideas are hallmarks of an effective team. Frequent open communication among team members is essential.

An effective team will develop and utilize appropriate resources to facilitate individualized interventions. Sometimes the interventions are not typical of "normal" life and may need to be practiced and role-played for maximum effectiveness.

A team's effectiveness also increases if members accept each other as equals, share information openly, distribute responsibility appropriately among team members and avoid pride and pessimism. While parents seek team members who will be uplifting and eager problem solvers, professionals and other team members will appreciate parents who display similar qualities. Complaining does not motivate the team to work harder. We have often seen that team members are prone to withdrawing contact from negative or pessimistic parents. They may even align with the "poor child stuck in this family."

HANDLING PROBLEMS IN THE TEAM "DYNAMIC"

Pessimistic parents: When parents are discouraged and tired, they may be looking for a way to end the turmoil of the Downward Spiral and have the child placed back in foster care. Other parents may be seeking out-of-home treatment in the name of finding rest and relief. These parents may feel hopeless and helpless and be dismissive of interventions. They may even resent their child's cooperation with other team members. To confront this problem, it is even more urgent to guide the parents toward the Trauma Lens Paradigm Shift, while offering respite and reframing the child's behaviors through the trauma lens.

Lack of training: Team members are instrumental in keeping the family and child safe, projecting healthy beliefs and preventing the recapitulation of the child's N-IWM. Sometimes children have disruptive behaviors, because of a fracture in the team. An uninformed or less-trained team member can inadvertently promote disruptive behaviors. When examining the child's behavior, be mindful of the possibility of problems in the team dynamic: new team members, members who have not had recent communication with the team or members who overly sympathize with the child. If a team member lacks the education to be effective, proper resources must be made available promptly. Educating the team may be as uncomplicated as informing a teacher regarding which interventions are most likely to work or informing Grandma regarding ways she can help during an overnight stay.

Making a mistake: Draw upon healthy group dynamics when confronting a team member who has made a mistake. Confrontation is inherently somewhat painful, as is admitting a mistake. Here Dan Hughes' acronym *PACE* comes into play. That is, when the confrontation is done with Playfulness, Acceptance, Curiosity and Empathy, the "processing" of the mistake can actually promote greater team cohesion.[23] When the group uses PACE to address a problematic behavior or a mistake, they are able to learn more, because there is no evaluation or judgment. PACE prevents defensiveness. With empathy, the outreach to the erring team member can include a reminder that no team member nor any parent is perfect. Everyone will be challenged by these children—even the most seasoned professional. Sometimes it is helpful to offer resources to the member and sometimes it is necessary to bring in another professional to intervene. A divided team will be ineffective at best. Partnerships with caring collaboration will provide a healthy environment for the child's healing.

Not using team members: Many times families do not trust professionals sufficiently to assemble a team. They may have been previously judged and criticized. They may fear that their child will hurt team members. They may doubt the therapeutic potential of team members. When these fears are legitimate, they can be confronted by special arrangements, such as safety plans. Again, an empathic understanding of the parents' dilemma may set the stage for introduction of educational resources, including the Trauma Lens Paradigm Shift.

Taking advantage of family and friends: Parents may forget to be thankful and reciprocal to those who volunteer to help. Thank you notes and offers to exchange "good deeds" will be appreciated and encourage others to stay involved. Thank you notes to professionals validate the hard work they are doing. When parents write thank you notes, they will naturally reflect on successes achieved by the team, including themselves, and thus become "self-encouraged."

ROLES AND BOUNDARIES
WITH PROFESSIONALS

When the family begins working with a new team or team member, clearly defined expectations and responsibilities must be determined at the outset. State regulations and agency policies offer guidelines for mental health professionals and should be used to meld the team function to the needs of the family.

Parents often feel great gratitude for a job well done. They may seek any opportunity to express their thankfulness. Agency policy will set the boundaries, but parents will sometimes struggle to find ways of expressing gratitude within those boundaries.

Primary caregivers in particular will feel like "targets" of their children. Mothers feel drained between trying to parent the disruptive child while fulfilling their other responsibilities as wife, daughter, neighbor and employee and at the same time advocating with agencies and schools. In the natural balancing of these roles, we all temporarily give more effort to areas of our life that are currently producing the most pressing problems: "The squeaky wheel gets the grease." However, this natural balancing skill, left unchecked, becomes a liability when the squeaky wheel never stops squeaking. Feeling powerless, she will naturally look to others for a source of power. The professional may look like a knight in shining armor coming to her rescue.

Firm boundaries prevent emotional over-involvement, misuse of power and over-dependency of parents. Maintaining a therapeutic relationship involves pointing out the parents' power and ability to control the environment. They must understand that they cannot physically control the child, unless the child is small enough to safely physically control. That period in a child's life is really quite brief. But most parents work with the delusion that that period is much longer than it actually is. In the parenting of a typical child this delusion works to the extent that it allows our nonverbal communication to be much more persuasive. This delusion can have very dangerous repercussions when striving to parent a child with early trauma. However, parents can control themselves and the home environment and that will help the child. Team members, even professionals, can sometimes foster this delusion of physical control of the child. This leads parents to lose focus on where their true power lies. If the parents have abdicated power or had their power removed by a system of critical, judgmental service providers, they need help to regain their sense of power.

Respite services are a good example of providing extra help for the parents without obscuring boundaries. Good respite systems reinforce the parents' authority with their child. Respite families clearly define themselves as team members serving a carefully defined role, which is *not* substitute parenting, but instead temporary relief and rest for the child and parents during their arduous journey toward healing.

Professionals must be aware of personal emotional "triggers" throughout the team process. Unresolved past traumas, attachment issues or relationship difficulties will surface during interventions with the traumatized child. Even without these lingering personal matters, facilitating the recovery of a child with early trauma and attachment disruptions can be extremely discomforting at times. Unresolved personal emotional issues can make this impossibly discomforting. Sometimes these personal issues can be dealt with by frank team discussions, but they may instead require some reflection with an individual therapist.

Above all, the professional must develop the ability to "leave the case behind" at the end of the day. This is not the same as being emotionally unaffected or empathically shielded from the child and family. Instead, professionals should think of disengaging temporarily from their work for the very purpose of resuming it the following day, refreshed and rested, ready to be more helpful to the family than ever.

SPECIFIC TEAM MEMBERS

Therapist: The first professional team member should be the family therapist. The perfect therapist will have a background in child development, developmental trauma, grief and loss, attachment, domestic violence and addictions and a familiarity with the fundamental principles of social work. Unfortunately, the perfect therapist is as available as the perfect parent. Nevertheless, social work educators Stephen Erich and Patrick Leung recommend that therapists at minimum be trained in the psychodynamics of attachment and childhood trauma in order to be able to assist the parents with knowledge and skills for effective behavioral strategies.[24]

Parents should pursue clinicians with advanced training in trauma and attachment. Treatment goals and a treatment plan will be formulated. Subsequent sessions will pursue the identified goals. Since the child's behaviors may be quite dangerous or fear-inducing, parents may ask that the first goal be to help the child to stop disruptive behaviors. Nicole Cox found that professionals working with the child to improve behavior might not improve the parent-child relationship. "Improvements" may be fleeting if the treatment plan is behavior-focused.[25]

Other parents ask therapists to help their children to develop coping skills to manage anger, so that they will stop harming themselves or others or damaging property. Of course, safety is always paramount. But outpatient therapists are limited in their ability to affect safety outside their office. Other team members may be assigned to help with this goal.

Yet another treatment goal parents ask for is teaching the child to use new coping skills as a substitute for aggression and dangerous behavior. This too can lead to parental disappointment. Remember that parents expect their child to develop skills that can be used when he is dysregulated.

They want their child to realize when emotions are becoming too intense, to then shut down the emotion, open his "toolbox" of skills for an alternative activity such as listening to music or taking a walk and continue that activity until calm! When the parents reflect on their own anger management skills, they may notice that their brains don't shift easily from anger to a replacement activity. Imagine driving your car and seeing a policeman in your rearview mirror with lights flashing and siren screaming. One does not quickly shift from the fear response to a replacement activity. In short, these coping skills are not accessible under heightened emotional stress. We will discuss later how "scaffolded practice" and enhanced cognitive awareness are employed to empower the use of coping skills.

Therapy for a child with early trauma must be "dyadic" (i.e., focused on one-on-one relationship dynamics) and relational, as opposed to a focus on behavior management training. Because of their child's relentless disruptive behavior, parents may develop indwelling anger and resentment toward the child and consequently withdraw from the child. Thus, the parents themselves become traumatized by the child as well as by society's harsh critique of their parenting "failures."

Therapy red flags:

- Traumatized foster and adoptive children may not have access to the same therapist for long-term treatment, because of frequent moves and changes in their health insurance status. But treatment is built on a trusting relationship. These children are already untrusting of their foster and adoptive parents to meet their daily needs. How can they confide their most scary life events to a stranger? And if they do allow themselves to trust the therapist enough to share deep, hurtful feelings only to have the therapist leave, what are the chances that they will allow themselves to be vulnerable with a therapist again? Before the child is introduced to a therapist, reasonable expectations for long-term availability should be established and any residue from prior losses of therapists recognized and accounted for. Therapists and others involved in the treatment should never lose sight that true long-term healing will be done primarily within the parent/child relationship.

- Therapists may blame parents for the child's problems. Educational psychologists Michael J. Scheel and Traci Rieckmann found that some parents feel inferior to the experts working with their child.[26] They perceive that the experts appear to have more success with their children, setting up a competition between parent and therapist.[27] Scheel and Rieckmann noted that these parents may be hesitant to interact with the treatment team or be proactive in the treatment. Cox validated the findings by describing a "custody battle of therapy."[28] If the child is participating in individual therapy sessions, a relationship with the therapist may exclude building relationships with the parents who, after all, are the "forever family."

- The therapist may not have sufficient boundaries or training to work with this population of children. As we have noted, these children may be superficially charming and engaging, with many subtle survival skills. Some have histories of charming neighbors for food, manipulating teachers for lunch or clothing and lying or stealing to obtain food or escape danger. They can be masters of avoidance. Therapy requires children to become self-aware of their problems and that they need to be addressed. They must see the therapist as someone who can help and not as one who can either be duped or totally mistrusted with vulnerable feelings.

- Working with a child in the isolation of a therapist's office may prevent healthy attachment from occurring with the parents, rather than encouraging it. A superficially charming and engaging child may appear problem-free as she describes a mean parent who withholds necessities. Unwittingly, the therapist may support the child's N-IWM, believing the notion that the parents are abusive. Families are systems and children are part of the system. If parents are not involved, vital members of the system are ignored. Lasting change then may not occur. Real family life issues must be addressed and resolved. The individual receives treatment, but the system that created the problem (the birth family) or the system that is currently trying to parent (the foster/adoptive family) are not taken into account in the treatment.

ALLIED MENTAL HEALTH PROFESSIONALS

Parenting a relationship-avoidant child with a past of severe abuse and neglect is an all-consuming task. The stress of loving one whose goal seems to be to stay unloved begins to overwhelm the family. Some states have professionals to assist the family. For example, in Pennsylvania, families can gain access to two-clinician teams formally referred to as Family-Based Mental Health Services (FBMHS). These teams are to collaborate with the family to design and implement the necessary treatment plan and strategies. These relationally-focused efforts, when done properly, facilitate a caregiver relationship in which attachment-disordered children can heal. Realistic therapeutic goals are attainable when coordinated by well-educated team members. It is imperative that the team be educated in child trauma, so that every member understands the nature, symptoms and treatment. As the members become educated, each will realize how emotionally (and sometimes physically) dangerous and difficult it is to live with a child with attachment issues.

The effective FBMHS team reviews the treatment plan frequently and revises goals and methods accordingly. It often appears that these children have defective cause-and-effect thinking, when in reality what is manifest is the effect of a N-IWM. This enables the child to feel more comfortable with negative results than with positive success—thus, the appearance of a cause-effect thinking disability. These teams also need to be mindful of the constant lapsing into a power struggle between parent and child. Valuable time can be lost if the day is spent in a battle for control.

Working closely with the mother is particularly vital. She is usually both the primary target of the child's disruptive behavior and the one to whom the child needs to attach. Her emotional and physical health must be guarded. Otherwise, her ability to transform the relationship will diminish. A "tag team" approach is routinely facilitated by the FBMHS team, who also assist the family in providing a safe and nurturing atmosphere. This helps to eliminate dangerous acting-out behavior that otherwise would necessitate more extreme and restrictive treatment measures. In sheer economic terms, many tax dollars are saved if the child does not end up in prison, a psychiatric hospital or homeless. Healing will enable the child to become a productive member of society.

Sally's Family

Jane never had time to find a support system. She regretted that she never married; that would have allowed for at least an evening tag-team. She relied on a paid babysitter and professionals to support her, but they did not work evenings. After years of struggling on her own, Jane was determined to begin building a team. She started with a local adoption support group, where she found another single parent, Dave. They met to brainstorm ideas. Jane's church had a teen group on Wednesday nights. Dave and Jane met with the group leader and explained their children's behaviors. The leader assured them that the group was well-supervised and could manage those behaviors. Jane allowed Sally to attend the group. Dave offered to keep Sally every other Friday night while Jane went out with friends. Jane returned the favor. They shared resources, helped during crises and supported each other in meetings with school staff. When they shared their success with the adoption support group, others offered to exchange assistance. They developed a list of what parents offered and what they needed and set up a "barter" system.

SUPPORT GROUPS

Talking to other parents who have a child with attachment issues and early trauma gives validation to parental frustrations, as well as information on the difficulties one may encounter in parenting and treatment. Parents need to "normalize" their experiences. Sometimes parents with traumatized children report that the typical parent does not understand their family. These parents then get "good advice" on how to parent their child. This lack of understanding and empathy leads to isolation and disconnection from others.

We advise parents and clinicians to check for foster and adoptive support groups, local mental health support groups and trainings. Increasingly, faith-based agencies are becoming involved in the foster and adoptive process via sponsored support groups. Some families find support through internet sites: blogs, chat rooms, message boards and resources. The "surfer" must use caution when using on-line resources, as must the parent attending a support group. Groups or websites that focus on recounting negative behaviors will further drain energy and morale from parents. Also, parents are at risk for beginning to anticipate in their own children the dreadful behavioral escapades they read about on-line or hear about at group. Thus, they slip into a mode of "waiting for the next shoe to drop," hyper-alert and fearful. Sound familiar? This perfectly mirrors the child's N-IWM. They cannot enjoy the present without fearing the future. Encouragement, useful tools, resources and interventions are what parents should look for in order to keep up their morale and continue their healing work.

EDUCATION

Trauma and attachment research has only begun to flourish in the relatively recent past and remains underemphasized and underutilized in graduate medical and mental health training programs. Therefore, parents continue to find professionals who are only vaguely aware of the impact of early developmental trauma and its effect on attachment disruptions. Parents may come across as "stubborn and overly focused on pushing an agenda" when asking professionals whether they are educated in their child's disorder. But after all, professionals are obligated to provide the most effective treatment possible to meet the child's needs. Thus it is not unreasonable for parents to ask professionals about their training and treatment methodology.

Sometimes professionals delay or even refuse to read the child's history, with the idea that they do not want to prejudice themselves against the child. So they develop an understanding of the child devoid of the critically important early developmental background. This is a set-up for the development of simplistic, futile behavior modification approaches lacking a relationship focus. Knowing the child's history, the informed professional will be able to identify the child's preoccupying need for control, the triggers of that need, the conditions under which the child can be safely maintained and other safety concerns.

With sufficient education, team members can avoid shaming the child. A professional who lacks understanding may create a behavior chart with a reward system that is shaming when the child fails to comply. Further, some professionals insist on reviewing the child's success or failure with the charts in the child's presence. With awareness of the N-IWM, though, the professional will understand the futility of reward systems and will understand why the child gets a feeling of empowerment and control by defeating the system.

Teams can access or develop a small library of resources or a bibliography of resources in print and online. These can then be readily available as new members join the team. This shared body of resources furthers the "team-ness" by helping all team members to speak a common language and share a common theoretical basis for their work.

Sally's Family

Jane began a lending library at their support group by donating her extra books. Other families followed her lead. Now families were not just bartering for services, but also had resources to offer those outside the group. Dave's son had a new caseworker who lacked education in trauma. Dave invited her to the group. This very vocal group was happy to share their experiences and give her a short lecture on trauma and the impact on the child and family. The caseworker left the meeting with more insight and a trove of resources with which to deepen her understanding.

VALUE AND REFRAMES

The team can support the family in many different ways. Just by directing the child back to the parent instead of directly meeting the child's needs is therapeutic. Validating the child's worth and the parents' trustworthiness and narrating the environment are therapeutic interventions that are healing. Team members can have at the ready these repeated messages for the child:

- You are safe.
- You are lovable.
- These parents love you.
- These parents can be trusted.
- As a baby, your needs were not met, which created unhealthy parts that are causing you to make poor decisions.
- The unhealthy parts make it hard to have fun with you.
- The healthy parts make it fun to be with you.
- You can overcome those parts that are causing you trouble.
- You are strengthening the healthy parts and staying out of trouble.
- The unhealthy parts can develop and grow to match your other abilities, so that you can have a happy life.
- Your healthy parts are developing and growing; it is so much fun to watch you grow up!

You will find handouts in chapter 15 regarding these team topics: Team Responsibilities, Team Cautions, Working With Professionals Diplomatically, Interagency Team Meetings, Service Flow and Records.

CHAPTER 6

The Healing Embrace of the Child and Family

Humans tend to use old models to accomplish new goals. Change evokes fear and must be marketed and sold. Without buy-in and a means to sustain change, it will not occur or last. This book offers a fresh look at the community that surrounds foster and adoptive families: their "village." This fresh look is through the Trauma Lens.

Time is of the essence. The villagers must act quickly to learn new skills. According to *Adoption.com*, "Professionals have expressed concern that recent public and private initiatives to increase adoptions and decrease time to adoption might lead to inadequate selection and preparation of adoptive homes."[29] Without adequate preparation, the parents may begin a Downward Spiral as they institute "normal" parenting techniques. This Downward Spiral perpetuates ever more disruptive behaviors.

Parents facing a future of living with a child who has dangerous and frightening behaviors have few options to address the issues. Recently, NBC/Reuters investigated *The Child Exchange, Inside America's Underground Market for Adopted Children*. This frightening but real internet "exchange" offers ways for desperate parents to give their adopted child to other "parents" willing to take custody of the problematic child, as if children are "commodities that can be traded or discarded."[30] This clearly violates the core premise of adoption. If appropriate services arrive too late, parents may withdraw emotionally from the child, may be excessively punitive and may threaten the child with removal, also known as adoption disruption. In essence, the child may become afraid that his or her new parents may recreate environments similar to those of his or her early trauma and abandonment.

Families must count on the villagers to provide an accurate history of the child, training in trauma, attachment and child development for parents and professionals, accessible and affordable professional services, support groups and subsidies.

For this book's purpose, the village will be specified to include: the agencies that link families to waiting children, those who educate the children and the community resources with whom families are involved in daily life.

THE VILLAGE

1. Foster Care or Adoption Agencies

Families may begin their involvement with foster care, since it does not imply a permanent commitment. The family must be licensed after receiving child abuse clearances and meeting training and housing requirements. Other families may proceed directly to an adoption agency. Adoption agencies may offer American-born children or specialize in international adoption. The cost for adopting children out of foster care is less than international adoption. Some families seek a specific child by exploring websites with waiting children.

2. Educational Facilities

Most families are likely to use their local public school. Others choose smaller or specialized educational systems with the idea that their child will be more successful in a smaller school or with specialized assistance. A still smaller number of families attempt to homeschool their adopted child. Homeschooling a foster child requires special permission from the governing agency. Permission may not be granted due to the inability to measure learning success and the focus on learning social skills.

3. Community Resources

Families are linked to religious, scouting, sports and special interest groups. Many count on these resources to help their children learn social, athletic, musical and recreational skills. The Letters to the Villagers we provide in chapter 19 contain information and resources that parents can use to help the community be aware of possible disruptive behaviors and positive ways to interact.

These resources are valuable assets that enrich the lives of foster and adoptive families. If the village is ill equipped to understand and intervene with the children's behaviors or lacks ways to support the families, the village may be of little help or even detrimental to all. Let's look at fresh ways to help the villagers help the families. But first, we'll have co-author Faye's perspective.

FOSTER CARE AND ADOPTION AGENCIES

Everyone enters the foster and adoptive journey in his or her own way. Humorously, I continue to blame my sister for mine. Some may be forced by infertility to begin the journey. Others make a conscious choice to add a foster or adoptive child to their family. Kinship care brings extended family into the journey as they begin caring for family members' children. Each journey follows varying paths depending on the agency the family chooses. Agencies differ in the qualities their parents must meet, training requirements and available children. Public agencies usually offer foster care, are government regulated and may have older, harder-to-place children. Children may be adopted through public agencies with less cost than private adoptions. Employee turnover in social service organizations is high, with large caseloads and low pay. Children may have numerous caseworkers while in care. Private agencies may provide both foster care and adoption. If the family seeks a child through international adoption, the cost increases dramatically and the process is highly regulated by both countries involved.

Foster and adoptive agencies are routinely caught in the bind of too many difficult questions and too few satisfying answers. Children need families and families must be willing to accept a child into their home. Parents state they want to know the child's history and possible disruptive behaviors. How much of the child's history is available to share with potential families and how much should be shared? What will scare a family away? How can you prepare a family for disruptive behaviors if those behaviors are minimized or denied? Where is the balance?

More than one foster or adoptive family has judged a previous foster family as inadequate and voiced that they did not know how to manage the child. The family was too weak and permissive or too demanding and lacked love. If you only "tightened up" or "lightened up" the rules, then the child would obey.

Or the new family may declare, "All the child needs is love" and structure, routine, time, consistency, healthy food, an education and rules. Misdirected parents become driven to make this child fit into their family and may further slide down the slippery slope by pressuring the child to represent their family's values.

Ideals are ideals. Never would I have expected the future to change so dramatically when adopting a little boy. We were successful parents until he entered the home. The following years were difficult and scary. Often we worried about everyone's safety. We learned that compassion without preparation could place our lives in fear.

That was a long twenty years ago, with many twists and turns, blessings and problems. The road has been more than rocky, more comparable to a path with hidden landmines. We have changed and grown in ways that would never have occurred without Allan in our family. Each family member's life trajectory was impacted by his presence. The birth siblings remain close even though miles and continents separate them. They are cordial to Allan and are not interested in a close relationship at this time. His lifestyle continues to reflect his birth family's values.

—Faye Hall

HOW A CHILD MAY ENTER INTO FOSTER CARE: CHILD PROTECTIVE SERVICES

911 Operator: *"911, what's your emergency?"*

John: *(sounding very upset) "I found a little boy wandering the street without a coat on and it's cold. I have seen him around the neighborhood before, but it's unheard of for him to be out in this cold."*

911 Operator: *"Okay, what is your name, sir?"*

John: *"John Grange."*

911 Operator: *"John Grange. How old are you, John?"*

John: *"Forty-nine."*

911 Operator: *"Forty-nine?"*

John: *"Yes."*

911 Operator: *"Your address, John?"*

John: *"He's crying and cold, what should I do? He wants his mom."*

911 Operator: *"I will dispatch an officer, sir, but I need your contact information."*

John: *"I live at 344 North Main Street."*

911 Operator: *"You live at 344 North Main Street. Where are you now?"*

John: *"268 South Main Street, I was coming home from work and he's standing outside of a dark house. It's cold! He won't stop crying. I need help!"*

911 Operator: *"You are at 268 South Main Street?"*

John: *"Yes."*

911 Operator: *"What is his name and how old is he?"*
John: *"Corey and he says he is four."*
911 Operator: *"Sir, do you know where his parents are?"*
John: *"I'm sorry, I don't; he says his mom went looking for Larry. He's cold and crying. Could you hurry, please? I don't know what to do."*
911 Operator: *"I will dispatch an officer. Can you stay with him until the officer arrives and provide the details?"*
John: *"Yes, I will wait. What else can I do to keep him warm? I gave him my coat."*
911 Operator: *"An officer is five minutes away. He will put him in his car and call Child Protective Services."*
John: *"Thank you. Please hurry."*

Corey's Family

Corey regretted going outside and looking for his mom. If he had just waited inside, then everything would have been all right. She told him to stay inside. This was his fault. Why didn't he listen? She would come home soon. Corey knew his Mom had to get Larry from the bar most Friday nights or he would not work on Saturday. Saturdays were important: that was payday.

Tonight felt different. She left before dinner and was gone longer than usual. He was afraid something had happened to her and he might need to help. Corey's fear increased so fast thinking that his Mom could be hurt. It was just like when Larry tried slapping her. Corey would sometimes get between them. Larry did not care that Corey was only four. He yelled that Corey caused their problems and hit him. Corey always doubted what was the right thing to do when Larry was angry; try to stop Larry and get hurt or watch Mom get hurt? Corey hated Larry.

Corey was angry at himself for not finding another way to get food or a place to get warm. He should not have asked this man. Why did he call the police? The man could have given him some money or food or a coat. The policeman might arrest Mom and Larry when they come home. If Mom knew the policemen were searching for her, then she might never come home. What would happen if he could never see her again? Maybe he should run, but the man kept holding his hand. His hand was warm, which was nice, but what was going to happen? This couldn't be good.

Children are egocentric and believe they cause events to happen. They bear the burden of culpability with thoughts of *If I had only...*or *I should have...*, which may prevent stranger involvement that leads to foster care. This emergency call typifies how authorities remove children from frightening, dangerous and chaotic environments. Children may be found wandering the streets, admitted to an emergency room for parent-inflicted or neglected injuries or removed from a home with filth and deprivation. Neither poverty nor wealth can predict a parent's ability to care for children. Some parents may be handicapped by physical or mental illness and/ or addictions that inhibit their abilities.

Unknowingly, Child Protective Services and law officers may inflict more trauma on the child by minimizing the child's fear and pain and by offering "new homes" until their parents can retain custody. With good intent, public officials are forced to comfort and help manage the children's overwhelming emotions, but the children's fear naturally increases when these authorities are involved.

Since children learn from modeling and experience, it is not unusual for children to fear the police, because their parents' activities include drug use or other illegal actions. Imagine the child's experience when the parent acquires the drug and demands secrecy. The child is taught that police are dangerous: someone with power and control that can "ruin" lives. Children may be instructed to lie, fight back or flee as defensive strategies to maintain their sense of safety.

Typically, law enforcement personnel transfer the child to the local Child Protective Services for investigation and placement. The child will be transported to a temporary foster home until the court decides the child's immediate future. A neglected and abused child incites empathy and sympathy in everyone. Agency workers and foster parents may try to make up for the child's trauma by going overboard with gifts and leniency, with the philosophy that this child just needs extra love. Seasoned foster parents understand that copious love is not enough, that this child also needs routine and structure. Corey was placed with Rebecca and Danny, who leaned heavily toward the structured side.

Corey's Family

When Rebecca answered the phone, she was surprised to hear the on-call caseworker asking if she could take an emergency placement. The police had picked up a four-year-old standing on the street without a coat. The police were looking for his parents, who had not yet been found. At seven o'clock, the caseworker rang Rebecca's doorbell. Standing next to the caseworker was a tiny, dirty little boy. Rebecca's heart broke with the sight of this child. She welcomed him into their home and handed him his basket of toiletries. He asked, "What time is dinner?" The caseworker reminded him that she bought him food on the drive to Rebecca's. Corey stated, "I forgot." The caseworker told Corey to be a "good little boy" and she would be back soon to get him when his parents were found.

Days went by without any word on locating his parents. Corey knew not to tell Rebecca that he was afraid his mother would not come to get him. He also knew that Larry could have hurt Mom. Corey followed most of Rebecca's commands. It seemed like all she did was tell him what to do and would not stop talking when he didn't obey. She was always explaining why people do this and why people do that. He did not care why people did anything. He was used to doing what he wanted most days while Mom slept, fought with Larry or visited neighbors. If they did not have enough food, he went with her to the neighbors. They gave him food.

As weeks went by, Rebecca became more concerned about Corey's eating. For a little boy, he did not stop eating. One day when he was outside with her birth children, she started changing the sheets on his bed. As she pulled the bottom sheet off, a myriad of snack wrappers tumbled to the floor. How could he have taken these snacks and when? Rebecca reviewed her close supervision and could not discover what she was missing. He must be up during the night when the family was asleep. She hadn't thought that he could not be trusted during the night. "What else could he be doing at night?" she asked herself. How was she going to stop this? She must explain to him that he cannot be getting up at night and that he eats enough during the day to last all night.

Agency staff and their foster parents do a disservice to the children and families they serve without specific trauma and attachment training to provide the Trauma Lens Paradigm Shift and an understanding of the Trauma-Disrupted Competencies. No child should be warehoused with placement in a foster family that does not have adequate training.

LESSONS FOR CHILD PROTECTIVE WORKERS AND FOSTER PARENTS

Training

1. With training in early trauma, staff will be more likely to accomplish the Trauma Lens Paradigm Shift that will enable them to see the child's behaviors as expressions of a negative working model. This paradigm shift is necessary to adequately provide placement permanency and support the foster or adoptive family.

2. With training in early trauma, staff will be more likely to understand the Trauma-Disrupted Competencies (TDCs) with which they will be able to understand the child's behaviors in all their complexity.

3. Staff will be mindful that early trauma affects children's brain structures, making it extraordinarily difficult for them to process even simple information at times.

4. Staff will be responsible for adequate and appropriate training for the parents. Agency staff will provide training in each TDC and help parents view the child's behavior through the trauma lens.

   a. Staff will be aware of the foster and adoptive parents' struggles in parenting a child with early trauma. Agency staff will allow the parents to be "real" and understand foster and adoptive parents' need to appear competent.

   b. Agency staff will watch for minimization of the child's behavior problems. If the parents describe their distress, agency staff may refuse further placements with this family due to their "incompetence." Pre-adoptive parents must present their "unconditional love and acceptance" for the child. Parents know the agency can disrupt the placement if the parents seem inflexible and demand the child be perfect.

5. Staff will support parents by listening to the parents' distress and use their expertise in exploring the child's behaviors through the trauma lens.

Lessons about the Children

1. Children tend to be aligned with their birth family regardless of abuse and/or neglect. They want to go home. Home is predictable even if unsafe. If a person speaks negatively about the child's parent, the child may exonerate the parent and accept total responsibility for any problems.

2. The child needs to experience all adults as working together for his or her best interest.

3. As the child travels through foster care placements, the staff may feel a sense of obligation and responsibility for the child. The child may perceive this staff as a "weak link" and use the staff's emotions to extort goods.

4. Staff turnover is high in social service agencies and the child may experience numerous caseworkers. It is therefore critically important to assist in the transitions by introducing new staff and expressing trust in the staff.

Lessons for Foster and Adoptive Parents

1. Foster and adoptive parents will question their agency's training policy and ask for support in training and resources.

2. Foster and adoptive parents may have to offer training materials to their agency staff.

3. Foster and adoptive parents may have to insist their agency staff help with additional resources.

4. Pre-adoptive parents may have to insist on future resources after the adoption is finalized.

5. Do not withhold important trauma history from the new foster parents. Help them become aware of the child's triggers and ways to assist the child when triggered. Provide resources to the new parents to ensure the child is receiving the best care possible.

6. The foster and adoptive parents are a healing agent for the children. The children may lack emotional regulation skills that were not facilitated by their original caretakers. The foster parents are now placed in this role.

7. The children may have developmental delays that prevent them from functioning in a manner expected for their chronological age. Use their emotional age to figure out expectations.

8. Do not speak negatively of the birth parents. The child is genetically connected to these parents. If the parents are bad, so is the child.

9. Foster and adoptive parents are the children's advocates and must be proactive in services and educational placements.

EDUCATIONAL FACILITIES: EDUCATORS

Coming home from school one day, Allan exclaimed, "I can earn washers (small metal disks) for good behavior and use them to buy things at the school store. I don't have to be good, because Dad has a drawer full of washers in the garage I can use instead." I surmised that the token system might not be a good idea and made a mental note to alert the teacher. Homework quickly became the next hurdle. The family valued academics and insisted that Allan spend time each night completing his assignments. Night after night, Dad and Allan battled over homework. Most nights, Allan never completed the work.

I felt comforted when school staff gave him two days of in-school suspension as a consequence for his defiance. He did not comply with the teacher during class time and each evening detention staff asked me to "make" him complete the schoolwork. Allan was given an extra day of suspension as a consequence for non-compliance. He declared that the in-school suspension classroom did not have water.

He complained to me that he had nothing to drink and could not go to the bathroom all day. When I dropped him off the next day, I discussed the lack of water with school staff. A staff member was bewildered and declared, "And I thought Allan was my friend!"

As Allan learned that he could persuade school staff with his lies, his behavior at home became more dangerous with increased aggression and defiance. I did not think it could get worse until he started playing with fire. He was drawn to matches and enjoyed the family's fireplaces. Now, he was starting fires in other places. I knew the family lacked safety if he was attracted to fires and was up during the night. Something had to be done.

—Faye Hall

As with the staff in Allan's school district, educators are optimistic and see many windows of opportunity for learning. They love to learn and try to impart the same love in their students. Generally, students approach learning with similar curiosity. Even timid learners can be motivated to explore new information. Learning requires the development of emotional control, motor development, retention and analysis. Educators scaffold their curriculum to accommodate a range of learners and their maturation levels.

Unfortunately, the educational community is held accountable for students with mental health disorders that disrupt learning. Educators are in a predicament: their classrooms are for academics, not therapy. Children with a history of early trauma and attachment disruptions present unique challenges, as their learning and behaviors will be unpredictable with differing results. These children will present differently to various school staff members and their responses to situations are very hard to both understand and predict.

Early trauma creates a need for the child to feel safe in all environments. This leads to a child who learns to "read" adults and uses the information to sway adults as needed. Just as Allan was able to have school staff supply his clothing, other students lead staff to buy breakfast or lunch, snacks and toys. Nothing touches an educator's heart more than a child who tells his story of abuse and portrays the current parents as also mean. Imagine hearing from a child that he had to eat dog food to stay alive while with the birth family and just that morning had to miss breakfast because of not finishing chores in time to eat before school. As educators come to know these children and their families, they may infer that these parents are just as bad as the child's abusive birth family. The educators will be further challenged since they are mandated reporters of abuse. Foster and adoptive families are warned that these children frequently make "false allegations of abuse" and dread the investigations many have had to undergo.

With foster care placements, this may lead to removal of the child and/or other children in the home before the investigation is conducted. Sometimes educators are puzzled and concerned about parents' behaviors and attitudes. The parents may seem punitive and inflexible. They may be overly concerned about the child's appearance. These parents tend to express that the child is representing their family and must dress in a particular style. Still other parents may have no concern about the ill-clothed child with poorly fitting clothing or no coat. A seemingly unconcerned parent may have given up on trying to keep the child in good clothing with nightly baths. These despairing parental attitudes may then affect their approach to monitoring homework, peer relationships, school functions and even meals.

BEHAVIORISM

Educators use behaviorism to reinforce and "consequence" students to improve academics and behaviors. To manage the masses, students are taught how to operate in a school setting via their handbook and classroom rules. Pre-school students understand the color system of who gets to go out for recess (usually those on green) while the students on red miss recess. Classrooms are full of posters that identify where to sit, when to wear a coat outside and what work needs to be completed before the end of the day. The students know what will happen if they don't comply. Every student hears about the kid who had to go to the principal's office.

Special education classes usually add token systems to reward students for improved behavior with prize boxes or classroom stores. Just as children with early trauma feel safe by reading adults, the children may use behaviorism to make the environment predictable. This does not mean the child will work for a prize. It may be exactly the opposite. A negative consequence or restriction may reinforce the child's negative internal belief system.

Lessons for Educators

1. With training in early trauma, school staff will be more likely to have the Trauma Lens Paradigm Shift that will enable them to see the child's behaviors as expressions of a negative working model. This paradigm shift is necessary to adequately provide a good education for the child and continue supporting the family.

2. With training in early trauma, school staff will be more likely to understand the Trauma-Disrupted Competencies with which they will view the child's behaviors differently. The

accommodations will more accurately address problematic behaviors and barriers to learning.

3. Educators will understand that the child's brain is wired differently and may not be ready for learning during some circumstances. (Not infrequently, these children require neuropsychological testing in order to identify specific disrupted brain circuits.)

4. Encourage and assist the parents in building a support network. Schools are increasingly offering training to their staff in mental health. With that enhanced understanding, staff can suggest or provide resources to the family and connect them to community resources.

5. The child may have little sense of self and struggle with stating what he or she likes or dislikes. Some may tend to mimic other students or seem like a chameleon changing with circumstances.

School rules

1. School staff will be more successful if they provide unambiguous instructions. Leave no wiggle room and use clear directives to eliminate possible arguments.

2. Given that the home is now a place of healing with increased parental nurturing, educators should not ask the parents to punish the child at home for school behaviors. Parents are encouraged to be empathic and offer comfort for their child, not administer consequences for school behavior problems. The child with a N-IWM will only interpret that as a conspiracy between bad teachers and bad parents.

3. The child will be looking for the "weakest link" in school staff. This weak link will be the one the child uses to feel safe by asking for items, privileges and a "special" relationship. Some school staff have expressed that they would "take this child home with them because they have such a good relationship." Don't fall for this trap.

4. Use behavior management to provide consistent consequences. Express sadness without anger and be empathic. Express confidence that the child will be successful in the future.

5. Children with early trauma will use their skills to escape uncomfortable situations. They may lie to protect their sense of self. These lies tend to be very believable, leaving adults to question what the child's life must be like. Do not accept the

child's reasoning or make allowances without talking to the child's parent. Believing the child's lies will delay his or her recovery.

6. Provide little unstructured time. These children may be flooded with trauma memories and to avoid the memories, a child may become disruptive. Other children may have developmental delays and may not have the ability to occupy themselves.

7. Watch for "It was an accident" or "I just found it on the playground." Both remove the child from responsibility. Stealing is common; book bags, purses, lockers and jackets may need to be searched frequently. Do not allow the child access to your personal property.

8. Hold the child accountable for academics and peer relationships. Give the child opportunities to correct work and repair relationships. You are building a child's ability to handle distress. Enforce all school rules. Repair may include apology letters, completing a chore for another and cleaning up after an incident.

Lessons about the Team

1. Ask for feedback from the child's mental health treatment team before completing the Individualized Education Program (IEP). Problematic behaviors are usually present in all school environments. If a child can successfully read in science class but not language arts, reading may not be the problem.

2. Communication between all team members is vital. Include team members when communicating progress and problems. Ask about successful interventions that have been used in other environments.

3. If a child is in foster care, the foster parents are vital team members. Foster parent cooperation may be dependent on agency policy. For a healing environment, all the adults in the child's world should attend team meetings and agree on common goals and procedures.

Lessons about Parents

1. Parents will feel more supported if the school staff will intentionally build a relationship with the parents and increase communication. Do not depend on the child to carry the communication back and forth between school and home.

2. Successfully educating these children is dependent on a healthy working relationship with the parents. The parents will seem to be the child's target for animosity and anger. They are healing agents in the child's life and need support from school staff to continue their difficult and sometimes dangerous work. The child's recovery is contingent on adequate village support for the parents.

3. Redirect the child back to the parents if the child asks school staff to meet his or her physical needs and solve personal problems. These children have learned to go to caseworkers and multiple strangers to meet their needs. They must learn the skill of relying on parents to take care of them.

4. If the parents seem to be inflexible and fearful, help the parents form a support network. The child may be increasingly dangerous in their home.

Safety plans

1. Safety plans are often needed to help the child maintain or regain emotional regulation. Some school staff will assign an adult to accompany the child to the gym during a mid-morning break for a protein snack and quick run. Other school staff may allow the child to take a break from relationships, sit quietly and read to regain regulation. Long bus rides can be problematic. Parents may supply activities, toys, books or small electronics to occupy the child. Some children need to sit near an adult or the bus driver to remain regulated.

2. Recognize that these children may have unknown trauma triggers that can spur disruptive behavior. If children are asked to draw their family tree or study genetics, memories of their early history will occur. Functional Behavioral Assessments (which attempt to determine the antecedent for a problematic behavior and the appropriate consequence to extinguish the behavior) are not always successful, because of the unknown triggers that can precede a behavior.

3. Some children's abuse was sexual, which may lead to sexually acting out at school. Additional safety measures are needed to keep everyone safe. Be watchful for any sexualized behaviors. Some children should not be allowed to go to the bathroom with other children. Others must use the restroom in the nurse's office. Watch for any predatory behaviors toward younger children.

Lessons for Parents

1. Parents must realize the school's difficult situation. The school is to educate children. Do not let the child's behaviors become a barrier between home and school. Do not try to change the school's behavior management model. Children must learn from society what homes cannot teach.

2. Parents must accept that they are their child's advocate and may have to educate school staff. Educators may not be as willing to accept mental health information from parents as from other team members. Parents must be willing to form and use a support network.

3. Parents are responsible for homework time and space. Parents cannot make their child learn. Parents may need to reduce their expectations for the child's academics even though they know how smart their child is. It is not unusual for these children to have a disparity between grades and IQ.

4. Parents need to avoid supporting the child's negative internal working model. Each negative comment will cling to the child's sense of self.

MENTAL HEALTH
TREATMENT PROVIDERS

Behavior problems increased at home and at school. By Christmas, David and I arranged for a psychological evaluation for Allan. The evaluator identified his behaviors as being too dangerous for him to remain in the home and recommended treatment at a residential facility. The prescribing physician grimly stated, "Good luck; these kids don't make much progress." Allan was accepted at a facility across the state. Each day when he came home from school he asked if his letter came stating when he would leave. These were not unhappy times for him. It was as if he were getting ready for a trip.

Finally the day arrived. We loaded our large van with suitcases and ski equipment. Our intention was a short family vacation after Allan was admitted to the treatment facility. The treatment staff welcomed the family as the intake paperwork was completed. We toured the large campus and met the day staff in his "cottage." He quickly adjusted to his new surroundings and was content as the family drove away.

Twice a month, David and I or the girls and I made the long trek across the state for therapy sessions and off-campus visits. It was not unusual for Allan to ignore us when we arrived. He rarely greeted us and sometimes refused to go off campus with us. Therapy was distressing. Many times, he sat under a table refusing to talk. I found comfort in the support group for families with children in treatment and in my relationship with Allan's therapist. A kindred spirit sometimes develops between parents and therapists, which leads to empathy for each other's experiences and the sharing of resources. I grew emotionally and intellectually while Allan grew physically. After eleven months of treatment at fourteen and a half years old, Allan was a young man. He was six feet tall and two hundred pounds. The balance of physical power shifted. Allan was much larger than we were and could do serious damage if he lost control.

At discharge, Allan began treatment with a specialized outpatient therapist. Each two-hour session included time for me to review the week with the therapist and discuss treatment goals.

—Faye Hall

The therapist needs to be well versed in understanding the enduring brain and behavioral effects of early trauma, the many ways in which the negative internal working model (N-IWM) that results from the trauma causes difficulty in here-and-now relationships and the special needs of parents and other caregivers who are responsible for healing the child. Just as importantly, the therapist must be very skilled at empathic attunement to the child and parents and adept at recognizing and responding therapeutically to the appearance and reappearance of the N-IWM in the therapy session and in stories shared about the home scene. To repeat, the characteristics of PACE (Playfulness, Acceptance, Curiosity and Empathy) are what the parents should look for in a therapist.

Treatment Goals

1. **Safety:** Safety is always the first goal, but outpatient therapists are limited in creating safety outside their office. Other team members may be assigned to help with this goal.

2. **Improve the parent/child relationship:** Since the children's behaviors may be quite dangerous or fear inducing, parents may ask that the first goal be to help their child stop the disruptive behaviors. Nicole Cox found that professionals working with the child to improve behavior may not improve the parent-child relationship.[31] Lasting effects may be fleeting if they are behavior focused. Other parents ask therapists to help their children develop coping skills to manage anger so that

they will stop harming themselves or others or damaging property.

3. **Emotional regulation skills:** Parents frequently ask that their child learns to use coping skills to stop the aggression and dangerous behavior. This expectation can lead to disappointment. Programs are known for "equipping the child with a toolbox of skills" that can be used when dysregulated. Ideally, the child will recognize when emotions are becoming too big, shut down the emotions, open the toolbox for an alternative activity like taking a walk or listening to music and carry out that activity until calm. When parents are asked to reflect on their own anger management skills, they may notice their brains do not shift easily from anger to a replacement activity. The normal development of self-regulation skills begins with parent/child co-regulation. Treatment will include teaching parents how to co-regulate with their children. Identifying and learning to use coping skills follows co-regulation and involves scaffolded practice and more cognitive awareness.

Within two months of being home, Allan's aggression had escalated to dangerous levels. I called the local mental health agency for more support. I asked for staff who would be able to help us maintain Allan in our home. Four months later, staff was hired. We adjusted to a staff member being present in our home forty hours per week. Actually, we were happy to have more stability and a sense of freedom. During the months of waiting for this extra help, Allan became more defiant and refused to cooperate with family plans. The girls were unable to attend their piano lessons, as Allan would go off and hide if he didn't want them to go. I could not leave him unattended with his whereabouts unknown. He would run away at other times, turning up hours later. With his physical strength, he was potentially dangerous when refusing to comply.

With the stabilizing presence of the staff member, we established enough of a sense of calm and order that some therapeutic interaction became possible. If Allan was noncompliant, we and the staff member could help him to identify and express his distress. Special outings were planned to help Allan learn to trust us and work with us. The staff member attended therapy sessions with the family in order to coordinate treatment goals and interventions between therapist and the home. Finally Allan began to make some progress in therapy. His world began to become cohesive.

—*Faye Hall*

Lessons for in-home treatment providers

1. Encourage and assist the parents in building a support network. Incorporate school staff, suggest resources to the family and connect them to community resources.

2. With training in early trauma, in-home staff will be more likely to have the Trauma Lens Paradigm Shift that will enable them to see the child's behaviors as expressions of a negative working model. This paradigm shift is necessary to adequately provide treatment goals and interventions for the child and continue supporting the family.

3. With training in early trauma, in-home staff will be more likely to understand the Trauma-Disrupted Competencies with which they will view the child's behaviors differently. The interventions and expectations will more accurately address problematic behaviors and barriers to success.

4. Recognize that the child's brain is wired differently and may not allow approaches utilized for children of similar chronological age.

5. The child may have little sense of self and can struggle with stating what he or she likes or dislikes. Some mimic others or change with circumstances.

Lessons about Parents

1. Parents will feel more supported if in-home staff will intentionally build a relationship with the parents and communicate frequently. All planning should be coordinated and include the parents. This is about building healthier parent/ child relationships.

2. Successfully treating these children is dependent on a healthy working relationship with the parents. The parents will seem to be the child's target for animosity and anger. They are healing agents in the child's life and need support from in-home staff to continue the difficult and sometimes dangerous work. The child's recovery is contingent on these parents.

3. Redirect the child back to the parents if the child asks in-home staff to solve any personal problems. These children have learned to go to caseworkers and multiple strangers (foster parents) to meet their needs. They must learn the skill of relying on parents to take care of them.

Treatment staff

1. In-home staff will be more successful if they provide clear instructions.

2. Staff may think the parents are unreasonable, punitive, angry, controlling and inflexible. This is the transference of the child's belief system to the parents. Many parents state they were never negative or angry before the child entered their home. As the maladaptive behaviors escalated, the parents became more fearful and controlling. They must have expert professional assistance to overcome the hurt and fear.

3. The child will be looking for the "weakest link" in the staff. This weak link will be the one the child uses to feel safe by asking for items, privileges and a "special" relationship. Some in-home staff have expressed that they would "take this child home with them because they have such a good relationship." Don't be taken in by this.

4. Use behavior management strategies to provide consistent consequences. Express sadness without anger and be empathic. Express confidence that the child will be successful in the future.

5. Children with early trauma will use their skills to escape uncomfortable situations. They may lie to protect their sense of self. These lies tend to be very believable, leaving adults to question what the child's life must be like. Do not accept the child's reasoning or make allowances without talking to the child's parent. Believing the child's lies will delay his or her recovery.

6. Allow for unstructured time. Increase the amount of unstructured time as the child gains self-regulation. Identify for the child the problems that may occur and help the child learn and use new skills. Their trauma memories may have been avoided until now. This is an opportunity for the child to convey his or her distress to the parent and accept comfort. Other children may have developmental delays and may not have the ability to occupy themselves.

7. Determine the child's emotional age and allow the child experiences that match his or her maturation. Do not be alarmed if the child plays with toys of a younger chronological age. Most likely, the child has developmental "holes" that must be filled.

8. Ask for feedback from the child's mental health treatment team before completing the treatment plan. Include team members

when communicating progress and problems. Ask for successful interventions that have been used in other environments.

Safety plans

1. Safety plans are often needed to help the child maintain or regain emotional regulation. Given that the child's parental relationship may spur disruptive behaviors, develop a safety plan with the parents. Engage the child if the child will co-operate. Emotional regulation skills may be the first goals in the treatment plan.

2. Ideally the child should learn to emotionally co-regulate with the parent before self-regulation. This means that the parent is self-regulated and willing to cooperate.

3. It is not unusual for parents to be angry and resentful of their child by the time services are in place. Help the parents realize their feelings and remind them that the child's actions are sometimes not the child's fault.

4. Recognize that these children may have unknown trauma triggers that spur disruptive behavior. Their early trauma occurred at home with parents they should have been able to trust. Working in the home, staff will witness these triggers and the child's responses.

5. Some children's abuse was sexual, which may lead to sexually acting out. Additional safety measures are needed to keep everyone safe. Be watchful for any sexualized behaviors. Avoid being alone with the child. Do not place yourself in any situation that could be misinterpreted.

Lessons for Parents

1. Parents must realize the staff are professionals. They are in the home to assist the child in achieving behavioral goals. Organize a cohesive treatment team around the child's problematic behaviors. These behaviors are indicators of the child's progress and treatment needs.

2. Parents must accept that they are their child's advocate and may have to educate service providers. If treatment staff is reluctant to accept mental health information from parents, other service providers may be needed. Parents must be willing to form and use a support network.

3. Parents are responsible for assisting with the treatment plan and following through with interventions and possibly do their own homework.

4. The parent/child relationship will improve with positive and supportive statements. When parents and staff review the child's behaviors, the child's negative working model will be reinforced if the child is present. Each negative comment will cling to the child's sense of self. Some parents think the child should hear about bad behavior to motivate the child to change. This routinely backfires.

5. Allow staff to challenge the child. Children must learn from society what parents cannot teach.

When families accept a foster or pre-adoptive child into their home, they have great expectations for the child. This child will be part of their family. They include the child in events with friends, extended family, the neighborhood and the church. To be good parents, they envision giving this child many opportunities such as music lessons or sports participation. Even agency workers will suggest that community activities will help the child learn social skills and explore new interests. Some children are not successful in community activities due to their trauma, developmental delays and inability to form healthy relationships. Without this recognition, parents may "teach," lecture, blame or rescue the child from continuing the activity. Other parents will continue with the "insanity" of expecting the child to "get it" sooner or later.

We are offering two fresh approaches:

1. Assess the child's emotional age and emotional regulation skills to determine if and when the child should participate in activities away from the parents, how long the child can tolerate "being with people" before requiring a period of detachment and to assess for other TDCs that may be a barrier to success.

2. Prepare the community resources for the child's presence with education in trauma, attachment, child development and ways to support the family and child. With understanding and interventions, the villagers can accept and manage the child.

If many of the ideas offered to the various villagers in this chapter sound familiar to you or even redundant, that's because we consider them fundamental to every interaction with these children of early trauma.

Thereby, they apply to literally all encounters with them in every corner of the village.

If social service agencies, educators, treatment specialists and community resources can share a mutual and realistic basic understanding of the unique differences between these children and others, we stand the chance of making some impressive leaps forward in providing coordinated and effective care of them. Then we villagers, all of us including our foster and adoptive children and their families, are the better for it.

CHAPTER 7

Special Environmental Considerations for the Attachment-Disordered Child

In preceding chapters we discussed the impact of child trauma and how to develop a supportive team. Once the team is in place, we must turn our attention to creating a healing environment. This unique environment must be thought of as a "Secure Base" for supporting attachment, emotional regulation and thereby promoting developmental maturation. The healing environment must provide attachment opportunities, demonstrate unconditional acceptance, encourage developmental maturation and identify stressors (either removing them or helping the child to increase their stress tolerance).

THE ENVIRONMENT: USING THE TRAUMA LENS TO CREATE A HEALING HOME

As referenced in earlier chapters, children with a history of early trauma and attachment disruptions were forced to attempt to control their environments in order to maintain safety, reduce their anxiety and meet their own needs. Integration into new placements can be enormously difficult. Many times, the first few months a child is placed in the home may be peaceful and pleasant—the proverbial calm before the storm. Over time, the impact of the early trauma becomes more apparent as maladaptive behaviors increase. Foster and adoptive parents may be blindsided when these behaviors erupt.

Co-authors Faye and Jeff provide training we call "Creating a Healing Home." We illustrate the fear and anxiety experienced by a child when integrating into a new family. We distribute a wrapped piece of chocolate candy to all attendees. As they begin to express their appreciation for the treat, they are instructed to unwrap the candy and find a stranger in the room to feed the candy. An overwhelming sigh is always heard in the room. Usually, men are more shocked than women, probably because of women's greater inclinations to nurture. Then we begin building empathy for the child's experiences by describing in great detail the move to a "foreign" environment.

This foreign environment consists of different parents, siblings, customs, language, food, odors and values. These strangers violate the child's privacy by offering to bathe the child and tuck him in at night. The parents instruct, direct, touch and soothe the child. The child is told by the ones who removed him from the prior placement or birth family that these strangers are safe.

It is understandable that children in the foster and adoptive systems experience anxiety and fear. To compensate (but sometimes overcompensate), many foster or adoptive parents try to comfort children with material possessions, activities and services. The children are kept busy and expected to appreciate the good things the family furnishes. For healing to occur, though, the home environment must contain healthy, attuned caregivers who offer a secure base, carefully designed and implemented.[32] Child trauma authorities Kristine Kinniburgh, Margaret Blaustein and Joseph Spinazzola specified two goals in "attachment-focused interventions: building (or rebuilding) healthy attachments between those children who have experienced trauma and their caregivers; and creating the safe environment for healthy recovery."[33] This new environment must have a well-defined structure and limits in order to provide opportunities for healing. The parents' paradigm shift allows them to see the child through the trauma lens and act accordingly when designing the environment. These parents will be more flexible, attuned and developmentally engaged with their child, thus giving the child more opportunities for healing with relational, emotional and developmental maturation.

THE ENVIRONMENT AS A SECURE BASE

As discussed in earlier chapters, the secure base gives children the foundation and freedom to explore the world with implicit and explicit knowledge: the family will welcome them home and provide comfort if needed. The environment must support the secure base by providing structure, nurturance and challenge. Structure is comprised of the daily routines and rituals parents develop and use to give order to family life. Nurturance is relational responsiveness, unconditional love and intimacy. Challenge is the parent's influence in addressing, reframing and restructuring the child's negative belief system. Each demonstrates parental security via trust, reliability, sensitivity and physical and emotional availability.

The secure base is strengthened by structure. Children with early trauma need routines and rituals to give order to their lives. Many times, previous homes were chaotic and unpredictable. Meals, bedtimes and even school attendance may have been erratic. Young children may have had to gather food for themselves and siblings. They may have begged from neighbors, stolen from stores and solicited food from school staff. One child reported taking cat food from a neighbor's porch for her and her sister to eat. A five-year-old remembered fixing food for her two younger siblings and being yelled at by her mother when she burned the food. Small wonder these children tend to have "food issues."

Bedtime routines may have been nonexistent. The child may also have been abused during the night or in the bathroom. Consequently, nightly baths, bedtime stories and tucking in may be scary and strange to many foster and adopted children. Children may be oppositional to "being told what to do," because they are fearful or have learned to set their own bedtime, eat when they want to or when they can find food and go to school if desired. This can easily set the child and parents up to wrangle for control.

EXAMPLES OF STRUCTURAL PROBLEMS
Amy's Family: Not Enough Structure

James and Lori adopted two-year-old Amy later in life. Because they were so thankful to finally be parents, they indulged her. She never had to ask for anything. Even her language was delayed due to her parents' "over-attunement." When her peers were learning their worth to the family by completing chores and basking in the joy and approval of their parents, she slept late and demanded that her mother meet her needs. She experienced herself as fearful and burdensome. Her activities consumed the family's expendable income. As a teen, Amy became even more demanding, responding with aggression when her parents were noncompliant. James and Lori struggled individually at times with worries about "spoiling" Amy, but they never seemed to agree about when to say "no." In every situation either James or Lori would act to avoid the fear that Amy would erupt aggressively.

Treatment goals

In this case, structure needed to be increased. Parents need to determine and set firm boundaries and limits. James and Lori need to increase the ways in which Amy can contribute to the family effort through chores. They can also foster her development of self-control through such simple interventions as urging her to use "I" statements.

James and Lori admitted that they lacked control of their home. They gave in to Amy's demands, thereby not teaching her how to live effectively within a family system. They agreed to concentrate on building a unified stance to keep Amy from "triangulating" them—playing one against the other. Through their effort, a plan unfolded to set rules and define chores, privileges and responsibilities for their daughter. They were able to hold firm to boundaries and withhold privileges unless earned. They would still grant privileges occasionally just as a gratuitous expression of affection. They would listen to her demands, but did not give in to them. Following through with firm boundaries was very difficult. But Amy eventually realized that James and Lori would not tolerate aggression or destruction of property when they called the police after she broke their front door.

When James and Lori lapsed and failed to "follow their own rules," they apologized to Amy and explained their motivation for lapsing with the rules (usually fear of her retaliation). As Amy began to experience the security of reliable structure, her trust in her parents grew and the demands decreased.

Corey's Family: Too much structure

Rebecca and Danny began fostering children soon after they were married. They set firm rules for all the children. Upon placement, each new child was given a toiletries basket, four sets of clothing and housing rules with a time chart. The family scheduled bathing, eating, homework, chores and free time. When Rebecca and Danny decided to adopt four-year-old Corey, they did not change their routine. Over time, Corey's behavior problems arose and increased. Knowing that he came from a placement without strong directive parenting, Rebecca and Danny added more rules to clarify and assist Corey in his recognition of the value of caring, involved parents. Of course there were consequences for breaking rules. They joyfully anticipated the time when Corey would finally wake up to the fact that they cared and were there to keep him safe and provide the best for him. When that happened, they reasoned, "He would stop senselessly violating our every effort to provide for his needs." But that time never came. No matter how much Corey lost, he continued to blame them. Corey was getting angrier all the time and his ability to make "good" choices actually seemed to decrease.

Treatment goals

In this case, Rebecca and Danny needed to decrease structure. They maintained most of the rules, while negotiating with Corey about some of the less important ones. They were able to increase intimacy with Corey. Together with him in reflective dialogues, they explored his fears about connecting to them. They learned new ways of interacting with Corey with fewer demands and increased close proximity. They even decided to have fun times together, whether "rules" were being broken or not. They did this because having those fun times was actually a big part of why Danny and Rebecca became foster parents in the first place.

The secure base is strengthened by nurture. We hear about unconditional love and acceptance, but few are tested to the extent that foster and adoptive parents are. Many foster and adoptive mothers report that they feel abused by their children. When mothers feel abused, they do not want to nurture their children. One mother stated that she could not look into her child's eyes because her anger toward the child was too strong. Another mother refused to play a game the therapist suggested, because of the child's recent defiance. These are not trivial difficulties, as "every positive, nurturing, attuned caregiving response that they provide for their children leaves an indelible mark on the child's developing neural networks."[34] It follows that the opposite is just as true. These two mothers are operating from a behavior/consequence model that indicates that they have not shifted in seeing their children's behavior through the trauma lens. Stepping back and viewing the child's behavior with the trauma lens, they would see a clear link between their child's maladaptive behavior and a history of early abuse.

Therefore, the paradigm shift is essential before nurturing activity begins. The "Creating a Healing Home" model uses nurturing actions which far exceed the norm. Love, care, intimacy, touch and affection must occur every day and not be dependent on good behavior. If parents cannot or will not nurture their child, interventions that create more empathy for the child must be developed and the parents' own trauma history explored. Until the block in nurturance is thoroughly understood, interactions with the child may promote the parents' belief that "this child is unlovable" and the child's that "These parents cannot be trusted."

Parental care, nurture and unconditional love will begin the healing process by building or rebuilding healthy connections between parent and child. Parents must have the internal strength and insight to continue these potentially painful interactions. Children may not easily accept nurture, may resist and avoid intimacy.

The secure base is strengthened by:

- Challenging the child's negative belief that this mother cannot be trusted by suggesting and acting upon the belief that this mother can be trusted.

- Challenging the child's negative belief that he is unlovable by suggesting and acting upon the belief that this child is lovable.

Security comes when our internal beliefs match our external world. Given that children with early trauma have developed an internal belief system of "I am unlovable, adults cannot be trusted and the world is unsafe," the naturally safe environment supplied by foster and adoptive homes in itself will provide no relief from that belief system and ironically can contribute to the child's fear. Children living with constant fear learn early to insulate themselves from the fear and anger. This self-protective process occurs so often and so quickly that children will lose the ability to feel fear. They report that "things just make them feel mad." Before the child can begin to experience security in a safe, adult-led home, both the internal beliefs and the fear that they generate need to be labeled and challenged.

Amy's Family

Amy explained to Lucy, her teacher, "It makes me mad that they give me too many rules!"

Lucy asked, "Which rule?"

Amy responded, "All of them!" Amy said that she was feeling very angry when asked to play in her room for an hour while Mom and Dad worked on taxes.

Lucy questioned, "What was the problem with being in your room?"

Amy proclaimed, "I just don't like being in my room!"

A surprised Lucy knew that Amy's toys and video games were in her room and that she liked being alone. "Why were you mad?" she wanted to know.

Her anger mounting, Amy responded, "I just don't know. I don't like it in there!" Amy was acting on her belief that her parents couldn't be trusted. She shared the confusing explanation to her teacher that she did not like parental rules or being in her room. Her underlying emotion was fear of having rules and of adults trying to control her.

STAGING AN INTENTIONAL ENVIRONMENT FOR RECOVERY

Lack of Intentionality

Parents bring children into their home through birth, through foster care and/or through the adoption process. The resulting home environment is rarely constructed intentionally, but instead is often developed "on the fly," instinctual and driven by parental needs. Examples of reasons people have children include: "That's what people do," "My biological clock was ticking," "My mom said it is time to be a parent" and "I was lonely." Without a sustainable motive for beginning or adding to a family, how can there be intentionality in its creation?

Internal and external pressures may influence the home environment. Each partner carries an internal parenting model and is driven to reproduce or correct it. The rules, possessions, activities and personal interactions become subservient to that intent. A parent may consciously or unconsciously attempt to enforce his or her model on the other partner. One parent may not support the other. Marriages can be destroyed if parenting models are not merged or intentionally developed.

Home environments are also subject to external pressures. Television portrays ideal and fantasy versions of family life. Movies create idealistic expectations of how children should behave. Peers pressure the child to fit into their groups. Parents may measure success by children's performance outside the home. Adoption and foster care agencies enforce directives and requirements that must be followed for the child to remain in the home.

Intentionality

Our *Trauma Lens* model is intentional and derived through seeing the child's behaviors, development and emotional regulatory systems through the trauma lens. It addresses deficits with interventions that encourage growth. If parents proceed trying to parent their traumatized child as they parent healthy birth children, the child's behaviors are most likely to worsen. During co-author Faye's parenting experience, she termed it "parenting backwards," because it seemed that strategies that worked with her birth children had the opposite effect with her adopted son.

Staging

Trauma psycho-education must evoke a paradigm shift in the parents for them to be successful. Through this new paradigm, a healing environment will be designed and executed. This environment will not be static and adjustments must occur as the parents attune to their child's needs. The process is similar to staging a theater production with props, cast and a script that balances structure, nurture and the challenging of old beliefs. The performance is dependent on each element. Choose cast, script and props carefully, as they are the family possessions, the relationships and the daily interactions.

Daily Family Life Is the Production

As with any play or performance, the actors and performers practice frequently with many errors. They don't stop, collapsing under pressure, but continue to perfect their roles. Parents must realize they have the same opportunity as actors in a production. They will fail at times, but their children will give them many occasions to practice their roles and perfect the production. On the road to relational recovery, the child must spend time with the family. This section will offer ideas to increase family time.

Specific ways are suggested to script relationships, possessions and activities so as to minimize excesses and create a balance in each. By thus intentionally adapting the environment as with a production, disruptive behaviors may be avoided and attachment bonds strengthened.

• The Characters

The main cast of characters contains the child and the primary caregiver (usually mother) who replicate an infant's early experience. Mother is the first responder, attuned and emotionally activated by the infant's cues. Attachment is about building a relationship. The parent will need guidance to maintain a balance of "normal" life while being a therapeutic parent. Activities must include mother more frequently than not, but not exclusively. Families usually include another parent, siblings and extended family.

All family relationships will be stressed during the therapeutic process. The parents' relationship reveals the strength of the "secure base." Mother will rely on her partner's support. Siblings will expect assistance when treatment focuses on attachment building between parent and child. The siblings may feel left out and that the world is not fair; their world seems to center on the child with the worst behaviors.

Respite for the family, especially mother, is necessary. Parents may be hesitant to use respite, because they fear later "payback" for sending the child away. But they need the rest to recover and sustain their therapeutic stance. Respite must be encouraged for the family's health. The best respite provider is well-trained and provides two different types: restrictive and reward.

A restrictive respite offers limited activities and distractions. This respite provider offers quiet activities in which the child must occupy him or herself. A reward respite is used as a positive encouragement to give everyone a rest from the hard work they are doing in therapy. The child is able to relax in a less intimate setting. All respite providers must redirect the child back to the parents by stating that all good things during the visit come from the parents. They should compliment the child for hard work well done and predict more success for the child.

Corey's Family

Birth children Sara, Andy and Lane were happy to have another brother, Corey, in the family. Corey was four years old when he joined them after six changes in foster placements. The first summer was fun, with many activities and vacations. But as soon as school began, problems did also. Corey refused to bathe, sleep through the night and eat regular meals with the family.

Rebecca and Danny began adding services to help Corey with his daily tasks. Corey had a special one-on-one aide who came three days a week. Corey had a weekly therapy session and a monthly doctor's appointment. His caseworker visited every week. The children's mother had to go to all the appointments and meetings. It seemed like she was never home or had time for them. Corey was the one causing trouble, but he was the one getting all of Rebecca's time. The family needed help!

Rebecca consulted a specialized team for assistance. She was given literature to help explain to the children why Corey acted like he did. The children were asked to be sad for Corey because of his history, but to hold to firm boundaries with him. She was directed to use a "reward" respite for Corey once a month. If Corey's behaviors were too extreme, he went to a "restrictive" respite. The birth children were allowed to go to their grandparents' home for special times without Corey. As the children found relief from Corey's daily behavior problems, they became more accepting of Corey.

Beware of times when Mom is excluded from activities. The child may feel unsafe, especially when anyone suggests that Mom cannot be trusted, is too tired or not willing to participate. The child can perceive negative intentions simply by Dad innocuously saying, "Your mom will not deal with this behavior. So I will take you to practice." Other well-meaning friends or family members may state that the child should spend the weekend with them, because "The child should have more fun and give everyone some rest." This may produce a "pseudo-feeling" of belonging and safety that interrupts the need to attach to the mother—that is, to lower the child's innate motivation to heal: "If I can do this without Mom, why do I need a Mom?"

Focus on primary relationships to avoid confusion for the child and activation of hyper-vigilance. Eliminate non-supportive relationships and reduce the number of people interacting with the child by combining as many roles as possible. Consider the relative necessity of social workers, therapists (mental health, speech, physical, occupational), behavior specialists, caseworkers, early intervention teams, respite workers, doctors and teachers.

When Corey joined the family at age four, his speech and motor skills were delayed, because of neglect in his birth home. His birth parents rarely interacted with him, keeping him in a crib most of the day. Rebecca and Danny gladly accepted all the professional help offered. They arranged weekly appointments with speech, occupational and physical therapists. During the appointments, Corey was lively and playful with each professional, but on the way home he cried and kicked the back of the car seat. Rebecca was always happy to put him to bed after therapy. But she began to notice that Corey was pleasant with others and angry with her. She felt jealous of each therapist, wishing he would be as joyful with her as with them.

A team meeting was held to determine ways to decrease the time Corey spent with therapists. The speech therapist provided interventions for the parents to use with Corey and offered to check in with the family monthly. The occupational and physical therapists combined their treatment goals to enable Corey and Rebecca to have one appointment per week. During the sessions, the therapist directed Rebecca in motor skills interventions with Corey. Corey began to enjoy her presence in session and also while doing the therapeutic activities at home.

THERAPEUTIC ATTITUDE

The process of ensuring safety and steering the traumatized child into more productive pathways is energy-draining. It feels like a constant battle for control. Parents must redefine their roles and take ownership of what they can actually control. Old paradigms imply that the parents' role is to control their children. The new paradigm states that parents control their home and children learn to adapt to the family rules. Parents control "if and when" they take their child to the park, purchase the "needed" new shoes and, in short, create and supply the child's world. All good things come from the parents. All of this is within the parents' control.

As parents regain their personal power, they develop a "therapeutic attitude," because they know who controls "when, how and what" things are accomplished. They cannot be coerced or threatened to provide good things. They will base their decisions on their energy level, the child's reciprocity or maybe just because they are "great parents" and decide to treat the child to the park. Using the Trauma Lens Paradigm Shift, they know why their children behave as they do and know how to address those behaviors. They feel confident.

Knowing the parental role and power and the impact of trauma does not mean that parenting comes easy. Therapeutic parenting is hard work, always challenging and requires much thought. It is impossible to always be therapeutic with the child. Adequate respite, even for an hour, is vital to refocus on the task. It is important to explain the temporary separation to the child to decrease fear of another abandonment. These messages are delivered with loving calmness. Needless to say, sarcasm or blame reinforces the N-IWM.

Some examples of hurtful statements are: "You have been so bad lately. I cannot take it anymore. You are going to stay with the respite family," and "I cannot stand you anymore. You are going away for a while."

Examples of helpful statements are: "I need time to restore my outlook," "I am gaining control over myself," and "I will take some time for myself."

• *The Script*

The script for the healing process contains empathic statements, humor and encouragement. The goal is to maintain the delicate balance of structure and nurture. Often the script must be memorized, considering that the words may not come naturally in responding to a child who, at best, pushes the mother away emotionally. Remember Faye's "backwards parenting" experience. Communication is more than just words. Facial expressions, body language, tone of voice and word choice must be fine tuned to eliminate anger or sarcasm. Many parents spend time rehearsing Dan Hughes' PACE model, which provides concrete interactional interventions to engage with the child. Learning and practicing new communication skills is necessary. The greatest benefit will be the ability to draw on this wisdom and new style of engagement in times of overwhelming stress.

Parents are wise to use statements about what they will do, rather than what their child will do. No matter what earlier generations say, we cannot control our children (although we may be able to move them about when they are young). We can control ourselves. Examples of "I" statements include: "I will take you to Grandma's when your chores are finished," and "I give cookies to children who eat their broccoli."

Amy's Family

James and Lori determined that it was useless to tell Amy what to do, because she was so defiant. Their demands just seemed to give her more rules to break. They began to use "I" statements instead. They practiced them after she was in bed at night. They enjoyed the time together in a strange way, while they gained new skills. They reduced their demands as they stated what and when they were willing to act. Amy found it difficult to argue with them, since they were not telling her what to do.

Children with early trauma learned to be hyper-vigilant to keep safe. They needed to know everything that was happening in their environment. Parents can take advantage of third party conversations to help their children accept compliments. Direct compliments may conflict with a child's negative internal working model ("I am bad"). Therefore, a parent may "stage" the intervention to describe to the other parent the behavior they wish to compliment. With the child within hearing range, one parent compliments the child and the other reacts positively. With practice, the "listening" parent can take the cue and expound on the compliment to reinforce the praise.

Sally's Family

Jane found she could not compliment Sally without escalating her negative behavior. One day while talking to her mother on the phone, Jane told her about Sally's improvement in math. Sally smiled as she listened to her mother's phone call. Sally accepted the compliment, because it was not directed at her and she did not have to respond to it.

Many children complain that they do not feel heard or that they do not have a voice. Parents often interpret these statements as "therapy talk." That is, as a parroting of jargon they heard in a therapy session. But what the child is usually saying is that he or she does not "feel felt." The parent is not having the same emotional experience as the child. Parents are encouraged to be empathic—"walking in the child's shoes" and responding with like emotional intensity and depth. By matching affect, the parent will enable the child to experience the parent differently.

Amy's Family

After attending a training session, James and Lori were determined to use affect matching with Amy. They practiced with each other. James described his commute with heightened emotion. Lori used her own experience of being in similar traffic in order to understand James' traveling travails. She responded with emotions similar to his—frustration, anger and fear. Then James shared funny stories and Lori matched his laughter with her own. Somewhat to their pleasant surprise, these practice sessions increased the emotional versatility of their communication with each other. The sessions became their favorite time in the day. They then focused on using this skill during dinnertime with Amy.

At first Amy was disturbed by the change in her parents. She tried to make them stop; she told them "they weren't being real" and to "stop acting like therapists." But the parents were undeterred and they actually seemed to enjoy sharing their day in this way. Eventually they noticed that it was not taking effort anymore and the interaction was almost automatic. Lori reported feeling "gypped" when it didn't happen for some reason. Amy became more emotionally attuned to her parents and felt closer to them. Dinnertime became a pleasurable experience for all.

• The Props

Traumatized and abused children tend to come from environments that lacked physiological and safety provisions. Many naïve foster and adoptive parents assume that the children will be thankful for their new abundance and express appreciation for the changed lifestyle. These children may not have a template for how to interact in an abundant environment or even find it valuable. This is often the first clash between the child's and parents' belief systems (Child's: "I am unlovable and my parents can't be trusted." Parents': "This child is lovable and we can be trusted."). The natural parental impulse to provide relationships, activities and possessions for their child must be held in check at first. To minimize conflict, the environment must be adapted. The props for this production cannot be costly or cherished pieces that could be damaged or destroyed.

Remember that the child's nature is to push the family away and recreate what is familiar internally and externally, namely a chaotic environment and distant, abusive or neglectful relationships. Until the child develops a positive belief system and healthy emotional regulation, he or she will be prone to damaging or destroying possessions. So irreplaceable and costly items should be removed and stored. What better way to push a mother away than to break her favorite lamp, vase or jewelry? Other family members may also be targeted and so their possessions must also be secured and firm boundaries established.

There is great value in limiting the quantity and quality of the traumatized child's personal belongings at first. The child is easily overwhelmed with all the choices of toys or clothes and picking and choosing can become a virtual battlefield. The child may destroy anything of value under the influence of negative core beliefs. By staging a minimal environment, parents can give the child's chaotic inner world the opportunity to calm down, with reduced trauma triggers. As clinical social worker Paris Goodyear-Brown points out, one of the parent's responsibilities is to "be proactive in scanning the environment for anything that may spike the child's post-traumatic anxiety."[35]

Brandon's Family

Bob and Deena were first-time parents of newly-placed six-year-old Brandon. They wanted Brandon to integrate into their home without needing to adapt the environment. Both believed that a child will comply when he or she knows the rules and will be thankful for a nice home. On Brandon's second day in their home, they outlined for him how he was expected to behave, the family rules and his boundaries. Although the first week went well, Brandon began to "forget" the rules and what he was not allowed to touch. By the second month Brandon had gone from "forgetting" the rules to telling Deena that he did not care about their rules. In the third month Brandon broke Deena's valuable figurines and rummaged through Bob's desk. Bob and Deena did not know how to make him respect their property. The family had begun the Downward Spiral. The family therapist referred them to a developmental specialist.

The developmental specialist advised Bob and Deena to assess Brandon's emotional age and prepare a corresponding environment. After some reading on child development, Deena determined that Brandon demonstrated toddler behaviors. They simplified their home, removing costly items and adding toys and activities to engage Brandon. They actually had to teach him to play. Bob and Deena's relationships with Brandon then began to deepen. He started to mature emotionally and became respectful of the family's possessions as he watched Bob and Deena model how to care for their belongings.

Limit props to decrease stress. Specifically, limit the number of toys, clothes, books and furniture. The first rule: Don't buy anything for the child that is not absolutely necessary. A parent's inclination is to rush out and buy everything for this "poor, orphaned child," out of a desire to shower the child with glorious presents as proof of his or her loving kindness. But parents must visualize first losing connections to one's birth family, then being moved from family to family and now facing placement with still a different family. We must always try to see the world through the child's lens. What is the most important *thing* for the child? Is it really a possession?

Sally's Family

Sally, who had just moved to her fourth foster family, talked relentlessly about the expensive doll she had to leave at the previous home. "The doll cost a hundred dollars," Sally declared. Jane wanted to order her a new doll to make up for the loss. She thought it would ease Sally's pain. She failed to notice that Sally was not saying she missed the family who bought the doll. If we were Sally, what *should* we grieve? A possession? These children have a relationship deficiency that another possession will not remedy.

Many children have unknown "trauma triggers" that instill fear and anxiety. In the past, the child's toy may have given the caregiver a means to punish the child. The toy may have been taken away and used against the child or destroyed out of anger. Some children were "groomed" with toys by sexual predators. Such memories may trigger feelings of discomfort or outright fear of the new caregiver. If the environment must be adjusted after the child already has too many possessions, these traumatic memories can become activated with accompanying emotional dysregulation. Extra precautions must be used in this process.

Most foster and adoptive parents want to enrich their child's life with gifts and privileges. They quickly realize that possessions become another source of interference in the development of relationships. Children tend to destroy the gifts in which parents have invested time and money.

Disappointment grows into anger as the parents see their gifts ruined. The wedge between the parents and the child drives them further apart. The child will not be happy with broken toys but will experience comfort as he or she "feels" the resulting distancing of the parental relationship. Statements like "Who cares anyway?" or "So what?", delivered with complete disregard for potential consequences, demonstrate the child's comfort. Often the "icing on the cake" is blaming the parents for the damage: "If you would have bought a different one..." or "That was never what I wanted anyway." Or maybe it's the professional peering out over the top of his glasses at the parents with the judgmental observation, "I noticed all of his toys are either broken or have missing parts!" In short, if parents equate the child's care of their gift with the child's affection for them, the gift may be used as a wedge to divide the relationship.

TOO MANY POSSESSIONS

Brandon's Family

Bob and Deena tended to use retail therapy to sooth their emotional distress. When Brandon joined the family at six years old, they had a reason to buy more to make up for his deprivation. Brandon was a difficult child to parent with all his behavioral problems. Because of the stress of parenting, Bob's and Deena's buying increased. The home quickly became filled with "stuff."

Brandon's possessions required him to repeatedly make bewildering decisions about what to do with his time, attention and energy. He was ill-prepared to apply the focus, adaptability to loss (of all the things he did not choose to do at the moment) and security (that nobody would take the possessions away) that were necessary to manage this "embarrassment of riches." He began leaving items all over the house. He had tantrums when instructed to pick up the toys. When other children wanted to play with one of his toys, he became aggressive.

By reducing the number of possessions, parents will eliminate the child's messiness, destruction of property, aggression and tantrums related to possessions, and relieve their fatigue, anger, hyper-vigilance and overspending.

Therapy was focused on reducing the number of toys to a few favorites, decreasing parental purchases, increased parental time playing with the child and the parents finding new ways to handle their stress. The parents' savings increased as they reduced their need for retail therapy. As Brandon continued to mature and gain emotional self-regulation, he was able to handle more possessions.

PERFORMING THE PRODUCTION: FAMILY TIME TO GROW THE RELATIONSHIP

In addition to the characters, script and props, relationships will only grow when the partners spend time together enjoying each other's company. Imagine dating but not being together or having fun with each other. This may entail limiting "extracurricular" activities for the child, such as music or art lessons, sports or involvement in other organizations.

Corey's Family

Rebecca and Danny happily signed Corey up for soccer. Corey also stated that he wanted to play the trumpet and so private lessons were scheduled once weekly. Danny led the local Boy Scout troop and Corey tagged along. The family was active in their church, allowing Corey to be in the youth group. Rebecca and Danny were pleased that they could offer all these opportunities. They were fulfilling their parenting dreams by treating him like their birth children and helping make up for the deprivation he had endured.

A busy summer was followed by autumn with still more activities. Rebecca began feeling like a taxi driver with a growing concern about Corey's grumpy attitude. He was demanding and aggressive when late for an activity or asked to complete chores. They had little family time. Corey enjoyed his time away from the family. Rebecca and Danny thought that if they explained the inappropriateness of his attitude, Corey would change. But explaining did not work and consequences were of no "consequence" to him. Corey's behavior problems increased. Rebecca and Danny felt like they were in a vortex pulling them farther and farther away from their parenting dreams.

The therapist convinced Rebecca and Danny to curtail Corey's and their involvement in outside activities until such time as their relationship was solidified. They actually discovered with Corey an enjoyment of board games that they hadn't experienced with their birth children. As Corey began to respond with some warmth to this play time with his parents, they were reminded of the "P" in Dan Hughes' PACE acronym: Playfulness!

In chapter 16 you will find an assortment of practical suggestions for adapting the environment to the unique needs of the attachment-disordered child.

PART 3

The Trauma-Disrupted Competencies

CHAPTER 8

Why Children Behave as They Do

There are simply too few articles that adequately describe methods for parenting a child with a history of trauma, abuse, neglect and abandonment. Psychiatric social worker and therapist Ellen Ryan suggested that parents must "learn and implement a unique and intense reparenting process aimed at helping the child have a second chance at attachment."[36]

We have approached this "unique and intense reparenting process" by examining how trauma disrupts healthy child development. Through this trauma lens, we identified six trauma-disrupted developmental competencies and the resulting behaviors and then designed interventions to help the child with healing. We kept the description short for each Trauma-Disrupted Competency (TDC), just enough explanation for understanding. Books have been written about each of them, so for those interested in more information we have listed other resources. Parents with children who have severe impairments find these resources invaluable for learning and training service providers.

Trauma-Disrupted Competencies

1. Negative Internal Working Model (N-IWM)
2. Emotional Response
3. Developmental Delays
4. Object Relations
5. Self-Regulation
6. Sensory Distortions

We will use the Jones family and Corey's story to introduce the Trauma-Disrupted Competencies. Long before the Joneses decided that Corey would join their family, Rebecca Jones and Corey's birth mother were having similar experiences. Both were in relationships, became pregnant and gave birth to beautiful, healthy infants. Both moms wanted their babies but personal histories, circumstances and lifestyles changed their destinies.

Compare Corey's entrance and journey into life to that of Andy, Rebecca's child. Corey's experiences are typical of many children in the foster and adoptive community. Notice the difference between Andy and Corey's relationships with their moms, their internal beliefs, their child developmental milestones and how they approached the world.

ANDY'S STORY

Pink. The cylindrical plastic wand definitely glowed with a pale pink dot. Rebecca sat down hard with waves of fear and pleasure rolling through her chest. She and Danny had delayed pregnancy until their finances would allow her to be a stay-at-home mom. Now, it was a reality. She had life growing inside of her, another human being! She felt afraid, knowing that they faced so many decisions and they could be vulnerable to pain and loss. Were her hormones already overwhelming her? Questions flooded her. What if she and Danny disagreed on names? Parenting styles? Nursery furniture? She and Danny would be having many long conversations. She imagined him being a great dad and, after all, he said he wanted a baby, but could they do this effectively? It was so strange to want something so badly but still be afraid they couldn't handle it.

Rebecca consulted friends about obstetricians and pediatricians. She scheduled her first doctor's appointment. The doctor was kind and confident that Rebecca and the baby were in good health. Afterwards, she stopped by the local bookstore. She wandered from aisle to aisle, perusing children's books and parenting books and even glancing over a few medical resources. She finally chose a book that would chronicle the baby's growth week by week. She wanted to get to know her baby before he or she was born, by being able to visualize growth and development.

The nine months seemed to both fly by and drag along, with the morning sickness, nursery decorating, name selection, baby showers, medical testing, childbirth classes, meeting with the lactation consultant and hospital tours. Danny and Rebecca pored over other resources that friends had shared and discussed many of the "what ifs" that new parents fear. They kept a calendar chart of the baby's growth. They argued over the details and solved the problems. A week after the due date, Danny's eyes felt filled with gravel when Rebecca woke him early one morning. This must be their big day. Panic filled him as he followed their fully prepared plan:

1. Phone the doctor; 2. Take a shower; 3. Put the suitcase in the car; 4. Make sure Rebecca was comfortable; 5. Drive to the hospital; 6. Become a new dad and mom!

Twelve painful hours preceded the miracle of Andrew Christopher's birth. His piercing scream scared his new parents. Rebecca quickly asked to hold him as the nurses finished his postnatal care. Rebecca pulled him to her breast and began to relax. Finished! He was here. She felt exhausted but at peace; he was healthy. He calmed to her touch and voice. Snuggling close to her, he settled down and slept.

Thus began a pattern that occurred repeatedly hour after hour, day after day. When Andy felt scared, he cried and Rebecca came and picked him up. She noticed that his cry tended to scare her until she could determine what was wrong with him. Usually noises, hunger, tiredness, boredom and dirty diapers were the causes. After she knew what was wrong, she could calm down and soothe him. He liked to snuggle close to her when scared. He seemed to calm down when she calmed down. Time after time, she explained what was happening to him in comforting tones. She loved to snuggle him close and look into his eyes. Her eyes spoke of the great love she had for him.

One day when she heard Andy screaming from the nursery, Rebecca rushed up the stairs and into the room, quickly crossed to the crib and gathered him into her arms. As she looked around, she noticed how the mobile at the end of the bed had swiveled off the bar and fallen half into the crib and half down the side. Even as she ran the scenario through her mind she began to calm down. At first her voice was excited and scared, high-pitched and fast. Then, her voice began to slow down and her tone lowered. She held Andy away from her chest and smiled into his upturned face. Andy, as if on cue, slowed his crying, looked into her face and smiled back at her.

Rebecca's body adjusted to the new demands. She found that her breasts began to swell and were tender between feedings. Often, she could tell Andy would be waking up soon just by the way her body felt. After some initial experimenting, the two settled into an oft-repeated and very comforting pattern. Andy would cry with hunger and, most times, Rebecca would stop whatever she was doing to take Andy to their favorite chair and "assume the position." Andy would look expectantly into his mother's eyes and begin to nurse. As the pressure reduced for Rebecca and Andy's belly was filled, they both seemed to share a moment of peace and contentment. Danny would find himself smiling at the sight.

Another time, as Andy rested contentedly in the playpen after feeding, Rebecca cleaned the kitchen. She heard him cry as she began her final task. She knew he was not hungry, but he probably needed to burp. Without thinking, she threw a towel over her shoulder and went directly to Andy.

She picked him up gently and told him he was feeling gassy. "It's okay; we'll take care of that right now," she said. Placing Andy upright with his head above her shoulder, she gently patted his back. In seconds, Andy's crying was interrupted as he spit up on the towel. She carefully wiped his mouth. Rebecca and Andy both giggled. Danny watched from his seat at the kitchen table as Andy was returned to the playpen. He asked, "How did you know what he needed?"

"I don't know," Rebecca replied. "It just sounded like he had a gas bubble."

Andy enjoyed being with his mom. She was his favorite playmate. Rebecca entertained him with peek-a-boo, rocking and reading to him and playing with his toes and fingers. He especially enjoyed peek-a-boo. As time went by, he learned to laugh as she hid behind a blanket and he began to look expectantly for her return. His face would brighten with that same joy when she walked into the room after a nap or came home from a shopping trip. Andy's brain was learning to hold a picture of Rebecca even when he could not see her. Later this would help him to make decisions even when she was out of sight. Her ability to demonstrate a full range of feelings in Andy's presence, while still loving and caring for him, enabled him to recognize that the same person can have differing feelings.

Before long, Andy began eating food. Rebecca never questioned why she talked to him all the time. It was as if she thought he could participate in a long conversation. She talked to him about being tired or hungry. She told him he needed sleep and put him to bed. She told him when he was cold or hot as she dressed him. She held up toys and showed him how to play with them. She expressed her fear when he was sick. She cried when he cried when left for a short visit with Grandma. She even laughed when he had a messy diaper. They shared their feelings about everything.

Andy's brain grew fast in those first three years. He learned to do new things every week. His attention span continued to lengthen. Shortly, a routine emerged. He would become fearful of some experience he was having while exploring the room. He would cry, Rebecca would feel his fear and she would then deal with that fear for them both. Then Andy would return to his learning. From infancy, Rebecca narrated his world for him and he depended on Rebecca to calm and sooth him. He gradually matured and learned to calm himself, but returned to Rebecca for confirmation of his safety and interpretation of his environment.

From the time he began to intentionally lift his head from the crib, Andy gradually mastered gravity. Without ever thinking about it, he just knew how to navigate gravity. This learning was acquired by experience in the limbic region of the brain before he had words. Much like with gravity, Andy learned other things via experiences. He formed beliefs about himself, his mother and the world. As Rebecca repeatedly responded to the "routine" of infinite experiences of meeting Andy's needs, he formed a picture of himself and Rebecca. Each time he shared his fear with Rebecca, his brain shifted from fear to contentment. Eventually, he knew by experience that he was valuable, that she was trustworthy and he knew he and his mom could handle anything together. Like his experience of gravity, Andy used this early learning about his mom for almost every decision he would make for the rest of his life. Choices would be right or wrong based on how they measured up to what he learned in those early relational responses. His brain would tell him how to feel (what emotions to generate) about his every situation, based on this "back brain learning."

It was what he knew about his mother that allowed his brain to calm enough to master holding a bottle, then a fork and eventually a pencil. Her very presence seemed to move his brain into a relaxed but attentive state that was just perfect for learning. In this calm, attentive state, he learned to define sensations such as full, hot, tired and hungry. As he learned the definitions of these sensations, he learned to evaluate the experience. Was it good and desirable or bad and something to avoid? Through his relationship with Rebecca, Andy acquired near-automatic responses to certain experiences. Hunger was to precede eating. Sleep was to follow feeling tired. Cold could be dangerous and was to be avoided. He learned to master new skills like potty training and taking turns. Andy didn't move into these skills independently. Rebecca was present, offered encouragement, evaluated readiness and provided the tools and opportunities to practice. Her actions reinforced his earlier learning. He learned that pleasing her and mastering new skills was good. A happy mom meant new opportunities and interesting experiences. If she was fearful or angry, his world shrank and opportunities dwindled.

COREY'S STORY

Pink. The cylindrical plastic wand definitely glowed with a pale pink dot. Sophia sat down hard with waves of fear crashing through her chest. She had wanted to delay pregnancy until Larry would commit to giving up drugs. But accidents will happen, especially when they got as stoned as last weekend. Now it was a reality. She had life growing inside of her, another human being. She felt afraid, knowing that Larry had not followed through with his empty promises. He preferred spending time with his lazy friends and getting high. Sophia was faced with too many decisions, each leading to vulnerability, pain and loss. Were her hormones already overwhelming her? Questions flooded her. What if Larry left her? How would she feed this baby? They did not have enough food or money for themselves, much less a baby. Larry said he did not like kids; he would not be concerned about names or nursery furniture. Fear washed through her again. At the same time, she could imagine having a family and someone to love her completely, like a child. She did not know who to talk to who would support her decision to keep this baby. Larry's friend, Lucas, had a girlfriend with a baby. Sophia had held the baby many times while she got high with the guys. She would try to call the girlfriend, but her number had changed so many times. Hopefully, she'd be happy to help with a newborn.

Sophia finished signing the paperwork with the welfare caseworker and asked for a doctor who accepted her new Medical Assistance card. She scheduled her first doctor's appointment, knowing she had to find bus fare each time she went. The doctor was kind and confident that Sophia and the baby were in good health. After the doctor visit, she stopped by the local mission store to ask for a clothing voucher. Her stomach would be expanding and she barely had enough clothes to wear to work at her cleaning job. Sophia had little information on how babies grow before they are born, but since she had helped raise her four siblings, she could take care of this baby.

Sometimes Sophia worried whether she was eating right. She barely gained weight and wondered why she bothered with maternity clothes. The Medical Assistance card allowed her prenatal vitamins, but like trips to the doctor, transportation to the pharmacy was costly. She was afraid the smoking would be a problem for the baby. The gang filled their tiny apartment with thick layers of gray smoke. They would probably have to quit that when the baby came. But for now it was good to relax and there was no point having that fight now.

The nine months flew by with morning sickness, medical testing and a hospital tour. Larry finally consented to the hospital tour. He grouched as he walked the hollow hallways, declaring he would not be there during the delivery, because he didn't like screaming women. They argued over the details and never solved any problems.

A week after the due date, Larry's eyes felt filled with gravel when Sophia woke him early one morning. Anger churned inside him as he heard her cry for help. She held her stomach and begged him to phone the doctor, but he refused. He had friends to meet that evening and needed his rest. Larry rolled over and went back to sleep. Sophia wanted her caseworker to take her to the hospital, but her office did not open until 9:00 A.M. Sophia gathered her last few dollars and called a taxi. She put her and the baby's few belongings in a plastic bag and waited by the curb.

Twelve painful hours preceded the miracle of Corey's birth. The hospital staff refused to give anywhere near enough pain medication. Her head and everything else hurt and she could really use more drugs, but Larry had never shown up. He probably would have been upset with how long it took anyway. She hoped he was okay. The baby's piercing scream scared his new mom and she quickly asked the hospital staff to make him stop crying. The staff suggested that she begin breastfeeding to calm him down. She and Larry had already decided that she needed to return to her pre-pregnancy shape by not breastfeeding. Besides, Sophia heard that breastfeeding was painful and he would be going to daycare anyway. The nurse placed him on her chest and offered a bottle for her to feed him. Sophia tensed, holding him stiffly in her arms. He would not settle or nurse from the bottle. She began to cry softly and requested the nurse take care of him. Sophia felt so alone and afraid. Before leaving the hospital, the staff taught her how to hold him and make sure he drank enough formula. She started to remember all this from her little sister, so it was no problem.

What she didn't remember was how often the baby "needed" her. The neediness never stopped, hour after hour, day after day. When Corey felt scared, he cried so Mom would come. Sophia did not want to pick him up. He was such a bother and made Larry mad when he cried. Sometimes, she would pick him up and demand that he stop crying. Larry could hurt them both. Right now, he was only hitting her when the baby cried. She noticed that his cry tended to scare her. He cried from everything: noises, hunger, tiredness, boredom and dirty diapers. Knowing what caused him to cry was not helpful; she did not have enough food or diapers for him. She had to water down his formula to stretch it until the Women, Infants and Children Program check came in. Sometimes she had to fight Larry for the formula. He had found a way to swap it for weed. Sometimes it was just good to have a way to escape and relax. Sophia and Corey never seemed to have pleasant times together. They both seemed to share the same fears. Time after time, she explained what was happening to him in fearful tones. It was often distressing to hold him and look in his eyes. He always seemed to be saying that she was a bad mom. Her eyes spoke back to him: He was a fearful thing and he might be right about her.

Corey did not enjoy life. He lay in his dirty bed day after day. When he began day care, he could not tolerate other caregivers and preferred being alone. He cried and fussed when held. The busy staffers had many infants to attend to and were more than willing to leave him alone. They even praised him for being so easy to "take care of." The center always had new workers. Each new worker was given the task of caring for whatever infants were being served at the time. Corey had few needs; dirty diapers and hunger did not cause him to cry. He could lay for hours with a faraway look in his eyes. As time went by, he did not learn to laugh like the other infants. Most staff didn't remain employed there long enough to notice. One who did decided she wasn't going to rock the boat. She just described him as "never a bother." Sophia found the center a relief. Larry was not as angry when Corey was at the center. He could stay there five days a week from 6:00 A.M. to 7:00 P.M.

Weekends were the biggest problem. Larry tended to get high on Friday night and stay high until Sunday. As long as he had his drugs, Larry would not hurt them. If he had no money, then they would be in danger. A few times, he hit Sophia and the neighbors called the police. Since Corey was such a "quiet" baby, the police did not know he was in the house.

Before long, Corey was old enough for baby food. Sophia could not understand why he did not want to eat. She mashed the food the best she could. Sometimes, friends gave her canned baby food. He tolerated "rich kid" food better. Sophia yelled at him for being a picky eater. She found that she was yelling more and more. No food or clothing and an angry Larry; when would their troubles stop? She did not have enough clothing for Corey that first winter. She could not help that he did not like the wool sweater and cried. He had to wear as many clothes as possible to stay warm. She yelled at him for crying during those early morning walks to the center. She could not help it that he was cold—she was too. Couldn't he understand that?

Unfortunately, Corey did understand his mom in his own baby way. His tiny infant brain knew she could not be depended on and he was not worth taking care of. They shared the same beliefs.

Corey learned about gravity like other infants, though Sophia didn't notice when he began lifting his head, holding and dropping toys or pulling himself up using the crib railings. She called for Larry to watch when Corey took his first steps, but he was not interested. Her enthusiasm was quickly squashed when Larry responded, "Big deal; babies do that all the time. He'll be getting into everything now! You better watch him or there'll be trouble." Sophia tried to be a good mother and there were moments when she and Corey seemed to enjoy each other.

So often, she just felt fear about not being good enough for Corey or Larry or her boss. Tired, exhausted and chronically fearful, she felt unable to handle the life she found herself trapped in. Slowly she began to value and crave Larry's few moments of bliss delivered via drugs. She was not even aware that as she increasingly indulged in this short relief, her abilities and motivations for parenting declined.

Corey's life experiences caused him to feel fear like all other kids, but when he cried out for Sophia's comfort, she was often absent, too busy or too wasted to go to him. Corey learned to turn his fear into a piercing cry of anger. His body would stiffen, his face would turn red and he would just scream his loudest. This second scream caused Sophia or the babysitters to attend when the first cry did not. Unfortunately, when he received assistance after this call, his caregivers were often scared and angry, resulting in Corey being yelled at and occasionally hurt. Sometimes his needs were met and other times they were not. Corey knew at the very center of his being that "not having a caregiver's attention" meant death. He quickly learned that an angry caregiver was better than no caregiver.

Corey had to learn the same things as other children in their first years. Being human, he learned them in the same ways. The constant equation of sensation produced fear and a "call out" to mom followed by connection to mom. Her response communicated to him that he was "bad," burdensome and without value. He learned that his primary caregiver was untrustworthy, hurtful and dangerous. And the world he was born into was full of peril.

While other children were gifted with an attentive and attuned mother, one who played peek-a-boo and hide and seek, Corey's mother would disappear for hours and days at a time. He never knew if she would come back. When she did, her emotions varied so wildly with whatever she was dealing with at the moment, he could never predict which mom to expect. His brain did not hold a permanent or consistent picture of a caring mom. He never believed Mom's presence would help him make good decisions.

Corey's brain focused on the here and now in order to survive. He used all his energy being safe and keeping his fear in control. Corey's brain never seemed to calm down. His growing brain continually added neural pathways to assist him in dealing with the constant fear. Little things provoked him into wild emotional responses. The shadow of an adult overhead could cause him to curl into a fetal position on the ground. A slight perception of injustice could lead to a screaming, raving tantrum. He was rarely in a relaxed, attentive state that promoted learning. Instead, he learned to scan the environment for sources of danger or advantage while trying to listen to the teacher.

Bereft of the connection to an emotionally-attuned caregiver and his or her narration of life experiences, he never learned how to analyze the environment through an adult's eyes. All his evaluations went through an immature brain. He learned to survive under stressful conditions. If he felt cold, it wasn't always something to be avoided. Hunger was a regular occurrence and he learned to address this as best he could. Things like stealing and hiding food, binge eating and "playing helpless and cute" were within his power and produced a feeling of security more often than depending on others. Corey's constant hyper-vigilance, combined with his learning to stress adults to get what he needed, resulted in an almost supernatural ability to pick up on nonverbal communication. He became a master at always keeping the adult responsible for his well-being at a certain distance from him. Too stressed and he would suffer, too close and he would feel in danger, too distant and he would feel abandoned. Oddly, he became fearful and dysregulated in the presence of his mother. He usually felt like he needed to control her.

Corey's need to control adults left little energy for learning and achieving developmental milestones. He never learned to enjoy chewing food. Holding a fork was a task that only slowed down his consumption. While other boys were learning to occupy themselves with toys, Corey never seemed to know what to do with blocks or a ball or when sitting quietly or playing tag with the other kids. He would abandon whatever he had in favor of finding and taking whatever game the others were playing. Other children's reactions were scary for Corey and often resulted in his hitting, running from or avoiding others.

As he grew, the constant nonverbal communication from adults and the consequences he was given reinforced his early beliefs that he was bad, his mom was bad and his world was bad. Sadly, truth be told, Corey's behaviors did fit his early world fairly well. Stealing and hoarding did get him food he would not normally get. Slapping mom on the leg did get her off the couch when words would not. It was really good to know when Larry was in a bad mood so that Corey could avoid him. This saved him from getting hit.

Corey's main motivation in life became trying to stop the unending feelings of fear. Many of the ways Corey learned to reduce his perception of fear allowed him to survive in the neglectful and perilous world around him. It was not until later when Child Protective Services removed him from everything he knew and placed him with strangers that his problems began. Corey went to live with Rebecca and Danny. Rebecca and Danny did not change their parenting style after the adoption. Corey was expected to maintain the foster child routine. Over time, Corey's behavior problems increased. He did not regulate his eating, always asking for food. Rebecca found moldy food under his bed and food wrappers in his closet. She discovered he went to the kitchen during the night for more food. Rebecca began hiding food and locking cabinets. Their birth children constantly complained about the inaccessibility of food, because of Corey. Rebecca and Danny added more rules to stop these behaviors. Corey broke the rules.

Now therapists and foster parents began telling him that everything he believed was wrong. How odd to hear that he needed to "depend" on adults to get his needs met. In the world Corey knew, adults would say similar things to keep him quiet and avoid taking care of him. He "knew" how to respond to them. In this new world, he seemed unable to make the right decisions or learn from consequences. He was simply making decisions based on what he already knew about the world. He was not confused or bothered when the adults grew angry and took things away. He did not enjoy the feeling of loss. It was not something that could be avoided. That's just the way the world was.

Early in life, Corey learned the survival tactic of avoiding fear by becoming angry and using threats and blame. He never even noticed that all he felt was mad. Adults wanted him to try to "win" rewards but, as he got closer to earning a reward, he would begin to feel uncomfortable inside. Rarely was he comfortable enough to attain an award. More often, he would do something that would either sabotage his getting the reward or destroy what he already had.

Therapists responded to this by telling the foster parents that they needed to make the tasks easier and "Every boy takes his new bike apart at some point." Somehow, little Corey's inability to handle fear became the "shortcomings" of the foster parents.

Using this story of two babies, we will now examine how each of the six Trauma-Disrupted Competencies arises from an abusive start to life.

CHAPTER 9

The Negative Internal Working Model

Corey's Family

Corey had to learn the same things as other children in their first years. Being human, he learned them in the same ways. The constant equation of sensation produced fear and a "call out" to Mom followed by connection to Mom. In Corey's case, an increase in fear led him to learn in the experiential portion of his brain before his brain developed the capacity for encoding memory in words. He was "bad," burdensome and without value. He learned that his primary caregiver was untrustworthy, dangerous and hurtful. And the world he was born into was dangerous, too.

Rebecca and Danny thought they were good foster parents and tried to encourage their children. They could not understand why Corey continued to say he was a bad kid. They told him over and over he was not bad. He just had bad behavior. Why didn't he believe them?

Children form their belief systems via interactions with their primary caregivers, usually with Mom. Belief systems are formed by repeated experiences long before rational thought develops and are used for decision-making prior to the onset of the child's use of words. Repeated interactions with gravity enable a child to "know" or predict what a toy will do before he makes sense of the action.

Children are biologically prepared to look to a primary caregiver to keep them safe, nurture them and provide an external view of themselves. This biological hard wiring is the perfect foundation for learning about self, caregivers and eventually the world. In an ideal situation, a "good enough" caregiver will provide an internal picture or belief in one's self as the most important thing in the world, the caregiver as trustworthy and the world as generally safe.

If this relationship is disrupted or maladaptive for extended periods of time, the child's view of himself, Mom and the world may be internalized as negative. Disruptions may be the result of a parent's absence due to working long hours, being placed in foster care, abandonment or parental addictions, mental health problems like depression, domestic violence and/or illness. Even medical problems like ear infections or digestive difficulties can render a caregiver unable to sooth an infant. Each forces multiple caregivers (babysitters) to take care of the child. Some children are further traumatized by neglect and/or abuse. These children tend to feel defective, empty, helpless and perhaps even without hope. This is the genesis of maladaptive beliefs—namely, the Negative Internal Working Model of self, others and the world. Noted Dutch psychiatrist Bessel Van der Kolk refers to "a torn map of the world" for these children in which they learned how to navigate the world through their early experiences with their caregivers: "These inner maps are remarkably stable across time." [37]

The core beliefs of the Negative Internal Working Model (N-IWM) are:

1. I am unlovable.
2. Adults cannot be trusted.
3. The world is unsafe.

These maladaptive beliefs influence emotions, decision-making, perceptions and behavioral reactions. They almost certainly affect sensory experiences, such as hunger, pain, heat and cold in particular. A person's belief system interacts with the environment and leads to actions without thought. For instance, people may not consciously evaluate a hole in the sidewalk for depth and breadth, but simply step across the hole when possible, all because of previous experiential learning that automatically informs one that it takes more effort to go down and then back up. Additionally, a person's belief system interacts with the environment and evokes emotions without thought. When walking down a woodland trail, most of us feel fear when facing a coiled snake. Our belief about snakes is interacting with the environment. The fact that most snakes are nonpoisonous (in the U.S.) and almost always trying to get away from us, takes a while (if ever) to assert itself into our emotional world. It is like that with IWM learning too. People will use their IWM to interpret events and others' motivations. How many of us would think the snake is looking for someone to bite while simultaneously observing that the cold temperature may be making him move very slowly, causing him to have more important things to worry about. It is like that with the IWM (beliefs about self, Mom and the world) too. The beliefs organize memory and information storage.

Corey's Family

The Jones family planned a picnic at the local park. The day started off with a family hike and race to the top of Cooper Cliff. Danny and Rebecca were amazed by how agreeable everyone was. There was some good-natured ribbing near the top, but it subsided quickly when Danny stepped in and everyone moved on. After a quick, pre-made peanut butter and jelly sandwich they were off to the lake. Being in the cool water on a hot afternoon was fun and, miraculously, everyone was pleasant. Meal chores were divided up and everyone was assigned a task. Rebecca allowed Corey to wrap the potatoes in foil and push them down in the fire's ashes. She chose his chore specially and he quickly complied, because he liked to poke around in the ashes. Rebecca made sure to thank him as they ate the evening meal. With the day going so well, Danny decided to "push their luck" with one final activity, a family movie. They stopped at the local store, briefly debated on a title and chose a movie. Traditionally, Corey would not agree with any of the selections the family made. Often, he became loud and aggressive, trying to force others to agree. With popcorn and soda waiting, unpacking was completed quickly and the family relaxed while watching the movie. Rebecca and Danny shared a congratulatory smile and wink as they watched the children nod off after a perfect day.

The next morning Rebecca noticed that Corey was not making eye contact, spilled his milk and yelled at Andy for bumping him even though Andy wasn't near him. Rebecca explored what was happening for Corey by being curious. Corey, with a red, angry face, yelled loudly that he was lucky to be alive! He had to keep himself safe from the family. He accused Lane of trying to trip him on the trail yesterday. Then, Dad threatened to throw him off a cliff if he didn't stop fighting. Mom did not put enough peanut butter on his sandwich like she did for the others. He almost choked on lake water and no one cared. He had to be the slave preparing supper and cleaning up. The final injury was they rented a movie he liked but could not stay awake after having to work so hard all day. "I hate this family! I wish I could leave," he cried.

The Jones family had spent a fun-filled day at the park, but Corey could only remember the events that supported his N-IWM. The positive elements of the day (that clashed with his IWM) were simply not recorded. His memory was impaired due to processing the events through a brain that believed others were evil and would harm him. He used his beliefs to make sense of social situations and perceptions of others. When his sister told him he had a good-looking shirt, Corey hit her and told her she could not have it! Automatically, children like Corey "know" that others cannot be trusted, meet their needs or keep them safe. This automatic knowing enables quicker decision-making in dangerous environments and, initially, keeps them safe.

The "knowing" generates a pervasive emotional climate of fear when interacting with the external world. The resulting behaviors allow these children to ease the overwhelming feeling of fear by constantly striving for the perception of controlling the environment. Humans are always about the business of proving in the outside world what they believe true on the inside. A N-IWM is maladaptive, because the children feel more comfortable (or less fearful) when adults are angry with them, emotionally distant and avoidant.

When faced with an external situation that does not match our IWM, the initial response is always fear. We would experience fear if a serial killer invited us to dinner. Our belief is that serial killers are "bad" and, therefore, dinner with them cannot be a good thing. We would refuse the invitation (if not call the police). However, in this example, we have "reason" to explain the emotion. What if the source of the emotion was unreasonable and/or unrecognizable?

Typically, we humans accept the emotion, supply an action to reharmonize the emotion and use our reason to justify it. Corey received a new toy from Rebecca. He immediately threw it down, told her it was not what he wanted and insisted she take it back. He could feel "safe," because his internal belief about Mom was demonstrated in the external world as she scooped it up and called him a mean boy. He felt less loss over the toy (than a child with a Positive IWM), because he never expected to have it in the first place.

The beliefs are independent of reason and are functioning at an instinctual level. Without trained, supportive adults, most children will not know why they have a particular feeling of fear. They may even be unable to label the emotion of fear. They are still struggling to answer the question, "Why did you do that?" Many a wild accusation has its origin in a reasonable brain trying to explain a behavior without access to its emotional world.

Imagine a child living with an addicted parent. The child may develop certain beliefs from the experience: "I have no value or my parent would take care of me instead of buying drugs. My parent is unsafe and unpredictable when on drugs. She yells, screams and hits me. She is gone for long periods of time and I am alone. The world is unsafe, because I am in danger when strangers come to the house and they hurt me." Van der Kolk describes how "this information is embodied in the warp and woof of our brain circuitry and forms the template of how we think about ourselves and the world around us."[38]

These beliefs force the child to adapt and react in a hostile environment. The child must find food, perform basic self-care tasks and protect him or herself from dangerous people. Children learn to lie, steal and fight to be safe. These children may have younger siblings to care for and protect. Normal childhood activities are foreign and illogical. The child's very struggle for survival is based on the ability to act on these negative beliefs without analyzing the decision—a back-brain, emotional response.

In the same way that our internal working model is formed by interactions with the primary caregiver, the nature of being dependent upon parents for survival entails reaffirmation by adults to continually sustain a child's belief system. Families share internal working models. Children look to (depend upon) adults to define life's experiences. Parents hold, contain and model how to deal with emotions. Being in close proximity, sharing good and bad experiences and sharing intense emotions tend to harmonize family members' emotional worlds.

Some of the strife that occurs when children with early trauma enter a family system is from the clash and merging of internal belief systems. Just because a child is removed from a dangerous environment, the child cannot simply "relax and allow the parents to take care of him or her." The child knows that parents allow bad things to happen. This child is wired to be on hyper-alert and reject others' care. Though the new parents may be smiling and acting in pleasing ways, they're still scary.

Before a child or family can work at creating a more P-IWM, the N-IWM must be exposed. With this exposure, emotions and behaviors will be labeled and redefined by adults. Parents will gain an increased ability to understand the child and control their own emotional world. The child may actually feel weaker as parents gain their own emotional self-control. As initially scary as this "weakness" is, this awareness eventually leads to the ability, focus and motivation to heal.

Families are confronted with the child's survival behaviors such as lying, stealing, hoarding, gorging, etc. Unsuccessfully, families and professionals have attempted to use traditional behavioral methods to control these behaviors as if they are consequences for poor behavior choices. This consistency reaffirms the child's beliefs about himself and the world. When stress causes the child to revert back to old behaviors to get his needs met, he instinctively believes the new parents are mean and dangerous, so that a consequence will support this belief.

Ironically, the child may use disruptive behaviors *to feel secure*. Just by using a behavior consequence model, parents reinforce the N-IWM with punishment and reaffirm the child's belief, conditioned by the N-IWM, that the parents cannot be trusted. Healing interventions come from "disrupting his negative attachment behavior" and focusing on "rebuilding his internalized view of himself and his caregivers."[39]

BEHAVIORS

Children with a N-IWM believe:

- "I cannot do anything."
- "I am not any good."
- "I should be given back."
- "No one wants me."
- "I don't trust my parents."
- "I don't need a parent."
- "I'll never win."
- "I don't care."
- "It doesn't matter."
- "Others cause me to fail."
- "There is no use in…"
- "If they really knew me, then they wouldn't invite me."

Children with a N-IWM…

- Have fantasies (having a chauffeur or three fancy automobiles) that they might relate to others as reality.
- Talk about how well they can do something (but have not tried) or places they have been (but have not visited).
- Tend to have many "accidents" and break things.
- Hide or lose things.
- Tend to be charming and helpful to strangers.
- Are comfortable when others are in chaos and may then try to be helpful.
- When parents are sick, they may act like parents or become afraid and clingy or withdraw.
- Destroy their toys.
- Sabotage their rewards.
- (Without choosing) automatically behave in ways that produce failure.
- Only want what they cannot have.
- Steal to get things, even if they don't want them.
- Perform erratically in school and with chores.

- Cannot ask for needs or wants, but may ask for fantasied or prohibited items.
- Don't verbalize genuine likes.

INTERVENTIONS

Traditional cognitive therapy is less effective for traumatized children, because the child may lack adequate developmental maturation and ability to regulate emotions. Adults must not expect the child to analyze behaviors cognitively. Cognitive tools are still useful to highlight the child's beliefs and behaviors. These tools will encourage reflection and cognitive maturation.

Most behaviors are the by-products of an emotional state. The ability to change quickly from an emotional state to cognitive processing will take time and patience. Bit by bit, step by step, the child will begin to become reflective of how behavior choices are affecting his life. Remember not to lecture or punish the child. These only allow the child to place the blame on someone else.

The first intervention is the Birth of the Belief System that forms the framework for the Trauma Lens Paradigm Shift. This experiential role-play is intended for the participants to see the world through the baby's eyes, which will make sense of their responses to others and the environment.

COGNITIVE INTERVENTIONS

Many parents and professionals will question cognitive interventions, because some children may appear to lack the ability to cognitively process information. The goal is to increase this ability. According to childhood trauma expert Alexandra Cook, "By early childhood, maltreated children demonstrate less flexibility and creativity in problem-solving tasks than same-age peers."[40] Cognitive interventions will decrease the emotional response and stimulate the brain to process information. Clinical psychologist David Wallin noted that reframing of difficult emotional experiences may modulate reactivity in the amygdala, the part of the brain that aides in the processing of memory, decision-making and emotional reactions and is part of the limbic system.[41] Linking the child's experience to his or her emotional experiences may build new neurological connections. Do not expect overnight success—*any* progress is success.

Cognitive interventions begin with creating the Trauma Lens framework for the child. Caring adults can explain some of the possible scenarios that the child may have experienced during his or her early years. Historic information, such as child profiles, adoption records or foster care reports, may be available. The child may share personal memories, but these may sound like case notes because the information may have been relayed by a Child Protective Services caseworker. Don't debate the child's information; just record it for later exploration.

Because of the brain's plasticity, families have great hope in helping children heal. When children can understand and use the idea that their early trauma disrupted how they view the world and themselves, they are more aware of their responses to triggers. Remember, the early learning was experiential and the new learning must be experiential with added narration and reflection. Parents are continually building their children up and providing opportunities for healing within a new familial relationship.

CHAPTER 10

Emotional Response

Corey's Family

Corey's brain focused on the here and now in order to survive. He used all his energy being safe and keeping his fear in control. Corey's brain never seemed to calm down. His growing brain continually added neural pathways to assist him in dealing with the constant fear. Little things provoked him into wild emotional responses. The shadow of an adult overhead could cause him to curl into a fetal position on the ground. A slight perception of injustice could lead to a screaming, raving tantrum. He was rarely in a relaxed attentive state that promoted learning. Instead, he learned to scan the environment for sources of danger or advantage while trying to listen to the teacher.

Rebecca and Danny tried to get Corey to do his chores. Every night they fought the same battle. Making it work was so difficult. As soon as they mentioned chore time, Corey started complaining and moved into a tantrum. Evenings were wasted and everyone grew more and more angry. Rebecca could not find any reason for him to be so upset—the chores were simple and easy to do.

Infants' brains develop from the bottom up and from the back forward. Growing brains add connections (synapses); these connections are pathways for signals to travel within the brain. Pathways are added and influenced in response to environmental stimuli and genetics. Because of this environmental influence, the brains of traumatized children develop to specifically address the everyday needs of a less-than-functional world. They develop with a means to survive in traumatizing environments. Their brains may have a higher tolerance for stress and possibly even a need for stress hormones.

When a human's emotions get too big, the ability to think is limited. That is why people say foolish things when they are angry. Stress reduces the pre-frontal cortex's management abilities and sends additional signals to the emotional part of the brain. The right prefrontal cortex of the brain is responsible for the various indispensable "executive functions" of the mind, including practical and moral judgment, impulse control and emotional regulation. Cognition can be lost if stress is overwhelming. Stress hormones inhibit thinking via shutting down connections to the pre-frontal cortex. As emotions overwhelm the intellect, humans say and do things out of character that are linked to fight, flight or freeze.

Brains developing in traumatizing environments have fewer firing synapses to the thinking part, as part of their growth/survival strategy. Thus they present with a more rapid loss of cognition than a child who grew up in a healthier home. For example, say you have two circuit boards, one with ten firing circuits and another with six. When environmental stress cuts off four from both they are now down to six and two, respectively, and a minute later stress takes away two more. The second brain is now completely isolated from cognition while the first circuit board still has four functioning. The ability to recover from these highly stressful episodes is dependent on the body's responsiveness to stress.

Additionally, anything that challenges or triggers trauma memories for children with a history of early trauma may evoke stress and prompt an emotional response. These children's brains are designed to thrive in traumatizing environments the same way ducks are designed for water. Putting these brains in calm, healthy families is often like the proverbial "duck out of water." They can waddle around, but thriving will be complicated.

> "Today, I had trouble with my braces. I had gotten up this morning pretty scared, which I covered up with anger. When I went to the bathroom, the bracket was there and I broke it because I was mad. After I broke it I felt even more sad, but when they had me put it back together I felt a little better."
>
> —Allan Hall

What does all this mean? Parent/child interactions will be emotionally challenging. It is very important to watch for patterns in how the child's brain responds to stress. This will help the parent to determine how to interact with a dysregulated child.

As these children integrate into a new foster and/or adoptive family, they need to connect emotionally but lack healthy brain pathways to connect. The behaviors generated by these emotional reactions tend to frighten the new family, which evokes negative emotions in everyone, thereby again reinstating the N-IWM that begins the cascade to a Downward Spiral.

Amy's Family

Lori returned to the kitchen after completing the laundry. She was infuriated when she saw that the entire batch of freshly baked cookies was gone. Amy, sitting at the table, had chocolate on her chin, her fingers and the book she was planning to read. Lori exploded. "Why did you eat all those cookies? They were for the party tonight. Now, we will have to go to the store."

At the end of the third sentence, Amy looked up and with a dull, slack-jawed look, stated, "I did not eat the cookies." Lori could not believe that Amy would lie right to her face with the evidence on her fingers.

"You're only going to make it worse on yourself for lying!" yelled Lori.

Now Amy exploded and threw the book on the floor. She ran to her room, screaming, "I don't know why you never believe me!" She slammed the door and buried her face in the pillow. Lori was left wondering how Amy could have that kind of emotional reaction when she clearly ate the cookies. Yet, the eyes and ears of a mother told her Amy believed she was innocent.

Having previously learned about the impact of trauma, Lori realized that Amy's emotions were triggered by the guilt of stealing the cookies and the anger in Mom's voice. At that point, Amy's brain quit thinking. It would do Lori no good to try to talk to her now. Lori picked up the book and cleaned up the cookie crumbs.

At times of extreme emotional distress, cognitive interventions like lectures and rationalizing are useless. Amy was having an emotional reaction to being called a liar. Her prefrontal cortex had shut down. Amy's brain, having developed in an environment of domestic violence, learned to handle high-stress situations with fight, flight or freeze instead of thinking. This kept her alive during dangerous times in her birth home and was still operational. Even though it was years later, her brain was reacting to a high-stress situation by keeping her safe—she fled the environment and isolated herself.

One annoying response that frustrates adults is "I don't know." Even if the answer is obvious, traumatized children typically respond with "I don't know." It is possible that, in a heightened emotional state, the child simply does not have the ability to think at that moment. Call it brain freeze.

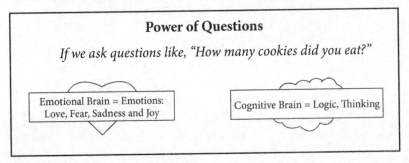

Power of Questions

If we ask questions like, "How many cookies did you eat?"

Emotional Brain = Emotions:
Love, Fear, Sadness and Joy

Cognitive Brain = Logic, Thinking

SIMPLIFYING A BRAIN INTO TWO PARTS: EMOTIONAL BRAIN AND THINKING BRAIN

"I Don't Know."

The child may feel fear immediately due to expecting a negative consequence, shame for eating too many cookies or fear of hearing the parent's angry voice. Immediately, the child's mental processes react to the stimuli, subjugate the cognitive component and offer an emotional reply. The emotional part of the brain will respond with: "I don't know." Obviously, the child knew how many cookies (or if it was too many), but the information cannot be retrieved from the cortex. In the past, this method protected the child. By not accessing the information, her body language automatically projects, "I don't know." The automatic emotional/cognitive response inhibits the feeling of shame and the fear of consequences for poor choices. The sequence produced a positive effect for the child in an environment where shame and consequences were erratic and maybe painful. The circuit must be recognized and circumvented for healing.

If we ask questions like: *"What did you like about...?"*

- The child can feel fear that her response could be used to manipulate her.
- The child can feel fear of the information being used to target her for punishment.

The child reacts to the question immediately and responds emotionally. The emotional part of the brain will respond with "Nothing." The cognitive information is not available because of the fear involved; the answer is buried in the cortex and unavailable. Even too much "happy" can cause loss of cognition. The children seem to become giddy, often reverting to younger "infant-like engaging" behaviors. Sadly, in relation to "happy" events, with this loss of cognitive experience of the happy moment the child can lose the memory of any enjoyment and thus the motivation to repeat whatever behavior contributed to the happiness!

Behaviors: Fight, flight, freeze

1. Fight
   a. Aggression
   b. Intimidation
   c. Posturing
   d. Hostility

    e. Arguing
    f. Lying
    g. Exaggerating anger

2. Flight
    a. "Who cares?" (denying implications)
    b. Hiding
    c. Withdrawal
    d. Avoidance
    e. Impulsivity
    f. Exaggerated sadness/fear

3. Freeze
    a. Disassociation
    b. Verbal confusion, babbling
    c. Covering one's face
    d. Inability to make decisions
    e. Immobility
    f. "I don't know."

CHAPTER 11

Developmental Delays

Corey's Family

While other boys were learning to occupy themselves with toys, Corey never seemed to know what to do with blocks or a ball or when sitting quietly or playing tag. He would abandon whatever he had in favor of finding and taking whatever game the others were playing. Other children's reactions were scary for Corey and often resulted in his hitting, running from and avoidance of others.

Rebecca and Danny bought Corey a new building set his first Christmas with them. He happily opened the present and proclaimed he had always wanted this one. He tore open the building set's box, spread the pieces on the floor and reached for another gift to open. Rebecca warned Corey that he would lose the pieces unless he picked them up but that did not seem to matter to him.

According to Kristine Kinniburgh, Margaret Blaustein and Joseph Spinazzola, "Trauma derails developmental competencies across domains of functioning and across developmental stages."[42] Healthy child development depends on attuned and competent caregivers. An infant acquires social skills by interacting with his or her parents, who are the child's first playmates. These playmates help the baby learn that he or she is fun to be with and when to respond and when to withdraw in relationships. Parents teach their infant about lifestyles, distress tolerance, emotional regulation, morals and values. Parents help children master emotional and physical regulation through experience, modeling and co-regulation. They are the child's world. The infant's ability to trust his or her parents is constructed from every interaction with these parents.

Optimal learning occurs during calm engagement, when both the infant and caregiver are open to sharing the world together. "Within episodes of *affect synchrony* parents engage in intuitive, nonconscious, facial, vocal, and gestural preverbal communications," say Marion Fried Solomon and Daniel J. Siegel in *Healing Trauma: Attachment, Mind, Body, and Brain*.[43] This is the dance of attachment in which the infant perceives "oneness" with the caregiver. The caregiver is establishing a trustworthy relationship from which the child can explore and return for security. As the child matures, his or her explorations will go farther and take longer, but he or she continues to return to the caregiver for validation and security. Each time the child completes this cycle, the child learns greater trust in the caregiver and increases his or her own sense of competence. Exploration promotes curiosity, creativity, imagination and more exploration, skills needed to be a good student and worker and to enjoy life.

Development is incremental and sequential, each stage related to and building on the last. Disrupt one step and others may be incomplete, distorted or arrested. Not meeting a child's physical, emotional or relational needs is terrifying and could mean death for the infant. If the parent is dysregulated or frightening, the child may be further traumatized. The parent that should be taking care of the child becomes the source of fear. Trauma arrests development, leads the child to mistrust adults, forces the child to take control of the environment and meet his or her own needs.

Famous developmental psychologist and psychoanalyst Erik Erikson illustrated the difference between healthy children and children with early trauma.[44] In the following chart, we can clearly see how one child will be more successful than the other. Many parents asked, "Why does my child not take initiative and just pick up his socks that are in the middle of the floor?" Since development is incremental, their children did not learn to trust or develop autonomy. They learned mistrust and shame that is evidenced in their daily interactions. Without these basic relational skills, there will be no initiative or industry. By the time these children become teenagers, role confusion may occur. Families' values are further challenged as the teen attempts to separate from the family and form his or her own sense of self. The teen will struggle with questions of family identity, importance of values and which family he or she is most like. If the familial relationship with the foster and adoptive parents is not strong enough, the child may dismiss them and gravitate toward the birth family and peers.

Age	Healthy	Unhealthy
Birth to 1½ years	Trust	Mistrust
1½ to 3 years	Autonomy	Shame and doubt
3–6 years	Initiative	Guilt
6–12 years	Industry	Inferiority
12–18 years	Identity	Role confusion

Building from the bottom up, psychologist Andrew Maslow proposed his hierarchy of needs in his 1943 paper, "A Theory of Human Motivation," in *Psychological Review*.[45] The hierarchy illustrated the foundation children must have and the skills that will develop with that foundation. If parents examine their children's behavior by comparing which level the behavior is linked to, they tend to find the behavior originates from the first two levels: physiological or safety needs. The children become stuck on the two bottom rungs. Without this foundation, they cannot form healthy relationships or self-worth.

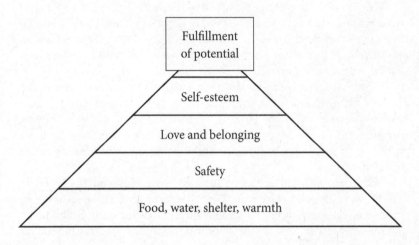

Maslow's hierarchy of needs helps villagers understand that they will not be successful with developing the child's self-esteem if the child is on the first two rungs. Interventions must be designed and used to firmly instill that the child will have all his or her basic needs met and he or she will always be safe (as much as the parents can achieve). Many parents express concern and anger over their children stealing food. Not understanding that the child is trying to take care of his "first rung" safety needs, families lock the pantry, hide food throughout the house and refuse to purchase certain items because of previous stealing. These interactions, delivered with parental anger, can actually cause the child to feel more fear and in-.crease his or her need for security.

Children will challenge the parent's ability to keep them safe. Parents place alarms on the children's doors, keep them in close proximity and arrange for increased supervision to enforce safety. It seems to be a never-ending battle between parents and children as to who will keep the children safe. The children insist that they are capable, given that they have not had trustworthy adults to care for them.

Allan's Family

> *Mom, if you find this, I have not run away. I have gone to the football game. I am fifteen, I DESERVE to go. Please leave the window OPEN for when I come back. I will not get drunk nor will I smoke. I will not cause any trouble.*
>
> Love, Allan

Parents teach their children basic life skills—holding eating utensils, drinking from a cup, when and where to go to the bathroom—simple tasks we all take for granted, unless you lived in deprivation and fear. Some children have worn paper towels as a diaper, entertained themselves with feces and spent days in cribs or playpens without adult interaction. Others were sexually or physically abused.

These children could not put their energy into exploring the world, playing with toys or even learning to crawl. Development will not automatically restart when the child is removed from the old environment and placed in a new home. The old, fear-laden environment was all the child knew and moving to a new environment is not itself a fear-reducing experience.

Children with early trauma may not have explored the world in healthy ways. Psychologist Jean Piaget believed that children progress through a series of four key stages of cognitive development. Each stage is marked by shifts in how kids understand the world. Piaget believed that children are like "little scientists" and that they actively try to explore and make sense of the world around them.[46] Children with early trauma may be "stuck" in the first stage, the sensorimotor stage, and still be learning through the senses. This means the child may touch, smell, taste and listen in extraordinary ways. They may eat odd and unusual items while refusing healthy food.

Parents may be annoyed and irritated by the behaviors, but they may be terrified by the danger of the child's ingestion of harmful items or amounts. Without healthy self-regulation, a child may eat too much or inedible items. While shopping, the child may touch everything. Some children walk up to strangers and smell them. They are always listening acutely and hyper-vigilant of danger.

Notice in the next chart that illustrates Piaget's four stages that, after infancy, the child moves into the preoperational stage. This stage is characterized by a lack of problem-solving abilities. What does this mean for parents? A developmentally-delayed child, regardless of the child's chronological age, may lack the ability to problem-solve.

	Piaget's Stage	Age	Characteristics
Infancy	Sensorimotor	0–2 yrs	Learns through senses
Childhood	Preoperational	2–7 yrs	Lacks problem-solving
Preadolescence	Concrete	7–11 yrs	Reversible thinking
Adolescence-adult	Formal	11+ yrs	No need to manipulate

The child's disparity or inconsistency between chronological and emotional/cognitive age poses parenting and educational challenges. Developmental delays may appear as behavioral inconsistencies that parents or professionals try to address with rewards and consequences. "Eat with a fork and you will get a reward," sounds good, yet the child may ask why he has to use forks, because he survived just fine eating with his fingers. Actually, he may be developmentally arrested at a time when learning was through the senses and eating with his fingers was the right thing to do. The Trauma Lens Paradigm Shift will help parents and providers make sense of the child's behaviors and set the stage for healing interventions.

Brandon's Family

Bob wanted to attract bluebirds to his family's backyard. So he decided he would teach Brandon carpentry skills by constructing birdhouses. They shopped for lumber, screws and nails. Both enjoyed the time together at the lumber store and celebrated their excursion with lunch at a fast food restaurant. Bob became concerned when Brandon wanted to play in the restaurant's indoor playground instead of talking about their building plans. "Brandon should have wanted to design the birdhouses with me," Bob said.

Saturday was the big day! They were constructing their first bluebird house with plans to attach it to the back fence post. Bob began by asking Brandon to gather the lumber. Brandon complained: "You only want me to help so that I can do the hard work and you have fun." Bob explained he had to have the boards to cut. Brandon wanted to cut, not gather, the boards. Brandon assured Bob that his last foster dad taught him how to use the saw. So, Bob handed him the saw and showed him where to place the blade. He knew there was trouble the minute he gave Brandon the saw. Seconds later, Brandon ran screaming from the garage, "Dad made me hurt myself!" The day was ruined.

That evening, Bob shared his concerns about Brandon's immaturity with Deena. She contacted their caseworker for information about Brandon's history and found that he had missed normal developmental milestones. Brandon was signaling them with his behavior that he was not ready for these activities. Bob and Deena reduced their expectations for Brandon and offered multiple age experiences. Instead of finishing the birdhouse project, Bob and Brandon played at the park, "built" a fort out of cardboard boxes and bought a small inflatable pool to splash in on hot afternoons. Bob enjoyed seeing Brandon's delight when he pushed him on a swing. Brandon used large crayons to decorate the fort. Bob taught Brandon how to sail boats in the swimming pool. Deena photographed the "boys" playing and scrapbooked the pages to help them remember how they were enjoying being Brandon's parents. Sometimes Brandon didn't want to play in the "younger way," especially when other peers were present. It was often a challenge for the parents to determine where Brandon was developmentally on any given day (or even at any given moment!). Mistakes were made and sometimes tempers flared. But eventually they all got better at communicating and enjoying their time together.

Like Deena and Bob, parents adapt their expectations and environment by adding toys and activities that span age groups. They offer unstructured time in which they invite the child to play with them. These times should be calming but short in length. Parents cannot force the child to participate, but only invite them. A developmental delay may not present in a consistent way. Children may be doing fine until stress increases or they may have a more profound deficit that renders them unable to react to their environment in an age-appropriate manner. Skills not mastered are not the same as skills not present. Both conditions require the child to re-experience the developmental stage for additional practice. The child's needs must drive the interventions. If the child perceives a "demanding parent," they will likely avoid the activity. It is challenging to accept a child at a younger emotional age. Parental attitude is important. There can be no shame or guilt about the experience or the child will not participate again. Parents have been known to thank the child for the opportunity to watch him or her grow up.

Behaviors that signal missed developmental milestones are:

- The child struggles with remaining focused through the task or activity.
- The child lacks dexterity to complete or perform a task or activity.
- The child argues or disrupts the activity before it is finished.
- The child enjoys playing with younger children or the toys of a younger child.
- The child regresses to talking or acting immaturely.
- The child cannot maintain peer relationships.
- The child is reluctant to begin a task or activity.

- The child cannot play independently.
- The child uses parallel play with others.

INTERVENTIONS

Developmental interventions can begin with and are as simple as playing with your child or snuggling together to share a few moments. Positive parental attitudes and motives are important for these activities to be successful. Approaching the child with the spirit of unconditional love and the knowledge that the child's behaviors are fear-based helps the behaviors seem less annoying. Setting the stage for the activities, inviting the audience and planning follow-ups can increase the possibilities for success. You are working to help your child mature and build his capacity for relationships. Without intentional, relationship-building interventions, parenting may be reactionary and less than proactive.

Many times the primary caregiver is challenged to plan proactive activities instead of being reactive to their child's behaviors. Parents' days may be consumed with "fighting fires" (sometimes literally) and lacking desire for intentional relationship-building activities, even though these connect and heal. Usually, as the relationship builds, disruptive behaviors will decrease.

Parenting during the infant months is sensory: touching, smelling, tasting, seeing, hearing and moving. The fun part of helping children heal is that parents and children will work together to make positive connections. As with a newborn, children may have a short attention span. So interactions are brief and pleasurable. If the child is defiant and refuses to participate, don't be discouraged: This is new! Only invite him to participate but continue with the activities. Acknowledge the fun you are having, not what he is missing. He will figure that out for himself. Children may not be able to identify their emotions, resulting in a fearful response to the intimacy of these shared activities. Be ready! Disruptive behaviors may come from this fear. Connections will build relationships; the relationship will produce compliance and reciprocity.

Cuddling is one easy way to recreate and repair the infant/parent relationship in the attachment cycle. The child can lay his head on Mom's lap while she sits on a sofa. If small enough, the child can be cradled in her arms. During this stage, the infant is calm enough for interaction but not sleepy. Mom must be emotionally available and invested in a positive experience for both herself and the child. The child can be fed or offered snacks or special drinks. Smiles, warm touches and soothing words are direct components of this bonding cycle. Quick, gentle hugs can be interspersed. The child's initial reaction may be to push Mom away, either physically and/or emotionally. Remember, your child may be reactive to relationships.

Plan a variety of activities for cuddling. Playing finger games, reading toddler books, chanting rhymes, playing with puppets, singing children's songs or listening to quiet music are a few ideas. Vary the time of day to prevent the child from sabotaging this special event.

A hesitant child may be discomforted during the first attempts to be physically and emotionally close to Mom. Five minutes of cuddling each day may be as much as the child can tolerate for the first week. Times can be lengthened as the comfort level rises. By monitoring the session, the team member can offer feedback and help the child reprocess the emotions later in the day. Reassure your child with: "Trust me," "You're safe," "No one can hurt you now" and "This mom will protect you with her life."

Oppositional children may try to hinder any attachment activity from occurring or may try to make the adult "pay" for desiring to play with the child. These children may be reacting to their fear: "If I become connected to this adult, I will be hurt." So they speak with their behaviors.

Possible Behaviors

1. Overtly defiant:
   - Refusing to cuddle or play
   - Becoming angry
   - Becoming aggressive
   - Not following the rules, actively

2. Passively defiant:
   - Moving slowly
   - Lacking communication
   - Saying "I don't know"
   - Not following the rules, passively
   - Forgetting the rules
   - Leaving the game frequently
   - Poor hygiene—to make others not want to be near

Parents who think about where their children are developmentally will spare themselves and their children a great deal of frustration and heartache. Children are enormously comforted when their parent is attuned to where they are developmentally and meets them where they are. In this way, rather than feeling the shame of not being able to do an activity, they "feel felt" and are far more likely to risk engaging in the activity with their empathically tuned-in parent.

CHAPTER 12

Object Relations

Corey's Family

While other children were gifted with an attentive and attuned mother, one who played peek-a-boo and hide and seek, Corey's mother would disappear for hours and days at a time. He never knew if she would come back. When she did, her emotions varied so wildly with whatever she was dealing with at the moment, he could never know if she was the same mom. His brain did not hold a permanent or consistent picture of a caring mom. He never believed his birth mother's presence would help him make good decisions.

It seemed that at least weekly, Corey's teacher called to complain about some misdeed. He stole food and asked the teacher to buy him clothing and toys. The teacher stated she could not buy things for her students. The teacher said that Corey acted like he did not have parents. Why couldn't Rebecca and Danny meet his needs? Maybe the foster agency should help this family manage their money.

Think about how you respond to a fussy toddler—peek-a-boo usually works. Babies quickly engage in the game with surprise and amazement. They laugh and smile as the adult is seen and then disappears, only to reappear once again. The toddler is developing object relations, the ability to begin to believe in the parent's existence when out of sight.

As children's brains develop, they gain the capacity to understand that things and people exist even when not in their perceptual field. The simple game of peek-a-boo starts out as "Oh no, Mom is gone," then, "Yay, Mom is here!" Eventually, the baby experiences "Mom is here all the time, even when I can't see her." It begins as the emotional fear of loss and the joy of reunion, ending with the contentment of constant presence. This skill assists with emotional regulation. Imagine, in the middle of the night, how the feeling of knowing that mom is present but not in sight is different from the fear that mom is gone.

Parent/child interactions affirm the infant's view of self, the caregiver and the world. For healthy development, the caregiver must be available and constant. Otherwise the child may perceive that the caregiver cannot meet his or her needs. One developmental competency accomplished through these parent/child interactions is object relations. This section will simplify object relations into two categories: object permanence and constancy.

Object permanence is the ability to realize that the caregiver may be in another location from the child. The child can hold the mother's image in his or her mind. Babies learn that Mom is present even when the baby cannot see her, as evidenced through increasing tolerance of mother's absence before crying in protest. Newborns are symbiotic with Mom, rarely leaving her side. As the baby matures, Mom does not immediately respond to the baby's cry. She calls from the adjoining room that she will come soon. The baby begins to "expect" Mom's presence. This process continues as the baby plays near Mom, looking back at her as the baby crawls away. Each check-in with Mom reaffirms her presence. She becomes "permanent" to the child.

Holding the image of our parent forces us to initiate behavior in relationship to our parents' expected reactions. Without the ability to hold an image of Mom and, eventually, others and things in our minds, all decisions would be made on the basis of only what would be in our visual fields at that moment.

The foundation for decision-making (right and wrong, morals) is because we know parents exist. To make decisions, we will consider how a given action will affect them. If a child cannot hold the image of a permanent caregiver, the child is alone in the world and has no important "other" to respond to any decision. The result is "I must take care of myself, no matter the cost, because there is no one else." Children who were not played with or whose early experience of Mom was that she went away and did not come back for days, are at risk of inadequately developing their ability to know things as permanent.

Object constancy is the concept that things can change states but still be the same. This often begins with the interaction with the primary caregiver. While children are born with the recognition of the primary caregiver, their perception can at times be radically different. An angry, fear-inducing Mom has different facial features, tone of voice, posture and touch from a happy Mom. This caregiver ideally has a full range of emotions but must still be able to care for the child's needs no matter what emotional state. The child will learn to recognize the caregiver as the same person whether angry or happy. The stability of the interactions links the mom in both perceptions.

The angry Mom will get the child a drink of water the same as the happy Mom. This eventually leads to the understanding, "She's the same Mom with different feelings."

Addicted parents, overly stressed parents or parents with mental health disorders may not be "stable" during these interactions. If Mom is too depressed or fearful and she is thus unable to get the drink, the child's development of object constancy may be disrupted. During infancy and early toddlerhood, a child's survival skill may be to treat Mom as if she is two people and develop different skills to get needs met from both Moms. Because object constancy is developed over time and through countless interactions with the primary caregiver(s), failure to achieve it leads to enduring difficulty with perceiving others realistically, rather than either "all good" or "all bad."

Both object constancy and permanency help the child organize "self" around the relationship with the primary caregiver. Mom will be the same person this morning as she was last night and she will be available when I need her. Lacking this organization, the child may feel unsafe, split his or her world into good and bad parts (black and white thinking), may become dysregulated if alone and/or return to old survival skills and try to control the environment to be safe.

Children with poorly-developed object relations may become part of the foster care and adoptive systems. These children may not go home to the same "Mom" or house that they left that morning. They may expect to return, but there is a consistent, underlying fear of never seeing loved ones again. Their moral development is arrested and, most likely, uses black-and-white thinking to classify the world. Each of these deficits complicates parenting these children.

Sally's Family

Every evening when Jane returned from work, Sally greeted her with great joy. Sometimes, Jane thought the greeting was a little over-exaggerated, but this was better than fighting with Sally. This kind of greeting continued throughout the evening. When Sally walked into the room, she said hello and that she was glad Jane was home. Jane was confused. Sally was not being sarcastic, but was she trying to irritate her?

Jane found her answer one night at her support group when the topic was object relations. She learned that Sally did not experience her as "permanent." To Sally, Jane appeared each time she walked into the room. It was instinctual to greet her again and again. Jane was able to help Sally mature by offering interventions to help her experience Jane as permanent.

Just as Jane was able to interpret Sally's behaviors and avoid conflict while offering healing, others can decode behaviors via object relations.

Absent parents may prompt children to become controlling to keep themselves safe. It is not just "Out of sight, out of mind" but "If I cannot see you, you do not exist." Think of the implications of "I am all alone" and "I must take care of myself; there is no one to protect me." How lonely and fearful the children must be! Additionally, the children may not "know" that a person can have two emotions at one time. They may fear that you cannot love them while you are mad at them. Children may internalize that parents stopped loving their children when they are mad. Imagine a child thinking, "Bad behavior causes Mom to stop loving me." This gives the child a tremendous amount of power and control.

Behaviors of a child who does not possess a mental image or internalization of a *forever-mom who will always love them* are:

1. The child will feel unsafe and use survival skills to operate in school. These past skills of fight, flight and freeze kept them alive. They will be hyper-alert.

2. The child may triangulate and split any relationships in the environment. Lacking a consistent conception of self or "other" makes chameleon-like changes a necessity. This creates stress and confusion while giving the illusion of control to the child. An adrenaline rush will be produced in the child.

3. The child will feel fear he or she can't cognitively explain. This may be expressed by anger and aggression. This acting out behavior is purposefully directed and will reduce the child's feeling of fear.

4. The child may display the inability to regulate emotions (i.e., have temper tantrums). A big response to small stimuli is due to the prevalence of non-defined fear.

5. The child may be excessively destructive to property, because the concept of "saving for later" isn't fully developed. This behavior reinforces the child's view of self, intimidates others, places him or her in control and puts distance between the child and others.

6. The child may portray a poor orphan to manipulate and control others.

7. The child may portray the perfect child to manipulate and control others.

8. The child may lie to control and withhold information. His conception of the world can't visualize a parent "finding out." His world is composed of separate, somehow unrelated experiences. It is also possible the child will not cognitively possess the information requested.

9. The child may steal from others, because he lacks the ability to think, "I'll ask Mom for one of these." Stealing is the only imaginable way to acquire.

10. The child may quit trying to succeed, because he lacks the motivation to please Mom. This confirms his belief, "I am not worth having a Mom who cares." Oddly, this behavior produces a feeling of comfort.

11. The child may be hyper-sensitive to stimuli when he feels he cannot control the environment. How often does a healthy child use Mom's remembered confidence in him, or the environment, to try new experiences?

To correct the child's capacity for permanence and constancy, parents are encouraged to play peek-a-boo games and use *transitional objects*. Transitional objects such as pictures are used to remind the child of the therapist when absent. Children can experience desertion when separated from parents.

TRANSITIONAL OBJECTS

Psychoanalyst Donald Woods Winnicott described a transitional object as a "monument to the need for this contact with the mother's body" that is "lasting, soft, pliable, warm to touch."[47] Use these interventions to comfort the child when Mom is not present. Transitional objects and interventions portray that Mom is present, available and in control, even at school, camp, church, etc. The message must be: She is always available for me. Be creative to provide for the child's needs. A few strategies that may be useful:

1. Create and permit a transitional object to be carried from home and kept with the child (a parent's clothing or jewelry, a stuffed animal, piece of a baby blanket).

2. Mom can arrange to call during the day.

3. Mom can arrange short visits.

4. Mom can share perfume with the child before he or she leaves home.

5. Mom can write and share notes and messages with the child.

6. Mom can supply treats.

7. School staff can keep a "mommy box" at school with extra supplies.

8. Place a picture of the family in the child's school desk.
9. Mom can place loving notes in the child's lunchbox.
10. Mom can write notes on snack items.
11. Mom can record stories for the child to listen to at bedtime.
12. Say a few words throughout the day to remind the child that Mom still exists, such as "I wonder what your mom is doing right now?", "I'll show this picture to your mom after school today," and "What will you and your mom do when you get home today?"
13. Narrate future emotions: "I'll probably be a little sad and angry during the game."

This list is useful for children with babysitters, in respite or in school. You may need to provide additional information to the substitute caregiver on why these interventions are required and how they can be reinforced.

Experiential learning

1. Discuss what others may be doing when they are not present.
2. Talk about your emotions when distressed because someone is absent.
3. Plan for the return of family members.
4. Act surprised when a child plays peek-a-boo.
5. Use puppets to leave and arrive.
6. Maintain self-regulation when others are late.

We never fully lose our delight at taking transitional objects along with us when away, nor our delight at an unexpected visit by a loved one. Thus, we have those wonderful pictures of our children or other loved ones in our wallets or purses and we are brought to tears when we see a video of a family surprised by the early return of their serviceman or woman. Mindful of our own such experiences, we can be ever vigilant for the appearance of difficulties with object permanence and constancy in our children and prepared to respond to them effectively.

CHAPTER 13

Self-Regulation

Corey's Family

Bereft of the connection to an emotionally-attuned caregiver and her narration of life experiences, Corey never learned how to analyze the environment through an adult's eyes. All his evaluatory processes were through an immature brain. He learned to survive under stressful conditions. If he felt cold, it wasn't always something to be avoided. Hunger was a regular occurrence and he learned to address it as best he could.

Rebecca was amazed at how much Corey could eat, more than a grown man. She was always telling him to slow down, chew his food and that he could have seconds or thirds. He was never full. Twenty minutes after dinner, he demanded a snack. Frequently, she found that food was missing when she fixed breakfast. She needed to talk to Danny about installing a lock on the pantry door.

Babies are born into a world they have no ability to navigate. Without knowledge or control of their own bodies, every sensation is a potential source of fear. They cannot regulate the constant influx of powerful sensory stimuli. In the extreme, overwhelmed and unprotected babies could curl into a fetal position and die. Fortunately, nature has provided the powerful, all-encompassing presence of a mother, who can intentionally modulate an infant's fear. Nature increases mother's power by the neural hardwiring of Mom and child to instantly share emotions. The neural connection between parents and children will aid in co-regulation, self-regulation and shared value judgments. Children watch their parents respond to the environment and reinterpret the information to know how to proceed in the world and form personal values and opinions.

THE BEGINNINGS OF CO-REGULATION

Infant brains are born with the capacity to recognize and differentiate "Mom" from the sea of sensory data streaming into their brains. Soon after birth, Mom decodes the complex tones in her baby's cry to determine the baby's emotional state. She will feel afraid when the baby is fearful, happy when the child giggles and sad when the infant is upset. Their attuned brains will share emotions. By sharing her baby's emotions, Mom can modulate her child's fears and begin a lifelong pattern of emotional regulation.

Baby feels fear, baby cries, Mom feels the fear, Mom picks up the baby and they feel the same emotion. Mom makes sense of the child's fear, calms herself down and then baby calms down with Mom, as they continue to feel the same emotion. Later, this pattern is reenacted when the toddler falls down, cries and crawls back to Mom. Mom has the same emotion as her child. She evaluates for any real danger and soothes her child with a smile and a pat. She encourages her child to return to play. The child relaxes and smiles. The same pattern will occur over the child's lifespan. Still more years later, the pre-teen daughter comes home from school angry and crying over "that boy" in school. Mom listens to her daughter's distress, feels the same emotion and then gently leads her in ways to handle the sadness and fear of adolescence.

BEGINNINGS OF PHYSICAL REGULATION

It is amazing how much babies learn through interacting with their caregivers. They help the baby connect being fussy (feeling tired) to "I am sleepy" and their toddler to being full, because he ate a banana and cereal. Parents intuitively define their children's world, make sense of the environment and narrate life's experiences. One adoptive mother stated that she never realized how much one talks to a baby until she was raising her child.

"No more," Mom said and put down the spoon. Laughingly, Mom patted baby's belly and put away the applesauce. Baby watched Mom intently and listened to her words. Baby's thinking brain was beginning to understand words. Mom labeled sensations like "full" and linked the word with the experience of eating. By interacting with Mom, the baby was learning "When I am full, I should stop eating." Each new learning experience rewarded Baby's focus on what Mom was doing and saying.

When a parent does not narrate or define the world, children must venture out with an immature brain and self-learned skills. Their interpretation of the world may lead them to lack value in using a fork to eat, eating regular meals, sleeping in a bed, using bathroom facilities, wearing a coat in the winter, resting when tired or crying when sad. These are self-regulation skills.

In a world of abuse and neglect, most likely the child did not hear the parents label the feeling of "full" nor was she encouraged to stop eating. The child may have learned the opposite: to survive one may need to gorge when food is available. A "gorging" child may in fact be completely self-regulated, but not in a normal sense. Frustrated foster parents may angrily remove food from the table and chastise the child for being "a pig!" This would be a complete mis-attunement. All the child's experience is now at odds with what the new parents are saying. If food was not always available in the child's early development, the child could easily interpret the parents' anger as them wanting more for themselves.

Bessel Van der Kolk states, "The children of unpredictable parents often clamored for attention and became intensely frustrated in the face of small challenges. Their persistent arousal made them chronically anxious."[48] Clinical professor Stanley Greenspan identified some children who have difficulty regulating "physiological, sensory, attentional and motor or affective processes and organizing a calm, alert or affectively positive state."[49]

Parents assist their children in physical regulation of:

- Elimination (Bathroom)
- Hungry/ Full
- Hot/Cold
- Sleep
- Energy Level
- Pain
- Attention

PHYSICAL REGULATION

It is not unusual for foster and adoptive parents to become frustrated by their children's dysregulated behaviors. These are children who go to school in the winter without a coat, defecate in their room or elsewhere, eat too much or not enough, hoard or hide food and complain of being cold in summer. Parents may try to teach children to wear a coat, toilet train or to eat regular meals. This is not about "teaching the skill" but about the child's ability to self-regulate. Some children are not motivated to learn these skills and place no value on them since they are contradictory to early traumatic experiences.

Sally's Family

Sally's biological mother used cocaine. In her early life, Sally's mom told her to "Keep moving when you're cold and ignore it; we don't have money for coats." Mom became angry when Sally cried from being cold. Mom bounced Sally up and down, rubbed her little hands and told her to get over it. Sally did not connect "cold" to bad, nor learn to avoid it or fix it by wearing a coat. Years later, Sally sweated when she ran to the bus stop in the new coat Jane had bought her. Without the coat, she could perceive the cold, but didn't feel the need to do anything about it. One day she stuffed it behind a bench at the bus stop. She noticed the teachers gave her special attention when she arrived at school without a coat. They were so concerned! Three days later the school called Child Protective Services, because Sally didn't have a winter coat.

Some children have eating disorders. A child may eat too much, eat inappropriate items or simply refuse to eat. Educated team members are necessary for a child with eating disorders to prevent the child from harming him or herself. Other children have disruptive sleep patterns. The children may not sleep during the night but instead try to roam through the house. Family members, as well as the child, may be in danger. Parents may need overnight respite to catch up on their sleep. As the child comes to trust the environment, he can relax and become more aware of his body and its functions.

Parents and children battle for control. Most foster and adoptive children have no real control over their lives. They are moved from home to home without volition. They are forced to follow everyone else's rules, whether they make sense or not. Parents and children get caught in battles trying to control what a child takes into the body and what is excreted. Parents perceive they can control what the child eats, which they may be able to do until the child is in the community without their presence and the food in their house is under lock and key. When a child enters school, eating issues may be reported. Children will "forget" their lunch or eat it on the bus so that others will provide extra food. Some will eat from the garbage can (a learned survival skill). Children have been known to eat out of garbage cans in the lunchroom, stealing food from the store and begging from neighbors, all while living with a family who provides more than adequately.

For the most part, parents must avoid making eating or going to the bathroom an issue, since interventions are practically unenforceable. Schools, babysitters, grandparents and neighbors may avoid or reject the child if they have to be the food police. Offer foods you want your child to have. If there is "forbidden" food in the home, the child will find it. The child may have no boundaries or consideration for other's possessions. Otherwise, a game of hide and seek will develop.

Bathroom time tends to be a problem, because of the privacy offered. Bathrooms must be toddler-proofed by storing all potentially harmful items out of the child's reach. Some families try to limit time in the bathroom, but find that difficult to enforce. Other parents try to control the amount of toiletries used, because the children may waste them (thus the Jones family's toiletry basket).

A dysregulated child is a child stuck in a state of fear, sadness or anger. The following behaviors demonstrate the child's inability to self-regulate:

- The child does not notice or adjust to energy or strength: does not sleep or oversleeps.
- The child does not notice or adjust to physical body temperature: cold and hot.
- The child has poor personal hygiene: oppositional to brushing teeth, bathing, clean clothing.
- The child has abnormal eating habits: eating too much or not enough, hiding or hoarding food.
- The child has unusual bathroom habits: defecating in odd places.
- The child does not regulate emotions: moves quickly into exaggerated fight, flight or freeze, has little body awareness of emotions, does not express or discuss emotions and does not seek comfort from a parent when distressed.

SELF-REGULATION: FOOD ISSUES

Parents frequently report that they become quickly frustrated by their children's abnormal eating habits—eating too much or too little, refusing to eat healthy foods, craving sweets, consuming non-food items and hoarding or hiding food. Eating is a primal activity with many meanings. Parents' emotions become activated when their children eat healthy meals; they feel like good parents doing what is right for their children. The converse is true when a child refuses to eat healthy foods, takes control of his eating or makes mealtime a battlefield.

These actions spur parents' fear—fear their children will not be healthy, that they cannot control their own home, that others will view them as bad parents or that the child has won the food battles. If a parent's fear is too great, he or she may make food issues larger by battling with the child. A war may begin, because the child is in a battle for his or her life (old survival skills). Many times desperate parents resort to punishing the child by removing specific food items, locking up food supplies and controlling meals. But these maneuvers only frighten the child at his or her most primitive level of existence. Lack of food equals death. We encourage parents to step back and determine what is best for the relationship with their child.

Imagine what your child may have experienced in the early months and years. Did he lack warmth or food, safety and/or healthy relationships?

While with the birth family or in previous placements, children may have charmed the neighbors for snacks, manipulated teachers for lunch and lied or stolen to obtain food. Each new placement consisted of different foods, odors and mealtime rituals. Imagine some of the "internal" images a traumatized child may carry. Think of the probability of neglect, of lack of food and a mealtime scene that consisted of yelling, anger and fear. Daniel Siegel noted that these implicit memories can become reactivated and "create a very unpleasant, disorganized and frightening internal world."[50] These images may be triggered and activated by harmless sensory input: sights, smells, tastes, touch and sounds. Food and mealtimes have many sensory triggers.

CHALLENGES TO PARENT'S SELF-REGULATION

What is the meaning of your reaction to your child's eating behaviors? Do your expectations and fears get in the way? Ask yourself if you are a good parent when your child:

- Overeats or undereats.
- Eats unhealthy foods.
- Eats only one food.
- Refuses a balanced diet.
- Is overweight or underweight.
- Disrupts meals.
- Withdraws from meals.
- Eats too much of the family's food.
- Hides or hoards food.

What prompts negative parental responses? Notice your emotions when you:

- Yell.
- Threaten.
- Punish.
- Withhold or reward using food.
- Shame a child for food-related behavior.

In summary, the bizarre self-regulatory habits of a clearly intelligent child with a history of early trauma are almost incomprehensible to us adults. We tend to believe that the brain and body of a healthy newborn is preprogrammed to automatically develop normal habits of physiological regulation as the baby ages. To a limited extent that is true—the human brain and body are prepared at birth to develop effective regulatory functions. But these functions will only develop normally if the pre-wiring is exposed consistently to healthy, emotionally-attuned experiences with caregivers. A child's "chronic arousal, coupled with lack of parental comfort, made them disruptive, oppositional and aggressive."[51]

Thankfully, the human brain is a very "plastic" organ—that is, it has a remarkable capacity to learn new responses. Our hope is that children who were hurt at a time when they were so helpless can still learn self-regulation with the help of devoted, understanding caregivers. As the caregivers provide acceptance of the child and new ways to attune, model self-regulatory skills and connect with their children, the children's defenses will reduce and they will build a new sense of safety.

CHAPTER 14

Sensory Processing Dysfunction

In this chapter we are discussing sensory processing dysfunctions not caused by a genetic, gestational or other physiological deficit in the child, but rather by traumatic early developmental experiences.

Corey's Family

Corey did not enjoy life. He lay in his dirty bed day after day. When he began daycare, he could not tolerate other caregivers and preferred being alone. He cried and fussed when held. The busy staff had many infants to attend to and was more than willing to leave him alone.

When Corey began to eat baby food, Sophia didn't understand why he sometimes refused to eat. She mashed up the food the best she could. Sometimes, friends donated canned baby food. Sophia chastised Corey for being a picky eater. She realized she was yelling more often. No food or clothing and an angry Larry—when would the troubles end? She did not have enough warm clothing for Corey to wear that first winter. He had to wear as many clothes as possible to stay warm. She got angry with him for crying on their early morning walks to the daycare center. She was just as cold as he was.

Rebecca and Danny wondered why Corey wanted to wear a coat when it wasn't really that cold outside. Their other children were happy with a sweatshirt when Corey wanted a coat and hat. Rebecca thought he would overheat while playing. She could not persuade him otherwise. At night he needed more blankets and complained about being cold. He even told his teacher that his house did not have enough heat. Rebecca was thoroughly embarrassed when school staff called to see if the family needed financial assistance.

The quality of a baby's sensory experiences and interactions in the environment and with the primary caregiver contribute to healthy development. Excited parents welcome a new baby with a well-stocked nursery. A crib, bedding, clothing, diapers, lotions, night lights, musical mobiles, toys, blankets and soft lighting furnish the room. The child's world is full of sensory input and parents are the supreme gatekeepers of this input. They are expected to maintain an environment rich in stimulation and continually monitor when the child is ready for new forms of stimulation and at what intensity. The relationship with the primary caregiver becomes the vehicle for a steady influx of sensory growth opportunities. Parents watch for the baby's sensitivity to fabrics, detergents, lotions and creams.

As the baby starts eating solid foods, parents try one food at a time to eliminate allergies or reactions. Parents manage all of the infant's movements. They cuddle, swaddle, bounce, read and rock. The baby is exposed to multiple sensory inputs throughout the day and learns that mom will keep the baby safe through each stimulus.

Now imagine a baby with unprepared parents who lack basic supplies. With few diapers, they are infrequently changed, resulting in diaper rash. Instead of a crib, the baby sleeps in a playpen in the living room. Overly-stressed parents are often preoccupied with their own interests and typically don't always interact with the baby for enjoyment and sometimes only when the baby cries. This baby can easily be sensory deprived.

Sensory deprivation can arise from lack of movement, little exposure to a variety of stimuli and too few interactions with the primary caregiver. A child who is left alone for hours, not picked up and carried infrequently by the parent could be sensitive to touch and movement. When normal sensory input occurs, this baby may stiffen and cry. Children without an adequate sensory "diet" may be overly reactive to fabrics, food and environmental changes, gravitate to the smell of urine and feces and reject physical touch.

Other foster or adoptive children may come from an overly stimulating environment with a constant blur of sounds, people and activities. These children may have little supervision, eat what is available, roam at will and have few hygiene skills. Their sensory system may be hyper-alert, with an accompanying need for more sensory stimulation that drives risk-taking behaviors. Adults commonly report having difficulty sleeping in a quiet country setting after living in the city. "The silence is unnerving," some state. This is similar to what happens when a developing nervous system has few prolonged exposures to "quiet." Without the exposure, tolerance is not developed. Now imagine this baby trying to sleep in the "unnerving quiet" of a new foster placement.

Amy's Family

Lori could not understand why Amy was so objectionable toward sleeping in her new bed. She wanted a "big girl" bed and now she had one. Every night, Amy cried for Mom to sleep with her, because she was afraid but could not explain why. Lori grew more irritable with each passing day that she had a poor night's sleep. And James was missing those few minutes alone just before bedtime when he and Lori would talk. No matter what they tried, Amy seemed unable to sleep without Lori lying next to her.

When they brought up the problem to the caseworker, they were told, "Oh yeah, the other foster family had the same problem." Subsequent investigation by the therapy team revealed that Amy's biological family was homeless and slept in a car for most of the time she was with them. By report, she slept in the back seat next to mom in the busy shopping center parking lot. Though Amy cognitively understood she was safe in her bedroom, her nervous system never developed the skills to self-calm in a quiet setting. When given a stuffed tiger with the sound of a beating heart and a white-noise-generating sound system, she dropped off to sleep the first night with a quick tuck-in by Lori.

Just as Amy does not have the skills to manage the quiet, other children lack skills of balance, modulation, vestibular and tactile systems, perceptive awareness, finger dexterity, weight shifting, stability, mobility and patience, all of which are required just to put on a pair of socks or brush one's teeth. Lacking opportunity to develop healthy systems, children can become frustrated and angry when challenged to perform a task for which they haven't been prepared by previous exposure or experiences. Children may be unaware of their body as it relates to space. They're confused about their personal boundaries. Carl Sheperis et al described the child's "difficulty modulating behaviors as evidenced by a tendency to invade other's personal space."[52]

In addition to the five common senses that develop with exposure, humans have other sensory systems: proprioceptive and vestibular. The proprioceptive system tells you where your body is in space. We know where our hand is in relation to our body even when we can't see it. The vestibular system monitors when the body is in motion. These senses are present at birth, but proper maturation of them depends upon adequate exposure and positive experiences.

Some organic sensory difficulties are hardwired at birth and may create a special challenge for mother in attuning to the baby and co-regulating. Some children feel the light, soft touch of a mother's fingers as fearful and uncomfortable. They may prefer deep pressure in strong squeezes or hugs. If the parent is uncomfortable with providing that deep pressure or doesn't understand the child's need for it, sufficient co-regulation and secure attachment may be threatened. This mis-attunement can create aversive experiences for the child. Without help, even a great mother can become a source of trauma to her infant when these sensory idiosyncrasies of the baby are not recognized and understood.

If a child has true sensory dysfunction, interventions should be prescribed and implemented by an occupational or physical therapist. Parents need to recognize the need for professional assistance, educate themselves and provide awareness for others (teachers, scout leaders, sports leaders) in the child's environment. Parents and professionals can guide children in selecting sensory activities that will enable them to reach and maintain optimal levels of arousal. The child's schedule may need to be adjusted to provide adequate stimulating developmental activities. The schedule must be balanced so that the child will not be over-stimulated and become dysregulated. Sometimes children may be able to maintain control outside of the home, but become dysregulated upon arrival home. Problem-solving strategies may be necessary to help the child become regulated without disruptive behaviors. Success, competence and control will be outcomes of these positive interventions.

BEHAVIORS

The child may exhibit a variety of behaviors to self-soothe and/or to help remain focused. These are typical and are not to be taken personally by the parent or overemphasized. Some may be irritating and distracting. Parents must consider why their child is using them and aid in helping the child to maintain calmness. Alternatives may be needed in environments like the classroom, church, etc.

Some self-soothing coping skills are:

- Whistling
- Tapping objects
- Body odor
- Shuffling feet
- Fidgeting
- Picking at the skin, nails, scabs or wounds
- Thumb sucking
- Hair pulling
- Rocking
- Head banging

Common Sensory Behaviors and Reactions

Hearing: May be sensitive to noise.
May not be able to filter individual sounds.

Seeing: May need to see everything in the environment to feel safe.
May be overwhelmed by visual distractions.

Smelling: May be comforted by familiar odors from the past.
Familiar odors may produce fear.

Tasting: Unfamiliar food textures may be scary.
Comfort may come from familiar foods.

Touching: May overreact to touch.
Light touch may irritate.
May crave deep pressure.
May touch everything to process environment.

Moving: May seek intense stimulation.
May be fearful to try new things.
May have difficulty paying attention.
May withdraw when overwhelmed.

Parental Responsibilities

- Educate self.
- Seek professional assistance.
- Professionals and parents help children achieve/maintain optimal sensory levels of arousal.
- The treatment team must determine priorities and goals to facilitate the activities.
- Examine and adjust expectations.
- Develop problem-solving strategies.
- Adjust the environment to reduce stressors.
- Adjust the child's schedule for therapy, transitions and interventions.
- Balance activities.
- Acquire sensory equipment and supplies.
- Implement prescribed interventions.
- Provide awareness to others.
- Inform educational staff of accommodations.
- Encourage the child's self-awareness.
- Employ sensory games with baby lotion, reciprocity and eye contact.

- Plan an adequate sensory diet, which is critical for children with disrupted sensory experiences. Equipment to facilitate the diet and scheduled time for the activities and experiences are required.
- Compliment the child on his or her bravery and patience.

The *Diagnostic Classification of Mental Health and Developmental Disorders of Infancy and Early Childhood (DC: 0-3R)* now includes "Regulation Disorders of Sensory Processing," which was expanded from "Regulator Disorders" to focus understanding and treatment on sensory processing difficulties. The experts recognized how commonly infants and toddlers suffer from difficulties in coping with either ultra-sensitive sensory input or lack of sufficient input. As we have in this chapter, they advocate for greater awareness of these problems by parents, professionals and all villagers, so that we can engage the children despite their sensory barriers and partner with them along their way to experiencing a more comfortable world.[53]

PART 4

Workbook for You and Your Traumatized Child

CHAPTER 15

Helpful Handouts

The following is a collection of handouts for your team that explain and summarize much of the information we have covered. It is our hope that presenting this information in a clear, concise manner will ease the way for new team members and help them to begin work helping your child more quickly.

HANDOUT: Changing the Negative
Internal Working Model (N-IWM)

The team can support the family in many different ways. Just by directing the child back to the parent instead of meeting the child's needs is therapeutic. Validating the child's worth and the parents' trustworthiness as well as narrating the environment are therapeutic interventions that are healing.

Examples:

1. You are safe.

2. You are lovable.

3. These parents love you.

4. These parents can be trusted.

5. As a baby, your needs were not met, which created unhealthy parts that are causing you to make poor decisions.

6. The unhealthy parts make it hard to have fun with you.

7. The healthy parts make it fun to be with you.

8. You can overcome those parts that are causing you trouble.

9. You are strengthening the healthy parts and staying out of trouble.

10. The unhealthy parts can develop and change to match your other abilities so that you can have a happy life.

11. Your healthy parts are developing and growing; it is so much fun to watch you grow up!

HANDOUT: Team Responsibilities

1. Keep all involved as physically safe as possible.

2. Have a working knowledge of attachment, trauma and child development.

3. Encourage parents with helpful ideas, plans and problem solving.

4. Facilitate planning time with the parents. The child needs to be in another "safe" place, e.g., bed, shower, reading, school, etc.

5. Model and encourage proper respect and behavior towards Mom.

6. Assess Mom's emotional state. Plan interventions to use on days when she is overwhelmed and emotionally unavailable. Remember the tag team approach.

7. During conversations with the child, encourage trust in Mom.

8. Guide the child into correctly interpreting parental expectations.

9. Assist the parent in maintaining sensory contact.

10. Understand that the responsibility for poor behavior choices is the child's.

11. Identify and support the child's ability for self-control and concede control to Mom (when the unhealthy part is in control, the child loses).

12. Identify and constantly reinforce the positive effects of cooperation (reciprocity) between mother and child.

13. Observe and respond to the child's healthy parts in the appropriate manner. Keep in mind the child may be uncomfortable with success.

14. Remind the child that he is valuable to Mom; remember, this is contrary to his core belief.

15. Be as flexible as possible to change activities, plans and expectations.

HANDOUT: Cautions for the Team

1. Team members working with the child must have a working knowledge of attachment, trauma, developmental milestones and therapeutic parenting.

2. Do not expect behavior modification techniques to change behavior.

3. Do not criticize the parents. Assess the parent's energy and emotional availability. Assist as planned. Determine the appropriate interventions ahead of time.

4. Adults are to be in control at all times. Control can be shared with a cooperative child.

5. Honest and frequent communication between adults is absolutely necessary.

6. Mother makes all decisions, in the child's eyes.

7. Mother, exclusively, may use components of attachment; e.g., touch, affectionate words and fun activities. If others are participating in fun activities with the child, use the idea of *funneling*: all good things come through/via parents.

8. Do not be drawn into the negativity the child brings with him.

9. The child is to be held responsible for poor choices but not "blamed."

10. Avoid anger and sarcasm.

11. Be aware of passive-aggressive behaviors.

12. The child may be triggered by sensory input that spurs fight, flight or freeze responses (neurological reactions).

13. Be aware that the child's behaviors can incite a loss of patience and empathy

14. Avoid coalitions and exclusions within the team.

HANDOUT: Working Diplomatically with Professionals

Enter the meeting with a problem that needs to be solved.
Leave the meeting with allies and solutions,
not with enemies and no solutions.

1. **Be accepting:** Accept responsibility for your behavior.

2. **Be accountable:** Follow through with your obligations. Expect the other team members to do the same.

3. **Be accurate:** Take notes at the meeting. Keep communication logs.

4. **Be assertive:** The goal is to find help for your child.

5. **Be calm:** Anger does not give more power.

6. **Be courteous:** Use your manners. Be remembered for your politeness.

7. **Be decisive:** Know exactly what you are asking for pertaining to your child. Clearly, with as few words as possible, write down the information before the meeting. Present supportive documentation.

8. **Be escorted:** Attend meetings with as many team members as possible. Encourage other professionals to be involved.

9. **Be factual:** Stick to the facts. Keep/bring supportive documents.

10. **Be firm:** When certain about the need, the intervention, the circumstance, etc., verify your stand by offering supportive documentation and/or the opportunity to consult with other professionals on the team.

11. **Be flexible:** Look for creative ideas and solutions. Brainstorm as a group.

12. **Be forgiving:** Others will make mistakes with this child, just like you have.

13. **Be giving:** Share resources with the professionals. Bring lists of materials

14. **Be honest:** Always tell the truth. Don't manipulate with half-truths.

15. **Be informed:** Know the facts.

16. **Be inquisitive:** Ask lots of questions. Compel the professionals to support their view, intervention or idea with documentation or research.

17. **Be kind:** Try not to be offended by decisions. Working with a child with these problems may be new to many professionals.

18. **Be observant:** Read body language. Know when to stop, whom to direct questions to, who is/is not comprehending the information, etc.

19. **Be open:** Let the professionals know about your home life. Be transparent.

20. **Be patient:** Remember how long it took for you to understand the need for precise interventions designed for this child.

21. **Be positive:** Do not project discord among the team to the child.

22. **Be practical:** A small change is a success.

23. **Be professional:** You are your child's advocate. Act, do not react.

24. **Be prompt:** You are with professionals who may be underpaid and overworked.

25. **Be respectful:** You are more likely to be respected in return.

26. **Be quiet:** Listen to their concerns, opinions and advice.

27. **Be sorry:** Apologize when you are wrong.

28. **Be supportive:** Encourage the staff. They must work within their system.

29. **Be thankful:** Acknowledge their time, interest, wisdom and guidance.

30. **Be unemotional:** Save your energy for parenting your child.

31. **Be wise:** The goal is a cohesive, supportive collaboration. Consult other professionals if you believe the recommendations may not meet the child's needs.

Don't be too hard on yourself. You are receiving "on the job training." This is new to everyone involved. You will have many opportunities to get it right.

HANDOUT: Interagency Meetings

Participants: parents, mental health professionals, therapists, educational staff and community team members. The child does not need to be present until the team has formed a unified position and treatment plan. If the child perceives disunity among the team, triangulation may occur.

- Measure progress.
  Repeat assessments.
  Request and present feedback from community team members
    (Boy/Girl Scouts, sports teams, grandparents, church, etc.).
- Write the treatment plan.
  Assess current behavior issues.
  Arrange for team members to attend therapy sessions.
  Focus on ways to build healthy relationships with the primary caregiver.
- Educate the team.
  Announce any current training sessions.
  Provide a resource list.
  Establish a lending library of resources.
- Evaluate the interventions used.
  Use feedback from all team members to analyze behavioral
    reactions to interventions.
  Determine if the success or failure of the intervention was
    dependent on the team member's information or ability.
- Plan future interventions as per direction of therapy.
  Consult with the therapist for current and future therapy direction.
  Determine additional support systems for child/family during this
    time.
- Air team problems (honesty is a must).
  Focus on the goal of preserving the family to aid this child's
    opportunity to heal.
  Remember the child's pathology may pull any team member off
    center. This is a team effort. All must work together.
- Evaluate the family's needs.
  Observe and listen to the family's needs.
  Address additional support systems.
  Validate their struggles.
  Rejoice in any progress.
- Evaluate the team's needs.
  Observe and listen to the team's needs.
  Address additional professionals needed during this quarter.
  Validate the intensity of the work.
  Rejoice in any progress.

HANDOUT: Service Flow

Research the flow of services for your county or state. Begin your inquiry with foster and adoptive agencies and the Mental Health Association. Check the phone book.

Service Flow for Pennsylvania

1. The child must have a Pennsylvania Medicaid card for many services.

2. The Medicaid card is not dependent on the family's income if the child has a mental health diagnosis.

3. An application can be filed at the Department of Welfare.

4. The child will have a caseworker with the insurance company who manages the Medicaid services.

5. Call your county's Mental Health Association for a caseworker to assist in finding and maintaining services.

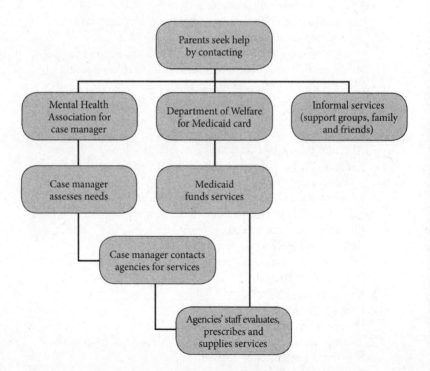

HANDOUT: Records

Keep complete and accurate records to share with the team. Carefully read all evaluations for accuracy and require that corrections be made if incorrect.

Sample files to be kept: with phone numbers, addresses, dates and outcomes

- Child's history
  - Birth/family history
  - Court records
  - Case notes
- Insurance
  - Private
  - Medicaid
- Physical health records
  - Doctor
  - Dentist
  - Optometrist
  - Medications
- Therapy
  - Physical therapy
  - Occupational therapy
  - Other

- Mental health records
  - Psychiatry
  - Psychology
  - Therapy
  - In-home services
  - Early intervention
  - Wraparound
  - Family-based
  - Outpatient services
  - Inpatient services
- School records
  - Report cards
  - Notes from teachers
  - Special education plans (IEP, 504 Plan, etc.)

HANDOUT: Team Communication

Use a sheet like this to keep track of all records for the child.

Date	Name	Agency	Phone #	Information	Follow-up

CHAPTER 16

Environment Interventions

Sports, scouting, music and dance programs present unique challenges. How much time should children devote to such activities? Parents must be intentional in how and where their family spends their time. Children can have too much of any good thing and it will interfere with family life. Too many activities, just like possessions, are problematic. Parents must assess their child's relational skills, emotional development, sensory processing abilities and physical abilities to determine readiness. These are all taught at home in the parent/child relationship. Society may ascribe social skills learning to activities outside the home. For traumatized children, these skills are experienced and modeled with/by the primary caregivers.

Checklist of Helpful Items to Have for Your Traumatized Child

- Clothing:
    - Buy the style of clothes the parents are comfortable with and set and hold firm boundaries:
        - "I'll be happy to buy these items for you."
        - "I know you want me to buy that shirt, but this one is more appropriate."
    - Avoid power struggles.
    - Use "I" statements; be empathic and acknowledge the child's preference.
    - Don't be sarcastic, critical or demeaning.
    - Buy coordinating clothes.
    - Be realistic and practical; buy durable fabrics and shoes.
    - Don't invest large amounts of money in clothing or shoes that may be destroyed.

- Toys and books: Assess your child's emotional age for appropriate toys and books.
  - Choose toys that have multiple uses (building, creative, thought-provoking).
    - Puppets
    - Dress-up clothes
    - Building blocks
    - Flannel boards and figures
    - Games for two or more players
  - Assemble a library with books to share and for relationship building.
    - Read-aloud stories, books on tape
    - Activity and hobby books
    - Relationship-enhancing stories (avoid stories in which children assume the role of an adult or illustrate that a child can survive without adults)
- Art supplies:
  - Soft modeling clay
  - Finger paint
  - Colored pencils
  - Variety of papers
  - Crayons
  - Drawing pencils
  - Stamps, stencils
  - Beads, pipe cleaners, felt, foam sheets
- Hobby supplies
  - Bird feeding, watching
  - Kite making and flying
  - Gardening supplies
  - Models
- Sensory equipment:
  - Fuzzy blankets (and other textured fabrics)
  - Lotions, massage oils with pleasing smells to identify with mom (e.g., vanilla)
  - Mini-trampoline
  - Jump rope
  - Rocking chair
  - Mats for tumbling, mazes, tunnels

DE-CLUTTER AND ORGANIZE

> Before you begin, leave pride and insecurity outside your child's room.

Since parents need to be trustworthy, carefully strategize before beginning the de-cluttering and organizing process. Do not invade the child's privacy while the child is gone and remove items, unless it is a safety issue. Decide how much input the child will have and when the child will be included. Be prepared for control battles with the child. Consider inviting someone from your support network to reinforce that "This mom can be trusted." Consider your child's developmental age and scaffold (divide into small chunks) the process. Only begin the project when you are emotionally energized with positive emotions.

Delving into the child's possessions will activate many triggers. Parents may think that, because an item is broken, damaged or old, it should be thrown away. This may not match the child's belief system. Store these in a container until emotions subside. Be aware that any item from the child's past may have some undetermined value to the child and may need to be kept. These are transitional objects with emotional connections. Enable the child to have access to these items even if they must be placed in storage containers.

If a child cannot have an item, the parents must be empathic and explain why, with deference to the child's N-IWM. Break the process into small chunks so that neither you nor your child becomes dysregulated. Watch for any escalation, stop the process and narrate the child's distress.

Step 1: Gather Large Boxes and Label One of Each: Store, Toss, Keep and Donate

- Sort items into boxes.
- Items to be stored can be separated into those that will be stored in the child's room or elsewhere (as in the attic). For storage in the child's room, label and designate placement.
- Assign places for clothing, shoes, backpacks and toys.

Step 2: Record the Process with Photos.

- Photograph the child wearing a beloved shirt, playing with favorite toys or demonstrating an athletic ability, etc.

Step 3: Repurpose, Rotate or Donate.

- Make a quilt or coverlet out of favorite outgrown clothing.
- Hang and display an outgrown clothing item.
- Make and decorate a keepsake box for memorabilia:
  - Include the child's name and picture on the outside.
  - Parents keep important originals; make copies for the child's box.
- Rotate stored containers of toys monthly or seasonally.
- Choose an organization for "needy" children to donate extra items.

Realize that even with the best storage system in the world, your child may try to disrupt the plans by not putting things away or by "recreating the system." Use these behaviors to identify his or her fears.

HOLIDAYS

Holidays are challenging for parents. Gifts, unstructured time, an increase in extended family and friends' presence and more personal questions may incite dysregulated behavior. Giving and receiving gifts is problematic due to the child's N-IWM. The child may fear he or she won't get the desired gift, because the parent cannot be trusted. The child may feel shame if not reciprocal or the parent may be angry if the child does not reciprocate. Even if the child receives the ideal gift, the child may fear the parent knows him or her too well and destroy the gift. The child may be overly possessive with gifts or passively unconcerned. Gift cards may cause fear in both the child and parent. The child may receive a gift card which he or she "wastes" on "foolish" items or the card may be "misplaced." The child may demand to use the card immediately and lack the patience to accommodate the parent's schedule.

Unstructured time is unpredictable and offers less stability. If the child does not trust the parent, then he or she is vulnerable to the parent's demands. These children tend to misread parental intentions and become oppositional and defiant. Unstructured time may increase the child's fear of the unexpected and prevent him or her from knowing what others will expect. The child may try to isolate to avoid interactions or become more intrusive to control others.

Allan's Family

I was feeling a little bit scared, because I didn't know what it would be like (going to visit Gettysburg, Pennsylvania) and after we got there I was aggravated, because nobody knew where we were going or what we were doing.

—*Allan*

The presence of extended family and friends can induce fear. The child may fear intimate questions, as they try to get to know him or her better. Family and friends may want to help the parents by offering suggestions, but may seem judgmental. They may offer to babysit, but the parents fear the child may manipulate them, be unsafe or embarrass the family. Just hosting guests creates fear. The child may be asked to change bedrooms, sleep in unaccustomed places or with others. The child may not trust the parents to keep him or her safe, so sleeping in a strange room or with others may evoke an emotional response and behavior problems. The child may struggle to remain age-appropriate for long periods of time.

Families will always celebrate holidays. Therefore, plans must be made to reduce stress and increase distress tolerance. Some helpful ideas are:

1. Parents can recognize the child's distress and discuss how they are managing the distress.
2. Parents can narrate the environment so that the child will know the parents understand the child's distress.
3. Parents can realize the child may need periods of de-stressing time away from others.
4. Parents can allow the child opportunities to regress if needed.
5. Parents can add structure to the days and encourage the children to trust the parents with the schedule.
6. Parents can arrange time for the child to be in close proximity as needed.
7. Parents can discuss gift-giving options and arrange ways to decrease anxiety.
8. Parents can develop a plan to house their guests before the guests arrive. The children can then practice the new sleeping arrangements.

BALANCING FAMILY INTERACTIONS

- Nurture: emphasis on comfort and care
- Structure: emphasis on rules and regulations
- Challenge: emphasis on challenging the child's negative internal working model (N-IWM)

In the environment chapter, we suggested "staging a theater production with props, cast and a script that balances structure, nurture and challenge of old beliefs." Parents tend to gather their skills from the way they were parented, leading them to lean more towards one style. The recovery process requires a new perspective and a balance of all three approaches to develop new, intimate family relationships.

Some parents gravitate towards a structured environment with overuse of rules and routines, creating the impression the parents are the directors of the production, not part of the production. Other parents dispense comfort and care to the extreme. These parents may appear weak and unable to handle the child's big behaviors. Few parents over-use challenge, since the home is not a therapist's office and daily life usually interferes with therapeutic parenting. However, it can be noted that if challenge is increased too quickly there may be an increase in problematic behaviors due to the unsettling nature of challenging the internal belief system.

The following charts are to be used to increase or decrease skills to achieve balance.

Nurture, Structure or Challenge

Where is your imbalance? Where do you need to refocus?

Increasing Nurture, Structure or Challenge:

To increase nurture:	To increase structure:	To increase challenge:
1. Enjoy your child's healthy parts.	1. Reinforce personal boundaries.	1. Redirect the child back to Mom.
2. See your child at his or her emotional age.	2. Prioritize expectations and assign chores.	2. Set circumstances so that Mom can be trusted.
3. Remember your child's traumatic past.	3. Pick your battles—do not focus on minor irritations.	3. Adults demonstrate that new beliefs, feelings, behaviors are possible and act upon expectations.
4. Focus on your role to help your child heal.	4. Increase consistency in responding to behaviors (but not necessarily negative).	
5. Begin parenting at your child's emotional age.	5. Increase consequences.	4. Reframe behaviors to internal working model (I am bad and I cannot trust my parents).
6. Respond with empathy.	6. Do not solve your child's problem.	
7. Touch frequently.	7. Allow your child to experience difficulties.	5. Link behaviors to emotions.
8. Smile and wink at your child.	8. Develop routines.	
9. Be in close proximity.		
10. Plan activities together.		
11. Be emotionally available.		
12. Connect with humor.		

Decreasing Nurture, Structure or Challenge:

To decrease nurture:	To decrease structure:	To decrease challenge:
1. Increase consequences consistently.	1. Recognize alternative motivations; not all negative behavior is malicious or intentional.	1. Reduce labeling.
2. Decrease nurturing activities.		2. Use planned ignoring.
3. Increase time away from your child.	2. Limit the number of household rules.	3. Give space to the relationship.
4. Make sure you have firm boundaries.	3. Soften the difference between success and failure.	4. Provide distractions (like books, playtime).
5. Allow and encourage your child to solve his or her own problems.	4. Use planned ignoring.	5. Respond to your child's emotional age.
6. Allow your child to experience difficulties.	5. Create exceptions: we will go to the park regardless of behavior.	
	6. Use "I" statements.	
	7. Make sure you use the "trauma lens" when reviewing disruptive behaviors.	
	8. Respond to your child's emotional age.	
	9. Have impromptu fun activities.	

CHAPTER 17

TDC Handouts and Interventions

THE NEGATIVE INTERNAL WORKING MODEL

The Jones Family's and Corey's stories, which introduce the Trauma-Disrupted Competencies, are the foundation of the Emotional Cognitive Trauma Model. Early in treatment, the staff uses storytelling to illustrate each baby's experiences.

Steps to role-play parent/infant emotional experiences:

1. Gather two stuffed animals or baby dolls.
2. Use the first toy to illustrate the needs and wants cycles as they are met by a nurturing, attuned caregiver.
3. Encourage the child to recognize:
   a. What learning occurs if these needs are met; what he believes about himself, his caregiver and the world.
   b. What feelings occur for mother and child.
   c. What behaviors occur between mother and child.
   d. What normal attunement occurs between mother and child.
4. Use the second doll or animal to illustrate the same needs cycles, but now identify cycles without closure. Project examples of times that mother may not meet the child's needs.
   a. What learning occurs when one's needs are not met? What does he believe about himself, his caregiver and the world?
   b. What feelings occur for mother and child?
   c. What behaviors occur between mother and child?
   d. What normal attunement occurs between mother and child?

5. Encourage your child to brainstorm how these beliefs and feelings affect behavior.
6. Transition from general to specific. Compare your child's specific behaviors or specific history to the feelings occurring.
7. Offer various circumstances and the baby's response. Some examples are: if the mother is loving and nurturing, if there is limited food available, if the mother is too sad to care for herself, etc. Highlight that everyone can have parts that are: healthy-sick, happy-sad, working-broken and old-new.

The *Two Babies Narrative*

1. Babies' brains are formed at birth with less frontal activity and more limbic activity.
   a. Emotions are functioning but the baby has little cognitive processing and no words.
   b. There are four emotions:
      i. Sad
      ii. Scared
      iii. Happy
      iv. Angry
2. Learning has to take place in the back (or limbic) brain without words and is used for the rest of our lives.
   a. A baby learns about gravity by experience (activity) in the crib.
   b. A baby learns about him or herself, caregiver and the world (internal working model) in the crib.
3. How does the baby develop a picture of self, caregiver and the world?
   a. What four things can a baby do?
      i. Eat
      ii. Dirty his or her diaper
      iii. Sleep
      iv. Cry
   b. What about the four things a baby can feel? (four emotions)
      i. What happens when baby experiences environmental stimulation like loud noise, cold or shaking?
      ii. What happens when baby experiences internal stimulations like pain, hunger, tiredness?
      iii. What does the baby do?
   c. Mom instinctively (hardwired to recognize) knows what a baby feels.

    i. How does a mother know to come? She is affectually attuned.

    ii. What does a mother do? She gathers the child up close to her body.

    iii. What happens inside of the mother? She evaluates the situation and calms herself.

    iv. What happens inside of the baby? The baby is linked to the mother in a co-regulating experience, so the baby calms.

  d. What does a baby learn when all of the baby's needs are met by an attuned caregiver? (Positive internal working model)

    i. I'm the most important thing in the world.

    ii. Mother is trustworthy.

    iii. The world is basically safe.

  e. What does a baby learn when the baby's needs are not met?

    i. A baby will survive by turning his or her fear into anger instead of dying.

    ii. Turning fear into "mad" so fast a baby doesn't learn to handle fear.

    iii. Negative internal working model:

      A. I'm bad.

      B. Mother is untrustworthy.

      C. The world is dangerous.

4. Closing Questions

  a. Three years later: How does each child get a drink of water?
   Baby Whose Needs Were Met—Asks for it
   Baby Whose Needs Were Not Met—Tries to get it for himself

  b. What does this baby feel?
   Baby Whose Needs Were Met—full range of emotions
   Baby Whose Needs Were Not Met—fear

5. Introduce Parts

After the *Two Babies Narrative*, focus on how the babies had many parts, like all humans. We have creative parts, less motivated parts, organized parts and messy parts. This concept will help the child (and the adults) have a healthier view of themselves and each other. Both babies had both healthy and unhealthy parts. Healthy parts want to make good choices, be creative, enjoy life, comply with adults and have good morals and values. The unhealthy parts decide to eat too much candy, not brush teeth, watch too much television and refuse to comply if uncomfortable. The baby with a mom who did not take good care of him had a hurt part, a part of his brain that learned to live in dangerous situations and survive. This hurt part learned not to trust adults and felt that he was unlovable and the world was unsafe (N-IWM). To help this hurt part grow up and be healthy, parents identify when the hurt part is making the decisions and the impact of the hurt part on the child's life.

The child's hurt part learned that his mom could not be trusted to take care of him and keep him safe. With new experiences with all the tools of affect matching, reframing, co-regulation and narration, the child will perceive how trustworthy this mom is. As the child's belief changes to "This mom can be trusted," this "trustworthy" mom can supply the child with the affirmation that he is loveable. The child will begin to form a new set of beliefs. The last belief is that the world is safe, which many of us doubt after watching a news program. Parents can only keep their child safe in the areas they control.

Allan's Family

> *Saturday we were in the car and I started whining about something, but I can't remember what it was. I was acting like a two-year-old, literally. But then the sixteen-year-old kicked in and I started laughing at how stupid I looked.*
>
> *—Allan*

Help the child realize that old beliefs and behaviors that worked in previous environments are not as successful in the new home. Be aware that the child will battle to keep his negative belief system that supports parents as untrustworthy. Use the following interventions to prevent or identify decisions made by using the hurt part. The handouts are helpful for a consistent environment when others are caring for the child.

THIS IS MY STORY

Some foster and adoptive children talk about their lives as if they have had more than one. Their birth family and each following placement seem to be a different life. There is no integration of the child's experiences. At one home, they behaved one way, following that family's rules, and at the next home they behaved another way, following that family's rules. One family may be Christian, the next Jewish. One year they celebrate Christmas, the next Hanukkah. Nothing is integrated or permanent. People come and go; nothing ever seems to be the same.

After children are exposed to the *Two Babies Narrative,* they may be willing to share their story. These stories may be filled with abuse, horror, abandonment, loss and sadness. Many emotions will be evoked for the child and listeners. The listeners must "be with" the child and can reframe the child's experience. Do not argue with the child. Be curious but not too questioning—this is not to be an interrogation session.

Before the child begins the story, discuss the emotions that could be generated and what kind of help the child may need. Describe what you will do to help. As the child tells the story, identify and note possible triggers in the current environment that create a reaction. List the child's strengths gained from these frightening events. Later the strengths and triggers can be used to understand the child's behaviors. This is the beginning of developing a coherent narrative in which the child makes sense of his or her history and integrates it into the present.

Goals

1. Just like the *Two Babies Narrative*, caregivers understand the child's experience.
2. The child will make sense of events as he or she tells the story and the caregiver clarifies and details emotions.
3. By having the caregiver be with the child and offer comfort, the parent can help the child co-regulate emotions. Parents can give the story a new ending and identify how they will prevent the trauma from happening again.
4. The child will connect past to present by linking previous strengths with current triggers.
5. When a child hears and sees others' emotional responses to the story, he or she will experience a deeper understanding of the trauma experiences.

Directions

1. After the child hears and integrates the *Two Babies Narrative* and has processed some of the information, invite the child to tell his or her own story.
2. Use good writing techniques: have a beginning, middle and end. Ask who, what, when, where, why and how questions to add structure. Use empathy and emotional co-regulation. Ask for clarification if the child remains regulated.
3. Ask how to help if the child has "big emotions."
4. Use empathy and show how the child's story affects you.
5. Attune to the child's emotional state; check to see if the child is "reliving" or "retelling" the story. Help the child co-regulate with the parent: the parent offers comfort and adapts to help the child regulate.
6. If the child seems to be reliving the story, identify his or her current safety level. The parent may need to offer more comfort.

7. If the child continues to be emotionally regulated, discuss the meaning of the story for both the child and the adults.
8. Remind the child of strengths gained during the events.
9. Identify present-day triggers and strengths that developed from the events.

The pleasant parts of the story can be written in a journal or scrap-booked. The past was not all bad and good things came from it. The birth parents were not all bad—they, too, had parts that were helpful and parts that were hurtful. The child will be healthier if he or she can integrate the birth parents' good parts.

Three categories of cognitive interventions

1. Identify the origins of dysfunctional behaviors.
    General: Demonstrate the link between the ways an infant and caregiver interact and the beliefs he develops about himself, caregivers and others.
    Specific: Introduce experiences from the child's history to verify his unhealthy parts. Highlight the child's own uniqueness and more socially acceptable parts.
2. Identify how fear (discomfort) is experienced when core beliefs are not represented in the external environment. A belief in gravity produces fear when suspended in the air or leaning over a railing at the Grand Canyon. A belief that guns are unsafe produces fear when a gun is pointed at you.
    General: Demonstrate how beliefs drive/explain the feelings and behaviors of everyone.
    Example: *"How would a boy who believed an adult was dangerous react/feel when that adult puts her hand on his shoulder?"*
    Specific: Use child's current behaviors to illustrate his unhealthy parts. Highlight the parts the child uses to "push" people away.
    Examples: 1. *"Why do you jerk away from your mom's touch? How do you explain this?"*
    2. *"How can you explain your fear of this mom?"*
3. Identify what is needed for corrective experiences to help the unhealthy parts become healthier.
    General: Identify how a positive experience produces positive belief in others.
    Specific: Identify how this child's experiences have produced/reinforced new beliefs.

HANDOUT: To encourage reflection and thankfulness

1. Encourage the child to say, "Thank you."

2. Ask the child to watch the recipient's response when he or she thanks someone.

3. Challenge the child to count the number of times he had reason to be thankful.

4. Engineer cognitive dissonance to challenge the old belief system.

5. Catch the child enjoying an activity. Record the moment with a picture or video. Later, remind the child of the earlier enjoyment.

6. Schedule fun events, not just as a reward or for a specific celebration.

7. Provide pictures (copies of photos) of the child enjoying the experience. Be aware that the response may be negative.

8. Allow the child to see other children enjoying themselves and earning rewards. *Do not encourage the child to do the same.*

9. Highlight observable differences between old family systems and new, without judging either system.

10. Verbally reframe and highlight the negative aspects of the child's life. Invite the child, with humor and empathy, to reevaluate his current level of fun.

11. Identify the adult's positive motivations: "We went to the park because I love you," "I wanted to see you have fun" and "I thought you would enjoy being outside today."

12. Define and promote the child's ability to hold and act on different beliefs (healthy and unhealthy parts).

13. Acknowledge, with humor, the child's ability to control others.

INTERPRETING CHILDREN'S BEHAVIOR

Parents are told to have insight into their child's world. Because these children have lived in so many different worlds, parents struggle with how to interpret their child's behaviors. The behaviors are clearer when viewed through the Trauma Lens. Here are a few examples.

Feelings

1. If the child is angry at losing a privilege, parents can reframe the loss as the child's healthy part growing, because he or she is sad about losing.

2. If the child is comfortable with having "nothing" (privileges, electronics, activities), parents can reframe the loss as the unhealthy part being satisfied with less and as if the child believes he or she does not deserve good things.

Behaviors

1. If the child is achieving goals, parents can reframe it as the healthy part growing.

2. If the child has good hygiene, parents can reframe it as the healthy part growing.

Feelings

If the child is:	Give meaning to the behavior
Angry at loss	Good; shows that a healthy part is growing
Comfortable with nothing	Old beliefs (direct at unhealthy part)
Desirous of realistic things	Proof of differing parts; healthy part can share desires
Fearful of something	Old belief; unsafe parent, self, world (direct at unhealthy part)
Happy about something	Good; beginning to let self enjoy things (direct at healthy part)
Sad about something	Very good; everyone feels this at times (healthy part's way of saying, "Let's not do this again")

Behaviors

If the child is:	Give meaning to the behavior
Achieving goals	New belief…getting stronger
Exhibiting good hygiene	I am worthy.
Exhibiting poor hygiene	I am not worth taking care of; I'll prove I am not worthy.
Failing to achieve	Fear of losing control of the environment (old beliefs)
Frustrating others	Fear of losing control of the environment (old beliefs)
Hurting others	Trying to export own hurt (old beliefs)
Lying	Fear of losing control (old beliefs)
Stealing	I can never earn it (old belief of "I am not worth it.")
Talking/crying (about hurts)	New way to handle (new beliefs)
Tolerating the mother's touch for a short time	Good new belief…courage
Truthful	I can handle it.
Withdrawn from the mother	Fear of the mother (old beliefs)

WORKSHEET: Cognitive Circle

A negative belief combined with a positive circumstance will produce fear.

Most children and parents have trouble initially understanding how the N-IWM (I'm bad, the primary caregiver is bad and the world is a dangerous place) interacts with the typical home environment and may produce a downward spiral in the parent/child relationship, with increased disruptive behaviors. Without this awareness, emotions are not recognized, circumstances and motivations are misinterpreted and the child's negative beliefs become the home's ruling force. Adults and children are encouraged to complete the following form together.

This Cognitive Circle exercise attends to the cycle of interactions that are present in families. No one acts without an impact on others. When a circumstance or behavior occurs that should be discussed and processed, the form gives structure without blame. The participants are asked to fill in the blocks with the circumstance, the underlying emotion, the precipitating responses and the belief about self. Thus, a visual guide to the experience will be crafted.

This visual guide helps parents and children be aware of the cycle, which they can now disrupt. Ideally, parents' perfect opportunity to stop or change the cycle occurs after the "I choose to act" block. PACE is a perfect tool to use, as well as matching the child's affect and using empathy for the child's predicament. The child will have a new experience of "People treat me as if I am a good kid who needs help with my emotions." Children will learn to disrupt the cycle by recognizing that their emotions spur behavior problems and they need to learn new ways to handle their emotions.

Example

Circumstance: The mother gives the child a fancy new glass at the supper table.

    Box 1: Identify how the child is feeling—angry, fearful, etc.

    Box 2: Identify the behavior. The child will act out the fear in a way that re-harmonizes belief and circumstance, i.e., "I broke the glass." Mom can still be the bad one if the glass breaks, especially if I cut myself on it!

    Box 3: Other's response—the repercussion is fear; i.e., "Mom yelled at me and called me a klutz."

    Box 4: Belief about self—The actions and reactions will support a belief about self. This circumstance reinforced the negative view of Mom: "When Mom yelled at you and called you a klutz…what does that say about you or Mom?"

Teach the child not to act on negative feelings. If the action had been, "I thanked my Mom and showed my Dad," Mom could have given him a matching plate to go with the glass. "If I have a cool new plate and glass, what does that say about Mom or me?" An alternative interruption starts after the "*People treat me as if*" box. If the child works to buy a new glass, he sends a different message back to himself and others.

This diagram can be used to...

- Help the child recognize fear-based emotions.
- Explain to the child why things "happen" to him.
- Explain the child's behavior to others.
- Help the child see how his actions affect himself.
- Demonstrate why negative responses to the child reinforce his negative belief system.
- Highlight one way the child reproduces his old N-IWM.

<u>COGNITIVE CIRCLE</u>

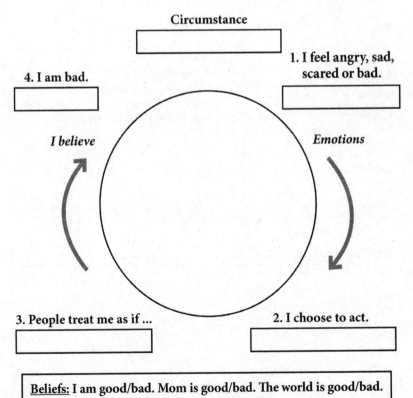

Circumstance

4. I am bad.

1. I feel angry, sad, scared or bad.

I believe

Emotions

3. People treat me as if ...

2. I choose to act.

<u>Beliefs:</u> I am good/bad. Mom is good/bad. The world is good/bad.
<u>Emotions:</u> happy, sad, scared, mad

CARDS OF COMPLETION

Oppositional children usually refuse to finish chores or perform the task as requested. Frustrated parents may give up on requiring the child to help around the home. Chores help identify the child's role in the family, build a sense of community and purpose and enable the child to feel successful. Using Cards of Completion keeps parents from questioning if the task is finished.

- Cards of Completion are used to reduce the child's ability to manipulate.
- Elements of the required task are broken down into small, manageable steps.
- The child must read the entire card and acknowledge completion.
- Children assist in compliance.

A Completed Example:

My Name: Sean	STEPS
Date: October 3	*Firewood bins are full*
Task Name: *Fill Firewood Holders*	*Living room floor is clean* *Wood pile is in order* *Tools are put in their proper places*

I have completed all items within this task the way that Mom likes them done!

Signature _____

Blank Cards for Your Use:

My Name:	STEPS
Date:	1.
Task Name:	2.
	3.
	4.
	5.

I have completed all items within this task the way that Mom likes them done!

Signature _____

My Name:	STEPS
Date:	1.
Task Name:	2.
	3.
	4.
	5.

I have completed all items within this task the way that Mom likes them done!

Signature _____

HANDOUT: Redefining the Mother to the Child by Team Members

1. Coordinate the entire team's efforts.
   a. Mother may give others "permission" to provide things for her child.
   b. Tell the child, "Your mom provided this can of soda."
   c. Remind mother to provide rewards (not in the child's presence) for others to use.

2. Do not answer questions that the mother could answer: "I know the answer to that, but healthy kids get that information from their mother. Aren't you lucky you have one now?"

3. Do not help the child: "No, I won't help you pack the car. Your mom said she would be here in a minute."

4. Revisit with statements like: "Good thing your mom remembered that" or "You have a great mom to do this for you."

5. Provide explanation and redefinition for the mother's actions: "Of course your mom said 'No.' What kind of mother would let a child who does not bathe go out with friends? They would laugh at you. You have a great mom."

6. Talk with the mother ahead of time. Try to help her avoid punishing and limiting decisions the child can use to reinforce his negative image of her.

7. Verbally highlight the mother's efforts (securing a team member, driving to therapy, etc.). All just for him. How would he explain that? Be prepared for a negative response.

8. Answer if the child asks a question to the mother in a general way without actually addressing her.

9. Play a game of naming good things the mother did for the child yesterday.

10. Have the child draw and label a good mom/bad mom.

HANDOUT: Direct the Child to the Mother

1. Your mom loves you.
2. Your mom does lots of good things for you.
3. What would your mom think?
4. Did your mom say you could do that?
5. Save that; I want to show it to your mom.
6. Please let me have that; I want to show your mom.
7. Let's take a picture of you for your mom.
8. Do you think I'm the one in charge? Your mom makes the schedule.
9. Why do you think your mom does that?
10. I bet your mom would be pleased to know you did this.
11. Let's call your mom. You can tell her how well you did on your test/play date/etc.
12. Your mom must have been thinking of you when she did this.
13. It takes a great mom to solve a problem like that.
14. Sometimes it's tough having a good mom like you do.
15. You make a lot of comments about your mom, but you have to admit she is a great mom.

IGNORING

Professionals frequently tell parents to ignore their child's less dangerous, but annoying, behaviors. Typically, positive behaviors are rewarded and disruptive behaviors are given consequences or punished. A child may view ignoring as "punishment," because he does not receive the desired connection with the parent. For children with early trauma and disrupted object relations, they may perceive that the parent is not available or is absent, which could prompt an increase in disruptive behaviors to force the parent to pay more attention.

For successful ignoring, a parent must be able to emotionally regulate, not be concerned about disruptive behaviors that may increase, identify the behavior to be ignored and what the adult will do instead of engaging with the child. The child must have some self-regulatory skills for planned ignoring to be effective. If the child is too disruptive or dangerous, the behaviors may become too unsafe.

Goals

- To affirm: "This is the mom you can trust."
- To affirm: "This child is lovable."
- To decrease disruptive behaviors
- To keep from being caught in a behavior/consequence cycle

Three ways to use ignoring

1. Ignore with no consequence, use to avoid the power struggle and the downward spiral:
   a. Prevents/negates sabotage.
   b. Enforces "I am good and I love you."
   c. Reduces "I am bad and you are bad."

   Example

   - "I know you threw that piece of paper on the floor next to the trash can, but I am taking you to the park anyway."
   - "Honey, look at those goose bumps on your arms. I can see that you are really cold." (ignoring the fact the child is not wearing a coat)

2. Ignore and label the natural consequence (this is not a punishment) to improve immediate behavior.
   a. Provides an opportunity for the child to reevaluate her approach to getting what she wants.

   b. Eliminates the need to provide an immediate consequence.

   Example

- "I hear your anger; please go to your safe spot. I'll talk to you when you are calm." (emotional regulation)
- "I see that you're drawing on the wall with a crayon. That will need to be removed before we go to the park this afternoon." (Parent does not take the crayon away or demand that the child relinquish the crayon.)

3. Ignore and label adult's boundaries, when adult needs to be separate from the child. Needs to be enforceable.
   a. Deliberate
   b. Time limited

   Example

- "I am going to sit here and drink my tea for five minutes. I will not respond to you."
- "I see that you are having a meltdown. Where do you need to be? I'll talk to you when you are calm." (Only employ once the child has achieved emotional regulation.)
- "You sound like you need a little time alone. I'll talk to you when you are calm." (Only when the child has achieved emotional regulation.)

HANDOUT: Helpful Statements

Parts:

"I" statements:

> "My baby part was really scared when that car pulled out in front of me."

"You" statements:

> "It seems like part of you wants to go and part of you does not."

"They" statements:

> "Look at that character on television! One part of him wants to do this and the other part of him wants to do that."

Fear or sadness underneath anger:

"I" statements:

> "I turned it into anger right away and yelled at the other driver."

"You" statements:

> "What are you afraid of? You look angry."

"They" statements:

> "That character is really angry! What do you think she is scared of?"

Link to trauma:

"I" statements:

> "When I was a kid, my mom was in five accidents. Now, I get scared easily when I drive."

"You" statements:

> "I bet you had to act angry to get your mother to pay attention to you."

"They" statements:

> "This is the fourth school Jimmy has attended. I bet he is afraid of being left out."

HANDOUT: Hurtful Statements

(Do not use these!)

1. Statements that attribute behavior to malicious intent:
   - "He just wanted to make me mad."
   - "He didn't want her to have fun."
   - "He gets a thrill out of seeing me angry."
   - "He hates it when everything is going well."

2. Judgmental statements, seeing the behaviors as "all good" or "all bad":
   - "She is always in trouble."
   - "She is always disrupting the family."
   - "She always leaves her clothes on the floor."
   - "That never worked when we tried it before."

3. Statements elevating anger (secondary emotion) over sadness or fear (primary emotion):
   - "I am just mad."
   - "There's no sadness or fear."
   - "He did that because he was angry."
   - "There is no reason for him to be sad or scared."
   - "He got mad, then he…"

4. Statements that ignore the impact of trauma and subsequent neurological impairments:
   - "He chose to destroy it."
   - "One of these days he is going to decide to change."
   - "He can do this whenever he wants to."
   - "He can do this to get what he wants."
   - "This is totally under his control."
   - "He may stop that and then go back to it in a few months."

5. Statements that blame the whole child and ignore parts:
   - "She just doesn't like to have fun."
   - "She cannot control herself."
   - "She hates to see others having fun."
   - "She's not happy unless she sees others suffering."
   - "If she would only be nice (or good, or fun or obedient)…"

6. Behavior management statements: needing consequences to motivate change:
   - "You cannot just let him get away with it."
   - "If there is no consequence, how is he going to learn?"

- "He'll get tired of this and then he'll do it right."
- "He cannot go to the park, because he broke the window. It would be like rewarding him."

7. Statements or questions designed to shame or "guilt" the child into behavior change:
   - "If he wouldn't be so hard-headed..."
   - "That's stupid."
   - "How many times must I tell you?"
   - "Do you think this time you will obey your mother?"

THE LEVEL SYSTEM

Behavior plans designed to leverage children into changing their behavior to earn a reward evoke doubt and questions in parents and mental health professionals. Behavioral plans tend to lose effectiveness within days, because of the fear engendered by compliance. Children lack parental trust from the influence of their N-IWM. At the inception of a plan, children, even teens, will approach it with great anticipation to achieve a reward. Both parents and children will imagine the end results. Parents envision improved behaviors. The child envisions earning the reward. However, the child's ability to "continually" imagine the reward is always being eroded by his or her own N-IWM.

As the days wear on, parents begin nagging and pushing the child for compliance and frequently remind the child of the promised reward. The child's resistance increases daily with many instances of "I forgot" and "Don't remind me again." Some children will misinterpret the parents' intentions and portray the parents as evil in developing a plan that was "too difficult for anyone to complete." Then, before its targeted end date, both parents and child toss out the plan with anger and animosity toward each other.

Due to these complexities, our level system joins together therapeutic interventions and behavioral techniques to achieve improved parent/ child relationships, emotional maturation and skill building. Additionally, the plan is built upon the idea that it takes twenty-one days to learn a new habit for sustainability. To begin, determine Level One expectations. Parents and/or staff identify behaviors that need to be improved and skills that need to be developed and determine a goal or reward the child would be invested in working toward. The child's input is important when identifying the reward or goal. Accurate identification of sincerely desired rewards is often problematic. Trial and error should be expected while a loving, well-intentioned parent tries to get to know a chronically fearful child who feels less safe the more he or she is known.

After Level One is completed, the child may not be ready to move to the next level yet. The plan must be restarted if the child is not compliant in other areas, as in borrowing without permission (stealing) or not returning others' possessions, not taking proper care of property or not conforming to family values. Watch for the child's saturation point of conflicting beliefs. His or her internal model will trigger fight, flight or freeze responses. It is important to recognize these triggering responses as part of the recovery process, not failure of the effort. Recovering children will need multiple experiences of both success (toleration of the fears generated by the conflicting N-IWM) and failure (giving in to the triggering fear). Encourage the child to reflect on the internal battle.

Allan's Family

> *I think I don't do the level system, because I don't think I can. Once*
> *I get going, I can go until I get stopped in the negative cycle; then I*
> *flounder around until I get tired of wallowing. So then I get going till*
> *the same thing happens. I think that once I get on Level Two, at the*
> *beginning I will be able to use that to propel myself forward like I used*
> *to be able to use hockey. But soon that will get old and won't work*
> *anymore or something could happen to make my life so miserable that*
> *I would either quit or move on. I think that if what's going on now*
> *continues I'll overcome myself in the end and win.*

> —*Allan*

A monthly calendar is provided to record the days that the level is maintained or lost. The child may experience "shame" if too much emphasis is placed on failure. Therefore, the calendar is kept by the adults and used therapeutically to help the child determine his motivations and beliefs. As the child functions more easily, the calendar will have the ability to motivate.

WORKSHEET: The Level System

LEVEL SYSTEM **GOAL:** _____

Daily Check-Up:

Name _____ *Date* _____

1. Check all completed tasks.
Level One:
___ Therapy Requests
___ Personal Hygiene
___ Clean Bedroom
___ Complete Homework
___ Family Chore
Level Two:
___ Attachment Activity
___ Reciprocal Chore/Card of Completion
___ Care of Personal Possessions
___ Additional Chore
___ Use of Family Resources
___ Family Values

2. I am on___ or off___ level.

3. Some of the difficult choices I made which had good results:
_____
_____
(If on level, skip number 4.)

4. I am off level because I chose to: _____
_____.

5. Identify and share emotions with one of your parents for today.

HAPPY SAD SCARED

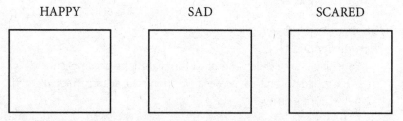

Steps to a Customized Level System

1. Determine requirements for the behavior to be completed.
2. Determine the length of the plan. It must be more than twenty-one days.
3. The level must be restarted if behaviors occur that are dangerous or violate family values.
4. A form must be completed each day, recorded on the calendar and kept in a binder.
5. Use a Card of Completion for each task.
6. Expect Level One to take more than twenty-one days and to restart more than once.
7. Determine how many completed forms are needed for success.
8. Determine your standard of when the plan must be restarted by the number of "off level days."
9. Identify for the child fears of accomplishment, lack of trust and ambivalence.
10. Don't make exceptions to or excuses from the plan.
11. If parents and child agree upon changes, changes are made and the plan is restarted.

Develop the Plan

The goal or reward must be determined and the behaviors that will be addressed in the Level System the child will accomplish. What is your goal and what behaviors must be completed? Next we'll take you through the form and provide examples and explanations for each step.

1. **Check all completed tasks.**
    ___ Therapy Requests
    ___ Personal Hygiene
    ___ Clean Bedroom
    ___ Complete Homework
    ___ Family Chore

Examples to choose:
Therapy Requests
Consult with the child's therapist for goals to be accomplished daily.
1. Child will share a present emotion (sad, scared, happy) during an event.

2. Child will identify which part of the brain he or she is making decisions with at any time when asked.
3. Child will notice when becoming angry and express the underlying emotion to his or her parent.
4. Child will move into closer proximity with parent when sad or scared.

Personal Hygiene

1. Child will bathe as parents direct.
2. Child will brush teeth twice a day.
3. Child will wear clean clothing.
4. Child will wear weather-appropriate clothing.

Clean Bedroom

1. Child will make his or her bed by a specific time.
2. Child will put clothing away in specific areas.
3. Child will keep bedroom floor clean.
4. Child will store toys in specific areas.

Complete Homework

1. Child will complete homework as school staff directs.
2. Child will complete homework in area parents assign.
3. Child will complete homework within time frame parents determine.

Family Chore

1. Parents will assign a daily chore for child to complete.
2. Parents will identify the steps to complete the chore.
3. Child will complete the task as parents direct.

Parents' Roles

Parents must be willing to help their child with the form and set aside time to listen to him or her share emotions. The child must complete the form at the end of the day: self-reflection is important. Parents will model how to reflect by talking about the day and become their child's cheerleader, not judge and jury.

2. I am on ___ or off ___ level.

The child will reflect on task completion.

3. Some of the difficult choices I made which had good results:

The child will reflect on overcoming and solving problems.

4. I am off level because I chose to: _____.

The child will identify why he or she may have lost the level for that day.

5. Identify and share emotions with one of your parents for today.

The child will share three emotions with parents that he or she experienced that day.

Level Two

Level Two was designed to continue chipping away at the maladaptive behaviors and to accentuate the weakening of old core beliefs. The child will experience a tightening of her self-control and transition into the realm of new family values. Internalization of Level One requirements will have occurred. Behaviors pertaining to hygiene will not be an issue. The attachment work in Level Two will be extremely difficult and many resets are to be expected. Patience and empathy for the child will encourage her. The parent is on her side. Do not become more invested than the child or her work will diminish to have the burden fall on the parent.

Level Two behaviors include all of the Level One requirements with less parent monitoring. Therapy requests include an attachment activity to be completed with the parent. The child will complete a chore with a Card of Completion. The child must improve and refine the care of personal items. Given that many parents complain that their children waste family resources (shampoo, food, paper products, etc.), the child will notice and monitor usages. A specific family value must be identified and monitored. Meeting these expectations, the child will be demonstrating improved decision-making, more age-appropriate achievements and distress tolerance. Each of these attributes increases the parents' ability to trust their child.

Level Two:

   ___ Attachment Activity
   ___ Reciprocal Chore/Card of Completion
   ___ Care of Personal Possessions

___ Additional Chore
___ Use of Family Resources
___ Family Values

Level Two Examples
Attachment Activities
1. Sit with either parent and discuss the day.
2. Work with either parent on a task the parent enjoys.
3. Share a goal and complete the goal (task, event, activity).

Reciprocal chore
1. Offer to complete a task for which either parent is responsible.
2. Complete a parent's task without asking (parent must be pleased; if parents are not pleased, child cannot mark this as completed).

Care of personal possession
1. Identify a possession for which the child needs to improve care.
2. Help child list ways parents can notice improved care.
3. Help child notice improved care.

Additional chore—Refer to Level One chores and add one of those.

Use of Family Resources
1. List the "resource" that will be monitored.
2. List ways parents will notice the resource is being used appropriately.

Family Values
1. List the family value that will be monitored.
2. List ways parents will notice the value is being supported.

The following example has both Level One and Two tasks filled in to illustrate what the form may look like. Remember once Level One is completed and the goal (reward) is earned, the child may not be motivated to attempt Level Two for some time afterwards. If Level Two is begun too soon, the child may feel pressured and manipulated. This intervention is to be used as the child has the internal strength to be successful and is motivated.

Completed Level System:
GOAL: To earn parent's trust to have a sleepover party

Daily Check-Up Example:

Name *Sally*   Date *3/14*

1. Check all completed tasks

Level One:

_x_ *Therapy Requests: Sally will identify which part of her brain she is in when asked*

_x_ *Personal Hygiene: Sally will brush teeth 3x a day*

_x_ *Clean Bedroom: Sally will make bed, put dirty clothes in hamper, put toys on shelves*

_x_ *Complete Homework: Sally will complete homework at the dinning room table from 6 to 7pm*

_x_ *Family Chore: Sally will vacuum living room everyday before dinner*

Level Two:

_x_ *Attachment Activity: Sally and mom will read a book every night*

_x_ *Reciprocal Chore/Deposit slip: Sally will wash dishes every night for mom*

_x_ *Care of Personal Possessions: Sally will put book bag on shelf after school*

_x_ *Additional Chore: Sally will take garbage out after dinner*

_x_ *Use of Family Resources: Sally will use less shampoo (1/8 cup)*

_x_ *Family Values: Sally will go to church without complaining*

2. **I am on _x_ or off ___ level. (If on level, skip #4).**

3. **Some of the difficult choices I made which had good results:**
"I did not want to do my homework tonight because the neighbors were riding bikes and I wanted to. I said to myself, 'finish the work faster so you can go play.' And I did!"

4. **I am off level because I chose to:** *(not applicable)*

5. **Identify and share emotions with one of your parents for today.**

HAPPY	SAD	SCARED
I was happy to have pizza for lunch.	I was sad when I remembered that I lost my blue sweater.	I was scared when the teacher said we would have a pop quiz.

Calendar

Month of: _____						
Sunday	*Monday*	*Tuesday*	*Wednesday*	*Thursday*	*Friday*	*Saturday*

EMOTIONAL RESPONSES

Rate the Distress

Here is a scale to help a child reflect on his or her degree of emotional response.

Degrees of Cognition

Full Cognition ⌐_|_____|_____|_____|⌐ Emotional Response

Decisions based
on thinking

Behavior based on
feelings (usually fear)

    This scale may be recreated on an index card and used to encourage the child to rate his or her distress. Parents can assist at the beginning and estimate for the child. Sometimes, when parents "guess" wrong, the child will correct them. The child will "know" the parent understands he or she is distressed and will be aware of his or her own distress; due to this, disruptive behaviors may be avoided. Just by reflecting on the amount of distress, the child's brain will move into cognition. Parents can align with the child to help mediate the distress when the child is more cognitively present. It is very important that the parent not minimize or deny the distress. Remember to use matching affect and empathy to connect to your child.

Rating Emotions

The first exercise helped the child rate the amount of emotional distress he or she had at that time. After admitted distress, parents can help their child identify the emotion. The child's ability to identify, express and process emotions is blocked by his defenses/fears. Some children may only acknowledge happy and mad without varying degrees. Number cards, scales, a number line and physical expression are concrete ways to describe the size of the emotion. In the future, parents can project the emotion to come, which permits the child to be more cognitive of parents' awareness and their vulnerability to trustworthy parents.

    Avoid intellectual (cognitive) conversations with your child when he or she is experiencing an emotional response. Keep it simple. Don't ask "Why" questions or questions that challenge the N-IWM like, "Don't you know better?" The child will feel interrogated and become more defensive, causing a deeper emotional response. Watch how you react if the child is not responding to you. Some parents increase the volume and inflection of their voice. Again, this propels the child deeper into the emotion, possibly removing cognition for hours.

Find the Emotion

Your child has admitted to being distressed and rated the emotion; now help your child express the emotion. Begin with empathic statements and curiosity to explore what is going on inside.

Examples

- "You looked really upset when I told you no. What was going on inside?"
- "I don't like it when my boss tells me no. Were you feeling that way too?"

If your child is not engaging, back down from the topic and offer other options with the opportunity to revisit when the child is ready. Children may not be able to discuss the distress until the next day. Parental patience is needed during this time. The goal is for the child to feel safe enough to share with the parent; therefore, the parent must be able to accept the child's decision. Sharing the information will signal that the child trusts the parent.

FIND IT IN THE MEDIA

Everyone knows that books, television programs and movies are full of conflict that leads to the story's climax. Without emotional characters, the plot falls flat. Who wants to watch or read a boring story? The media offer examples of how to do things right and how to do them wrong. Parents can capitalize on good (or bad) script writing to help their children understand the way the world works or does not work, reinforce their own values and beliefs and explain how other's emotions interfere or build relationships by the way characters interact.

For this intervention to be successful, parents have to be able to identify and reflect on the characters' interactions, emotions, values, behaviors and the results. Not everyone is comfortable talking during a movie or television program. Pre-recorded programs may be helpful, because they can be paused and restarted at the parents' discretion.

Ideas

- Highlight a character's emotional responses.
- Project the character's emotion as being similar to the child's.

- Link the emotion to the behavior.
- Link mad with sad or scared underneath.
- Talk about the character's values and benefits.
- Question the child, "Is this the way you felt the other night?"
- Note emotions that you have had lately, as well as behaviors and results.
- Identify a character's calming techniques.

PARADOXICAL: PROPOSE THE BEHAVIOR

Parents may fear that paradoxical interventions will make their children think tantrums and poor behavior choices are acceptable and this will encourage more disruptive behaviors. These parents often feel like another behavior problem can occur at any minute and want to avoid more problems. "Just let me have a moment of peace; why should I be asking for problems?" they ask. But remember that behavior consequences do not work effectively for these children. If they are encouraged to have a behavior, they usually do the opposite.

1. Before an emotional response:
   a. Prescribe the possibility of an emotional response.
   b. Practice what can be done.
   c. Practice your child's past responses and brainstorm together for other positive alternatives.

2. Prescribe the child's behavior that the parents do not want. Parents usually know a dysregulated child will have a temper tantrum, exhibit inappropriate eating habits and/or other problematic behaviors.
   a. Label the trigger.
   b. Prescribe the dysregulated behavior.

3. Before the trigger, suggest your child "perform" the problematic behavior or suggest the child take as long as needed to "work through the mad."
   a. "You always have a temper tantrum when this happens. Why don't you go ahead and have it now, so that it will not cause you problems later?"
   b. "Part of you will feel like arguing with me when I tell you we need to leave. Take as long as you need to work through it. We've got time today and it's a great chance to give you some healing."

4. Have a tantrum.
   a. Parents demonstrate what a tantrum looks like by having one. Make sure it is genuine and not sarcastic.
   b. Ask your child to score your efforts.
   c. Suggest he can do it better and practice.
   d. Celebrate success (your child complied with your directive).

TIME IN OR TIME OUT

"Time out" can vary from sending a child to his room, sitting along the sidelines during recreation, being placed in isolation or being locked in a room. It is commonly used as punishment for non-compliance, tantrums, aggression, lying, stealing, inappropriate mealtime behaviors and disruptive behaviors at school. Parents have relied on sending children to their rooms for years. Healthy children may learn to dislike "time out," because of the desire to be part of family activities. They self-regulate and ask to return to the activity.

Children with early trauma may find relief in being "sent away" from engaging activities. They may even use behaviors to prompt a "time out" if overstressed. During times alone, children have been known to violate boundaries by sneaking into other's rooms, stealing, damaging property or hurting themselves. Others may exit the home and run away. These children are demonstrating their power and control.

"Time out" may be used if:

- Safety is an issue if the child remains within the group.
- All parties can be safe during the separation.
- The duration is limited to a short period of time.

"Time in" is the preferred "consequence" for a child's behavior. The child is directed to sit near the parent for "a little mom time" to recover from problematic behaviors (tantrums, emotional dysregulation). "Time in" might even be reward-like: "Let's take a walk." It presents opportunities for co-regulation and matching affect.

"Time in" may be used if:

- The duration is limited to a short period of time.
- It's a recovery period for the child.
- It's a nurturing opportunity for the parent.
- There's no anger, threats, sarcasm or lectures.

Practice

A child may not participate as directed in the "time in" or "time out." For these oppositional children, practice time can be scheduled for the child to sit quietly in a chair near Mom. Parents can instruct the child to practice so the next time she has a tantrum she will not be distracted from the parent's directive. This practice time is more opportune if planned just before an activity in which the child is invested, like leaving for the park. The child can be directed to practice sitting quietly on a chair next to Mom. Use a timer as an impartial third party. The goal is for the child to learn to regulate emotions in the presence of an adult. Rocking chairs and bean bag chairs help the child emotionally regulate by giving the child sensory opportunities to rock or snuggle. If a swing is available, swinging can also aid in self-regulation.

EXERCISE: INCREASING REFLECTIVITY IN A CHILD'S EMOTIONAL COMMUNICATION

Ask the child to imagine a parent making the following statements. Encourage the child to identify the emotion, which is usually anger, and them ask the child to identify the underlining emotion, which is usually scared. To expand the child's reflective abilities, encourage him or her to think of ways the statement could prompt a "happy" feeling.

Statements

1. "Please take a shower."
   a. Mad or scared because child does not want to stop current activity
   b. Happy because child likes feeling dirty; will grow to desire being clean

2. "Brush your teeth."
   a. Mad or scared because child does not want to stop current activity
   b. Happy because child likes teeth feeling dirty

3. "Time to go grocery shopping."
   a. Mad or scared because child cannot relax
   b. Happy because child needs to get food

4. "I don't know where we are going."
   a. Mad or scared because child could be taken to foster care
   b. Happy because child is waiting for a surprise

5. "Your bus is late."
   a. Mad or scared because child will be late for class
   b. Happy because child has more "me" time

DEVELOPMENTAL DELAYS

HANDOUT: Ideas that may decrease oppositional behavior

1. Play with your child at the child's emotional age.

2. Invite your child to play with you, but don't insist.

3. Find activities that your child may be interested in.

4. Identify the length of time the activity will take (remember to match your child's developmental age).
   - Keep the time short.
   - Plan to finish while the child is still having fun.
   - Increase touch.
   - Narrate the activity.
   - Take pictures.
   - If the activity may be challenging, invite an audience:
     ○ To watch
     ○ To keep time
     ○ To keep score
     ○ To compete with the winner
     ○ To take pictures
     ○ To help the child process his or her emotions

5. Ask the child when he or she would like to schedule another playtime.

6. Ask your child what game he or she would like to play the next time.

7. Identify your child's fear:
   - Of playing with you
   - Of having fun with you
   - Of connecting with you
   - Of failing
   - Of succeeding

8. Do not play longer than planned even if the child begs—leave him wanting more. Be empathic: "I know how you feel; I am looking forward to playing again, too."

9. Offer the child the opportunity to display the photos or scorecards.

10. Don't insist that your child view the photos or scorecards until he is ready, because these may illicit strong emotions.

11. You can share your joy with others even if your child is listening. Don't draw him into the conversation unless he willingly participates.

12. Use relationship-building humor:
    - Laugh at yourself: Adults who have a healthy sense of self can identify and laugh at their "funny parts" such as being clumsy, having irritating or obsessive habits, etc. *"There I go again. Did you see me trip over the table?"*
    - Laugh at the funny things that others say, like on TV.
    - Share funny stories or jokes. As the child begins to participate in the process, the child can choose daily jokes to share from children's joke books.

13. Use your imagination:
    - Guess what will happen next while watching TV.
    - Wonder what odd foods would taste like—and then try them.

14. Benefits of using fantasy and imagination:
    - Life is more fun!
    - Imagination stimulates creativity: writing, art and music.
    - Imagination increases cognitive processing and reflective thinking.
    - Imaginative play encourages multistage strategies.
    - With practice, the child can visualize "I can be different."
      ◦ Cognition improves during play.
      ◦ After a child develops the ability to be reflective, additional interventions are possible. (Journaling, emotional processing, worksheets, games…)

HANDOUT: Playful Guidelines

- Avoid all control battles and have fun with the child.
- Use good versus evil and happy versus sad during play.
- Imaginative play must correspond to the child's emotional age.
- Label without judgment during play.
- Identify healthy or unhealthy parts of the characters during play.
- Be supportive of the child's developing imagination.
- Nurture the imagination. Work with oppositional characteristics.
- Brainstorm and recreate settings, characters and circumstances.
- Play devil's advocate.
- Participate in the child's fantasy.
- Exaggerate facial and/or emotional responses.
- Be silly.
- Use existing media: cartoons, tapes, movies, joke books.
- Be animated and enjoy the experience.
- Use field trips to create opportunities for imaginary thinking.
- Role-play a variety of behaviors, attitudes and characters.
- Value the child's opinion.
- Brainstorm with the child for creative ideas.
- Watch for mastery while playing, then identify it.
- Cautiously encourage the child to express thoughts, opinions and ideas.
- Allow fantasy, which comfortably removes the child from reality.

After the activity, revisit the play by expressing your emotions about the experience. Identify specific events that you enjoyed. Assemble and display game memorabilia. Create a scrapbook to display the pictures. Load the pictures into a digital picture frame.

Play is vital to creativity and flexible thinking. People with these skills are fun to be with, can solve problems and have new ways of looking at life. They are reflective and imaginative. They are the ones we call when we are stuck and need to see things differently. Success does not just mean good grades or acceptance to an Ivy League school; forming loving relationships and knowing you are lovable and safe is success for a traumatized child.

INTERVENTION: SENSE OF SELF

(to highlight positive attributes)

Children with early trauma lack a healthy sense of self. Parents are constantly "building their children" by helping the children learn who they are and the skills they have.

1. Outline the child's body on a large piece of paper with a marker or pen.
2. Write these questions on the side of the drawing:
   a. What are my best qualities?
   b. What are my favorite things? What are my least favorite?
   c. What do I believe about my family and myself?
   d. What do I want to do in life as a child and as an adult?
   e. What are my favorite activities?
   f. When am I successful?
   g. When do I find exploring fun?
   h. When am I good at solving problems?
3. Encourage your child to write answers to these questions on his or her outline over the following week. Do not direct where to put the answers.
4. Review successes. Reflect on the answers or non-answers.
5. Use empathy to explore why finding answers was hard. Talk about how fear keeps the child stuck. Link back to trauma and the child's inability to explore.
6. Parents should remain empathic and avoid problem-solving. Parents can use curiosity when a child is doing something that should be written on their body outline but not give a directive to write the answer.
7. Encourage the child to take small steps into exploration (when less fearful).
8. Offer to help if the child desires. Label the lack of desire as fear of the unknown or of the parents.

   Examples (both positive and negative):

   a. What are my best qualities? (loving, helpful, kind, funny, thoughtful)
   b. What are my favorite things? Dislikes? (Likes: Chicken noodle soup, cartoons, chapter books; Dislikes: tomato soup, scary movies, baths, wool clothing)
   c. What do I believe about my family and myself? (I am good at math but not science, no one loves me when I am bad,

Dad works long hours so he does not have to play
with me, my parents love me even when they don't like
what I do, Mom is disappointed that I am not
like her.)

d. What do I want to do in life as a child and as an adult? (I want
to be a baseball player.)

e. What are my favorite activities? (riding my bike and playing
soccer)

f. When am I successful? (I can do these things for myself; I set
this goal and achieved it.)

g. When do I find exploring fun? (I like to learn new things;
I am not afraid of trying; Don't ask me to try new
foods.)

h. When am I good at solving problems? (Knowing when to
walk away, deep breathing before I answer, stating how I feel
and seeking comfort from a parent)

Children who experience early trauma and attachment disruptions
do not have a secure base—a sense of safety that allows them to venture
out from the parent to explore the world. This exploration system shuts
down and development freezes. Sometimes, parents struggle to find positive characteristics. Children must understand why they did not develop
interests, realistic goals and a range of likes and dislikes or age-appropriate
desires. Beliefs about themselves may be idealistic or overly negative.

OBJECT RELATIONS

To correct the child's capacity for permanence and constancy, parents
are encouraged to play peek-a-boo. Transitional objects such as pictures
are used to remind the child of the therapist when absent. Children can
experience desertion when separated from the parents.

Transitional Objects

Psychoanalyst Donald Winnicott has described the transitional object as
a "monument to the need for this contact with the mother's body" and
"lasting, soft, pliable, warm to touch."[54] Use these interventions to comfort
the child when Mom is not present. Transitional objects and interventions
portray that Mom is present, available and in control. The message must
be: She is always available for me. Be creative to provide for the child's
needs. A few strategies that may be useful:

1. Create and permit a transitional object to be carried from home and kept with the child (Parent's clothing or jewelry, stuffed animal, piece of a baby blanket).
2. Mom can arrange to call during the day.
3. Mom can arrange short visits.
4. Mom can share perfume with the child before he leaves home.
5. Mom can write and share notes and messages with her child.
6. Mom can supply treats.
7. School staff can keep a "mommy box" at school with extra supplies.
8. Place a picture of the family in the child's school desk.
9. Mom can place loving notes in the child's lunch box.
10. Mom can write notes on snack items.
11. Mom can record stories for the child to listen to at bedtime.
12. Say a few words throughout the day to remind the child that mom still exists, such as "Wonder what your mom is doing right now?" "I'll show this picture to your mom after school today," and "What will you and your mom do when you get home today?"

This list is useful for children with babysitters, in respite, at school or being placed out of the home. You may need to provide additional information to the substitute caregiver on why these interventions are required and how they can be reinforced.

Experiential Learning

1. Discuss what others may be doing when they are not present.
2. Talk about your emotions when distressed, because someone is absent.
3. Plan for the return of family members.
4. Act surprised when a child plays peek-a-boo.
5. Use puppets to leave and arrive.
6. Maintain self-regulation when others are late.

SELF-REGULATION

Those working with the child can use labeling, reframing and modeling to help the child "contain" and validate his emotions. Emotional regulation can indeed be strengthened when left-brain resources (language, interpretation) are enlisted in the real-time processing of right brain bodily-based feelings.[55] Parents who match affect, use empathy, label emotions and offer comfort signal to the child that the parents are aware of what is happening for him or her and are available.

EXPERIENTIAL LEARNING = MODELING + AFFECT MATCHING + NARRATION

Activities that will increase your child's awareness of bodily functions:

- At mealtime, comment on sensations of hunger and fullness.
- Throughout the day, comment on the need to use the bathroom.
- Describe how it feels to have dirty hands and teeth.
- When tired, connect it to activities that made you tired and how it feels to be sleepy, etc.

Remember you are always being watched for your responses to the environment and for evidence of a healthy copying mechanism for sensory issues:

- Cold: "I am glad I wore my coat."
- Pain: "I have a headache. I am going to go lay down."
- "My sinuses were bothering me when I was sitting next to a lady wearing heavy perfume. So I quietly changed seats."
- "Wool keeps me warm but irritates my skin, so I wear a shirt underneath my sweater."

SELF-REGULATION ACTIVITIES

A. Opportunities to experience different states of regulation:
   - Take a walk in the park in the winter to experience cold.
   - Delay lunch to experience hunger.
   - Play red light, green light or act like a robot, with slow and fast motion.
   - Reflect on internal "engine" running fast or slow.

B. If needed, parents may assist by:
   - Taking a coat into school for teacher to provide.
   - Asking school staff to adjust recess times or means to expel extra energy.
   - Limiting the amount of lunch money if buying too much food.
   - Providing appropriate clothing to school staff or babysitter.

Three aspects of a child's existence that require self-regulation are emotions, physical perceptions and energy level. Adjusting the environment will allow the child to experience why a behavior change would be beneficial for him or her. In order to teach, experience and react to "cold," the environment must include the opportunity to experience cold. Parents cannot challenge or place their child at risk. Being "cold" cannot be a safety issue, as with any other intervention. The child must always perceive safety. If the child is not safe, this family will be like all of the other traumatizing environments.

INTERVENTIONS FOR FOOD ISSUES

Parent's Responsibility

- Calm yourself.
- Set boundaries you can keep.
- Parents decide what to eat, where to eat and when to eat.
- Document when the children want to eat and how much they eat.
- Assure your child there will always be enough: "We are the parents you can trust."
- Model and narrate your own eating experiences.
- Demonstrate food mindfulness.
- Express enjoyment of all foods and avoid drive toward forbidden foods.
- Demonstrate and narrate personal awareness of hunger and fullness so the child will learn self-regulation skills (body attuned to hunger and fullness cues).

Routine

- Establish structured meal times every two to three hours for toddlers and preschoolers and every three to four hours for older children.
- Keep fruit or healthy snacks available during the day. A future goal should be to avoid eating between meals and snack times.
- Provide healthy meal choices.
- Sit and eat meals together. Provide family-style meals so the child can determine his or her own portions.
- Encourage pleasant table conversation.
- Invite children to help plan meals, shop and cook.
- Children often eat more when stressed.
- Avoid locking kitchen cabinets.

- Allow a food stash to reassure food availability and decrease anxiety.
  1. Designate a drawer in the fridge, on a pantry shelf or in a storage container for your child's snacks.
  2. Write notes on the food containers to remind your child that "This is the parent you can trust."
- Provide snacks to school staff (or in the child's backpack) to increase your child's perception of security—again, write notes on food containers to remind child that "This is the parent you can trust."
- Don't take food from your child or limit food as punishment.

Your child may have an eating-related problem such as sensory processing disorder or a feeding problem. Signs an assessment may be needed are:

- Lack of maturation to experiment with food
- Limited ability to be reflective about eating
- Lack of dexterity in holding eating utensils
- Irritation by textures
- Chewing difficulties
- Inability to suck
- Oral-motor delays
- Messy eating
- Speech delays

SENSORY PROCESSING

Treatment

1. Label to normalize the experience.
2. Highlight negative effects of maintaining abnormal tolerances.
3. Use rewards and natural consequences.
4. Model ways you calm yourself.
5. Offer options from the following list.

During fight, flight or freeze states, the child is operating without the ability to think clearly. Calming interventions will vary depending on the child and his or her past trauma history. Use the five senses to spur healing. Calming activities such as singing quietly, rocking and being wrapped gently in a snuggly blanket and held by Mom may offer the safety needed to think more clearly. If physical closeness with Mom is a trigger, then an intervention to desensitize her touch may be needed. Mom can provide some quick touches, loving eye contact and physical closeness throughout the day.

To quickly change the child's physical state, play a game of tag, do jumping jacks or jump on a trampoline to achieve calm, reason and receptivity. Offer the child the following list and ask for him or her to pick three to experiment with first. Again, an evaluation from a trained professional is highly recommended for any suspected sensory issues.

Sensory Calming Techniques

- Rocking in a rocking chair
- Swinging
- Spinning on a tire
- Doing jumping jacks
- Doing push ups
- Jumping on a trampoline
- Blowing bubbles
- Running up and down the stairs
- Holding a personal transitional item (fuzzy blanket)
- Imagining a safe place
- Employing art/creative expression, e.g., clay
- Wearing a weighted vest (can be placed on the child's lap)
- Swaddling the child in a fuzzy blanket
- "Time in" near the teacher or aide
- Sitting quietly apart from the group with an adult
- Breathing exercises

Sensory Equipment

- Fuzzy blankets or other textured fabrics
- Lotions or massage oils with pleasing smells linked to mom (e.g., vanilla)
- Mini trampoline
- Jump rope
- Rocking chair
- Mats for tumbling, mazes, tunnels
- "Fidgets:" small, soft objects the child can manipulate (pull or squeeze) when stressed

WORKSHEET: Behavior Processing

The process begins with a recognized dysfunctional behavior. The origin describes a part of the child's development that was impaired. Our goal will be to correct the behavior by addressing the impairment which is fueling/driving it. To create a functional objective, specific behaviors will need to be incorporated with specific outcomes and origins. The technique is a corrective tool and the intervention is the way you will use the tool.

Example:

- **Behavior**—Child announces herself each time she enters the room
- **Origin**—Object relations
- **Goal**—To develop awareness that others exist when out of sight
- **Specific objective**—To decrease irritating communication
- **Technique**—Adjust the environment
- **Intervention**—Parents will welcome the child each time she enters the room

Instructions:

Use the information from the application worksheet

Step One: List details of the behavior.

Step Two: Theorize and assume (educated guess); then circle the origin of the behavior.

Step Three: Determine the general goal based on addressing the origin of the problem behavior.

Step Four: State a specific objective—the behavioral change desired.

Step Five: Circle the technique you plan to use and describe the intervention.

Step Six: After the intervention is implemented, evaluate the process.

Step Seven: Identify needed changes.

SAMPLE: Behavior and Intervention: Date: _____

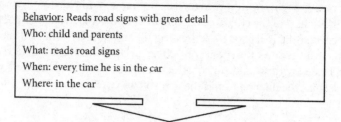

Behavior: Reads road signs with great detail
Who: child and parents
What: reads road signs
When: every time he is in the car
Where: in the car

Why? Origin of the behavior *(circle one):*
negative working model, developmental delay, emotional response, object relations, self-regulation, sensory issue

General goal:
Improve communication

Specific objective:
stop babbling

Techniques and Intervention:
Ignore by:
Time in with:
Model:
Adjust the environment: *Staff/family will label origins of babbling behavior as "self-soothing and need for control," Staff/family will set up "silent time" game with direct verbal promise not to ask Jimmy frightening questions.*
Educate the team:
Sensory:
Paradoxical:
Cognitive: *Staff/family can provide "if child can handle" reward*

Evaluation of intervention related to goal: *Jimmy was able to remain quiet for five minutes twice during half hour drive; represents ten minutes of improvement*
Changes needed?

Behavior Processing   **Date:** _____

Behavior:
Who:
What:
When:
Where:

Origin of the behavior *(circle one)*:
negative working model, sensory dysfunction, developmental delay,
emotional response, object relations or self-regulation

General goal: Specific objective:

Techniques and Intervention:
Ignore by:
Time in with:
Model:
Adjust the environment:
Educate the team:
Sensory:
Paradoxical:
Cognitive:

Evaluation of intervention related to goal:
Changes needed?

PART 5

Assessments and Letters to the Villagers

CHAPTER 18

Assessments

We created these forms and assessments to meet treatment needs, illustrate behavior changes, identify progress in meeting goals, determine mastery of parenting skills and provide information about the child. The scores are via parent and/or client report. The intent is to signify progress in our family-based program, not to be a standardized assessment tool or for diagnostic purposes. Others may find them useful for similar programs.

The rating systems are arbitrary. We used scales to signify change. When parents have the ability to reflect on their own and their children's progress, they are more likely to be hopeful that progress can continue. Ideally, the parenting attributes assessment will be completed pre-service and post-service to give the parents a feeling of being "capable" from the skills they have learned.

The notification forms help families identify their children's behaviors and needs and they can be used to inform camp counselors, coaches and babysitters. Some families prefer the Early Childhood Trauma form, because it does not classify their children by a mental health diagnosis. Other families may find other forms more helpful.

CHILD AND PARENT SKILLS ASSESSMENTS

Successful adoption or foster care placement is dependent on positive integration of children into their new families. The health of these relationships is dependent on each member's history and resilience. Forming relationships is difficult for many foster/adoptive children due to previous disrupted or poor attachments. Families need help in restructuring parent/child relationships, understanding behavior origins, designing healing interventions and co-regulating a dsyregulated child.

Many families enter treatment with the idea that learning a few new parenting techniques will change their children's behaviors and that the children will learn new coping skills that will stop the bad behaviors. If it was only that easy! Parenting a child with early trauma and attachment disruptions involves education in child development, trauma and attachment, personal exploration of one's own emotions, skills and lifestyle and the ability to communicate these skills non-verbally. The next assessments will identify skills needed to parent these children, as well as the child's skill level. Remember progress is progress. As Jeff has stated to many parents, "You are either moving forwards or backwards; you cannot stand still." Celebrate success.

Child Skill Assessment

Name:	Evaluator:		Date:

Scoring: 0–4 (Not present=0, Beginning=1, Developing=2, Functional=3, Healthy=4)

CHILD SKILLS	Definition	Score:
Secure Base		
Emotional regulation	Accurately identifies own emotions	
	Accurately connects emotion to experience	
	Verbally communicates to caregiver these accurate emotions	
	Accurately reads caregiver's emotions	
Parent assists in co-regulation	Attunes to caregiver's emotions	
	Modulates emotions (returns to comfortable state of arousal in a timely manner)	
Trusts caregiver	Perceives positive motives	
	Accepts complements or criticism	
	Asks for assistance	
	Seeks proximity to caregiver	
	Expresses distress when separating from caregiver	
	Uses transitional objects	
	Expresses comfort when parent returns	

(continued)

CHILD SKILLS	Definition	Score:
	Seeks and accepts comfort when distressed	
Communicates about inner life	Thought/wishes are healthy and realistic	
	Intentions	
Complies to rules and directives		
Imitates parents'	Values	
	Skills	
	Interests	
	Hygiene	
Seeks to resolve conflicts		
Safe Haven		
Emotional maturation		
Play	Plays alone	
	Plays well with others	
Relationships	Long term	
	Reciprocal—give and take	
Is curious, explorative and flexible		
Accepts challenges		
Respects other's boundaries	Physical	
	Emotional	
Inhibits impulsivity		
Projects accurate view of self	Strengths	
	Weaknesses	
Behavior processing	Is reflective about behavior	
	Can link emotions to behavior	
Acknowledges effects of behavior	Self	
	Others	

(continued)

CHILD SKILLS	Definition	Score:
	Offers positive behavior options	
	Changes to positive behavior	
	Accepts responsibility for behavior	

Parent Skill Assessment

Name: Date:

Scoring: 0–4 (Not present=0, Beginning=1, Developing=2, Functional=3, Healthy=4)

PARENT SKILLS	Score:
Secure Base	
Self-aware of own emotions	
Attunes to child's emotions, matches affect with empathy and co-regulates	
Identifies and labels own and child's emotions	
Regulates own emotions	
Models and communicates modulation skills	
Models range of emotions	
Remains in close proximity to child, especially when child is dysregulated	
Provides comfort if needed	
Behavior processing	
Labels negative or positive effects of child's behavior	
Uses curiosity to explore child's behavior, not questioning or demanding answers (PACE—see Trusts Caregiver)	
Uses reflective listening to hear child's story	
Matches affect when responding	
Links behavior and emotion	
Provides limits, choices and helps child own problems, plans and provides natural consequences without anger	
If asked, offers positive behavior options	
Reflective about child's behavior	
Trusts caregiver	

(continued)

PARENT SKILLS	Score:
Boundaries: Enforces personal boundaries, protects others' boundaries	
Communication: "Turns toward" the child, gives complements, rarely criticizes	
Emotional coaching: Projects positive and successful image of child	
Emotional container: Provides emotional safety, comfort, intimacy, child's emotions are not too big for caregiver	
Interactive repair: Willing and active to re-attune with child after conflict	
Narrates life experiences: Describes motives, events, behaviors and emotions	
Nurture: Lovingly provides for all the child's basic needs	
Personal joy: Models and rewards healthy values, skills, interests, hygiene, self-care, flexible thinking and creativity	
Regulates own behavior: Eating, sleeping, energy, temperature regulation (hot and cold)	
Safe Haven	
Maturation	
Encourages child to play alone, scaffolds time for child to play alone	
Engages child with emotional-age opportunities to experience new and novel information	
Gives age- and emotionally-appropriate responsibilities and opportunities to ask for assistance	
Encourages healthy relationships with peers	
Allows child to be in proximity of caregiver	
Acknowledges child's distress when separating from parent	
Provides transitional objects when separated	
Provides comfort and displays pleasure when reuniting with child	
Facilitates safe environments for the child away from caregiver (when possible)	
Teaches child ways to feel safe and maintain safety when away from caregiver	

Parental Relationship Assessment

Name:			Date:	

Scoring: 0–4 (Not present=0, Beginning=1, Developing=2, Functional=3, Healthy=4)

Parental relationship		Partner 1 Score:	Partner 2 Score:
Time with partner	At home		
	Away		
Agreement on	Chores		
	Discipline		
	Finances		
	Intimacy		
	Relationships with others		
	Religion		
	Time management		
Shared	Fondness, appreciation		
	Interests		
	Goals		
Communicates about inner life	Thoughts/wishes/intentions		
	Emotions		
Communication	"Turns toward" partner, gives complements, criticizes rarely		

Behavioral Rubric for Child

| Name: | | | | Date: |

		Beginning 1	Developing 2	Functional 3	Healthy 4
1.	Speaks caringly about family				
2.	Mother's touch is comfortable				
3.	Acts loving toward family				
4.	Understands "stranger danger"				
5.	Loving toward animals				
6.	Makes appropriate eye contact				
7.	Trusts parents				
8.	Asks for help				
9.	Accepts responsibility				
10.	Truthful				
11.	Has age-appropriate activities				
12.	Has age-appropriate friends				
13.	Feels guilty and makes amends				
14.	Cares for own property				
15.	Cares for others' property				
16.	Trustworthy				
17.	Shows appreciation				
18.	Shows reciprocity				
19.	Has normal eating patterns				
20.	Has normal pain response				

(*continued*)

		Beginning 1	Developing 2	Functional 3	Healthy 4
21.	Has normal sleep patterns				
22.	Has normal elimination (bathroom) patterns				
23.	Has age-appropriate personal hygiene				
24.	Has normal emotional responses				
25.	Shares feelings				
26.	Shares age-appropriate goals				
27.	Relaxed and calm				
28.	Has a good sense of humor				

Use this rubric to evaluate behaviors for treatment planning and identify progress for your child.

Reactive Attachment Disorder

My child, _____, has been diagnosed with Reactive Attachment Disorder (RAD, DSM IV 313.39). The disorder is attributed to a disruption in the attachment and bonding process during the formative years. These children have the process disrupted by: multiple caregivers, adoption, illness, neglect, abuse, addictions or depression of the primary caregiver. With the absence of this vital relationship, other difficulties occur.

Children with this disorder do not experience normal emotional development. Hyper-vigilance and control issues replace trust in caregivers and the surroundings. The child may become frightened if perceiving a loss of control of the environment. The reaction may be fight, flight or freeze. Talking quietly and not touching the child will assist in his ability to calm himself.

General Behaviors: developmental delays, poor cause-and-effect thinking, poor peer relationships, blaming, risk-taking, improper emotional reactions and triangulating adults to maintain control.

Behaviors toward strangers:

Charming	Surface compliance
"Poor me" attitude	Hyper-vigilance
_____	_____
_____	_____

Behaviors toward adults in control:

Lack of eye contact	Poor hygiene
Defiance	Aggression
Cannot be comforted	Passive aggressive
Controlling	Sensitive to touch
Targeting the mom	_____
_____	_____
_____	_____

For more information, contact:

_____

_____

Areas of concern:

_____

_____

Early Childhood Trauma

My child, _____, has experienced early trauma that has influenced his/her ability to form healthy relationships. Currently, mental health interventions are necessary to help him or her improve our parent/child relationship. With the absence of this vital relationship, future difficulties may occur.

Children with early trauma did not experience normal emotional development. Hyper-vigilance and control issues replaced trust in caregivers and the surroundings. The child may become frightened if perceiving the loss of control of the environment. His or her reaction may be fight, flight or freeze. Talking quietly and not touching him or her will assist in his or her ability to calm down.

General Behaviors: developmental delays, poor cause-and-effect thinking, poor peer relationships, blaming, risk-taking, improper emotional reactions and triangulating adults to maintain control.

Behaviors toward strangers:

Charming	Surface compliance
"Poor me" attitude	Hyper-vigilance
_____	_____
_____	_____

Behaviors toward adults in control:

Lack of eye contact	Poor hygiene
Defiance	Aggression
Cannot be comforted	Passive aggressive
Controlling	Sensitive to touch
Targeting the mom	_____
_____	_____
_____	_____

For more information, contact:

_____

_____

Areas of concern:

_____

_____

CHAPTER 19

Letters to the Villagers

Our desire is to provide the tools for dedicated parents and professionals to facilitate the healing of children. During Faye's years of therapeutic parenting, she needed more resources to become educated and draw others into the family's therapeutic efforts. We wrote these letters as tools to educate and spur commitment to her son's treatment and family support.

Parents are vital to healing and need support. These letters explain ten of the most common issues parents face when questioned by villagers and are designed to persuade team members to join the family in creating a healing home. They may be copied and given to villagers to explain what families are doing and how they can help. As these are coming from the professional community, they are written validation for the parents and the therapeutic approaches the family has been advised to pursue.

Validation is important while parenting in the trenches. You need as much support as possible.

May your adventure in healing begin.
—Faye, Jeff and John

1. Our Parenting Style

Dear _____,

Welcome to the world of therapeutic parenting for a traumatized child. Our child did not form healthy emotional relationships when young or lost those relationships, most likely with his birth mom. Sometimes, our kids are described as "just" having attachment issues. Our parenting must provide emotional co-regulation, unconditional love and connection to restructure the parent/child relationship.

Unfortunately, our time is not just spent parenting our child. We must coordinate, advocate, train, educate and finance services, not to mention continuing our relationships with other family members, running a home, having a career and performing community services which are parts of everyday life. Our homes have become training centers for professionals. Our schedules are full of appointments and meetings. We have a new vocabulary—MCO (managed care organization), wraparound (in-home mental health professionals), DSM-IV (psychiatrist's handbook), ODD (Oppositional Defiant Disorder), RAD (Reactive Attachment Disorder) and the list goes on…

Our spare time may be spent reading a new resource, going to another conference or trying to figure out our next step. Little time is left for relaxation or adult conversation—without "attachment" creeping into the topic at hand. Our minds rarely settle down. We become as hyper-vigilant as our children.

Some of the unique techniques that we use are attachment activities, cognitive reprogramming, sensory integration and paradoxical interventions. Some examples: 1. Our children may have missed some important developmental stages, so we provide them with opportunities to experience these stages. Consequently, our home may have toys that do not seem age-appropriate. The toys are "emotionally" age-appropriate. 2. We participate in activities that will build and reinforce our relationship. 3. We will not punish our child. We may describe his life in great detail to him. If he eats all the cereal, we will be sad that he could not trust his parents. We have to demonstrate that we are trustworthy. Please be patient with us. We will add interest to your life. We need your understanding and support.

Thanks for being there for us,

_____

2. Giving Our Child a Unique Opportunity

Dear _____,

Our family has been given a unique opportunity to offer our child a healing environment. This opportunity will have lasting effects on generations to come. Our child lost his most important first relationship, which impacts his abilities for future, healthy relationships. Our goal is to rebuild his ability to make healthy connections. We will model, mirror, reframe, identify and supply healthy relationships.

We wish we could prevent relationship problems from developing with all children in the world. Attachment parenting is such a benefit for both parent and child. Unfortunately, not all parents make the time, invest the energy, focus on their child's best interest or are emotionally available for their child. We have the opportunity to repair these missed connections.

We take into consideration past trauma, present behaviors and future goals. We must constantly weigh all decisions, interventions and emotional reactions. We need to be proactive, not reactive. Therefore, we must be deeply aware of our emotions at all times. Self-control, with loving emotions, must be conveyed to our child even with the chaotic behaviors.

Sometimes, people have implied that nothing is worth this much trouble. To us, our child is worth every effort that it takes for him to make progress. In some cases his success may be limited, but progress is progress. His emotional turmoil will be like a roller coaster ride. Over time, the peaks will be less steep and the level areas will be longer. As parents, we must not ride with him. We are his emotional coaches, his supporting team, the ones who have confidence in his abilities—he can succeed!

We are asking you to be part of the cheering crowd. Please support his successes and be empathetic for the setbacks. We all are praying that his ride will be short and that we can sustain though the process.

Thanks for being there for us,

_____

3. Fear motivates many of our actions.

Dear _____,

It does not seem reasonable to identify fear as a motivation. It may seem as if we are not trying to fix the problems in our home. Sometimes, we don't know which way to turn or what to do next. Let me describe our present life.

The stress is like emergency personnel waiting for the next call. These professionals never know if their next call will be a false alarm or a fatality. Their adrenaline levels rise with each call. Our family has the same adrenaline rush with each disruptive behavior. We are always listening for noises: "Where is he?" "Who is he with?" and "What is he doing?"

We may place an alarm on our child's door so we will be alerted when he leaves his room at night. His alarm may "accidentally" go off during the night. Many nights sleep does not come for us. As parents, our job is to keep everyone safe. Therefore, we have had to take extra measures so that we can project to our child that he is safe and we are trustworthy.

Isolation can be comforting. We are tired, our conversations are dismal and little emotion is left to connect with others. We try to avoid depression, isolation and fear—some days with no relief. Failure, grief and disappointment try to overwhelm us. We do not have the energy it takes to plan an evening out.

Our hope is that this will only last for a short time. We are seeking professional help. But your help is important to us as well. Our phone calls may seem frantic and our planning like micro-management, but we are doing the best that we can.

Yes, we do need a therapist. Some of us are fortunate to have that professional to assist us in processing these emotions and finding new ways to cope. If our family does not have a therapist yet, we may be afraid to confide in someone who may not understand. Imagine how unfit we feel. Please don't be judgmental. Support us in finding that special someone to talk to.

Thanks for being there for us,

_____

4. We need you to give non-judgmental support with insightful advice.

Dear _____,

Please care about our family. We are in desperate need of support and encouragement—it's just a different kind of support right now. We are seeking the best help for our family and child. There are few professionals who understand and can assist. At times, we feel so alone and isolated. We need you.

We have struggled to find the right professionals to form a cohesive treatment team. At times, we have had professionals criticize and blame us for our child's behaviors. Some have been patronizing and demeaning. Others have minimized our child's behaviors. (Of course, most kids don't clean their rooms—but not to the extent of urinating in the corners or ripping the drywall off the studs.) In the future, these professionals may ask for your assistance.

We know you may want to tell us to love our child more. It seems that if we would just love him more and be kinder, he would return that love and grow closer to us. That's the problem. If we showed him more love in normal ways, he would react against that love and not respond with reciprocal love.

On the other hand, you may want to advise us to become more strict. You may think that if we had more rules and didn't allow him to behave as he does, his behavior would improve. Unfortunately, more rules supply him with more opportunities to be defiant.

We truly have to walk a fine line between nurture and structure. We struggle daily to maintain an even balance between the two. When you don't understand why we do some things (and it's almost guaranteed you won't), please ask. We may refer you to other team members for further explanation. Don't be offended. Our emotions are raw. The other team members are to lighten our burden of parenting an emotionally-disturbed child.

For more information, please watch Nancy Thomas's video, *Circle of Support*.

Thanks for being there for us,

_____

5. Our child's early trauma disrupts his ability to form healthy relationships.

Dear _____,

Our wish and desire is for our child to have healthy relationships. We grieve that he has few, if any, friends. It saddens us as we watch him manipulate adults, especially our caring relatives and friends. Most of all, our hearts are broken that he cannot love us and accept us as his parents.

The fact of the matter is that he cannot trust people. This originated during his early months and years when his needs were not met. We are teaching him to trust, but it takes a long time. The first person he needs to trust is "this mom." Everything we do is centered on this notion. We constantly reframe his life in terms that support "this mom can be trusted." After he internalizes this belief, we will work on how lovable he is. He does not feel like anyone could love him since he lost his birth mom. He cannot form other healthy relationships until he believes that this mom can be trusted and he is lovable.

You can help him by reinforcing "this mom can be trusted" and "this mom loves you." All words and actions to support these therapeutic interventions will speed the progress along.

You may notice him trying to control you. His sweet and charming ways are an attempt to control adults. He may try to carry packages for you, do your chores, compliment you, hold your hand, run errands or even lead you to believe you would be a better parent for him than me. Please direct him back to "this mom." Phrases like these will help: "Let me see you do this for your mom; she loves you," "I know you can help me, but I am not your mom" and "You have a mom who loves you."

Thanks for being there for us,

_____

6. Our child may not experience temperature, hunger, energy levels or emotions like you and I do.

Dear _____,

During our child's early months (and years), he did not experience healthy self-regulation. Parents teach their children to regulate their emotions, temperature, energy, etc., by accurately and sensitively responding to their needs as infants. As the child experiences new circumstances, mom defines the meaning and mirrors the correct response.

Remember the many times as a child you heard, "It's cold; I'm going to wear a coat," "Come here, you look sad, let me hold you," or "I feel full after eating such a big meal." My child missed those opportunities. There were times he probably went hungry and was told to be quiet and stop whining. He may not have been dressed warmly enough (or was too warm) and does not experience temperature like we do.

So the impact of poor self-regulation is that sometimes I may look like a neglectful mother. He may go without a coat or eat too much or seem as if he hasn't slept in weeks. If we force the issue, he will become defiant. The best we can do is model appropriate behavior (how to dress in cold weather, even plan ahead for him to have a coat at school; he'll probably wear it to impress the teacher). We provide healthy food, but that does not mean he will eat our food. He may try to convince you how hungry he is so that you will feed him. Please share his stories with us or our professional team members.

He does not regulate his emotions well. He may not display the correct emotion for the circumstance. We may feel sadness; he may laugh. This is an opportunity for us to describe why one is sad. We identify, model and reframe the appropriate emotional responses. We cannot order him to be sad or happy. We do not minimize the feelings he displays.

His energy level varies from slow as molasses to the speed of light. Sometimes, there does not seem to be a reason. If it is a nice time for a Sunday afternoon nap, he can be flying around the room. We may ask you to babysit so we can rest at some point in the future.

Thanks for being there for us,

_____

7. Our child may have distorted object relations.

Dear _____,

Our child has problems with object relations which may be demonstrated by him becoming fearful and manipulative when he is not in our presence. During the early infant stages, his mom (or primary caregiver) was not consistent. He never knew if she would return. He learned to comfort himself and to not rely on others. When he is not with us, he returns to his survival skills as if we do not exist. Once, these skills kept him alive, but now they are a hindrance to his healing.

Anger and fear were part of the birth family system, so he relies on these emotions to motivate himself and intimidate others. He has limited ability to process emotions. He believes (emotionally) that people have one emotion at a time. So, he thinks that we cannot love him while we are angry with him. Sounds odd, I know.

Some of the things we do to help him are:

1. We will provide objects to help remind him that we are still in his life. He may keep an article of mom or dad's clothing or family pictures with him at school or have notes from us in his lunch box or we may stop in at school to see him. If he is at a friend's house to play, we may call to say hello. We may send a snack along with a note attached.

2. We model healthy emotions by identifying the times that we are angry with someone and reaffirm our love. Then, we explain how we will reconnect with that person. This is done over and over again.

3. When we are angry with him, we identify our anger and reaffirm our love for him. Again, this is done repeatedly. We try not to be angry with him; it can make things worse for all of us. Remembering the trauma he experienced helps us refocus on our task of being the nurturing parents who are needed for his healing.

Thanks for being there for us,

_____

8. You see different behavior from our child than we do at home.

Dear _____,

Our child presents himself differently to us than to you. Our child experiences fear when someone tries to be emotionally close, i.e., a loving family. He is so afraid of being emotionally close and losing control of the environment (which in the past has kept him safe) that he will do just about anything to "push us away." He uses behaviors to convey his fear.

You may see a cooperative and helpful child. We experience defiance, tantrums, aggression and even rage. Our love for him keeps us going through these times of turmoil. We focus on where the inner rage comes from—not having his needs met as an infant—and are empathic to his emotional states. Again, we identify and reframe why he reacts the way he does.

Our home will enable him to have healing opportunities. We removed some of the items in our home so that they will not become barriers between us. We have limited his access to television and computer games. These only allow him to distance himself from us. Healthy connections with his primary caregivers will help him heal. Imagine how a person would operate in a society if disconnected from others. Our jails are full of people without healthy connections. We want so much more for our child.

In our home, we have a balance of structure and nurture with interventions that challenge his beliefs that "This mom cannot be trusted" and that "He is unlovable." We do not shower him with toys because of his "deprived childhood." He has to learn to play first. So, he has the opportunities to experiment with art supplies, read appropriate books, use building toys, explore nature and participate in family activities. His choices may seem limited but that is all that he can handle right now.

Discipline is discipleship for us. When other parents use time outs for their children, we use time in. When he is trying to "push us away," we emotionally pull him in closer. Disruptive behaviors are managed with "Come sit near me, it seems as if you need some mommy time." Each of our interventions is well thought out and planned. We must be proactive, not reactive.

Thanks for being there for us,

_____

9. Our child may seem as if he does not have a conscience.

Dear _____,

This was scary for us to realize! During their early months and years, children are taught right from wrong. As a toddler begins to "toddle" around the house, Mom is constantly reinforcing which behaviors are appropriate and which are not. Many times a day, Mom has to say "No" to touching, pushing, climbing, banging, etc. She does this in a playful and loving manner. Her scoldings are mild and act more as a reminder to make the right choices. She may offer distractions and alternatives to the child.

The mom of a toddler designs the environment so that her child will not encounter danger. She removes costly or dangerous items, establishes boundaries and provides age-appropriate toys. The child experiences Mom returning him to the play area or removing toys that he may be using inappropriately. Her interactions are with love and care. She KNOWS he does not understand and her role is to guide this process. We KNOW our child missed this part and we are working to rebuild it. We must not get mad or be punitive. He is expecting us to be angry and punish him, because that is what he may have experienced in his birth home. His anger is linked to rejection.

Due to his past trauma, we are rebuilding his conscience but cannot force him to make good/right choices. He would become defiant if we forced the issue. Natural consequences are best. Going without a coat, one gets cold. Just as if one steals from a store, one must accept the consequences the store imposes. Our child may be young, it may seem unkind, but our child needs to make the connection between behavior and consequences. We cannot protect him and then expect his behavior to improve.

We will "allow" things to happen which we could have prevented. (We are not talking about safety issues—safety is first with us.) If he forgets his homework, we will not take it to him at school. If he does not take a bath, we will not "make" him take a bath. If he has problems with his friends, we will not intervene. (We may call the other child's parents to discuss the matter.) We will help him process why things happen and how he could prevent them next time. We will not generate the answers for him. Our goal is to motivate him to think and act accordingly.

Thanks for being there for us,

_____

THE UPWARD SPIRAL OF THE THERAPEUTIC PARENT

One of the most frequently asked questions by parents is "Why hasn't my child's behavior improved, since he has been in our home for years?" The Downward Spiral method of managing behaviors via consequences and rewards tends to reinforce the N-IWM instead of building relationships. The Upward Spiral highlights the "strange" parenting responses that do not consequence or reward behaviors, but rather increase emotional connections.

Beginning with the behavior and then moving downward on the spiral, when a parent lacks empathy and "punishes" the child, the child experiences the lack of safety and perceives a punitive parent who does not care. Each negative experience incites more negative experiences until the child is removed. Some marriages have dissolved with the placement disruption or adoption dissolution.

Beginning with the same behavior, parents may instead move upward by using the techniques taught throughout this book. With each response, the child perceives safety and parental care. After multiple repetitions (in jest, we predict a million), the child will have less need to use bad behavior to convey distress.

No parent wants his or her child to "get away" with poor behavior and this is not the intent of therapeutic parenting. Therapeutic parenting offers emotional connections, "reading" the child's internal states and understanding the child's intentions. Behaviors become an assessment tool to understand the child. Consequences may be given but the attitude and approach will be different.

Initial Disruptive Behavior:
Child Lacks Trust, Uses Behaviors to Express Distress

The Downward Spiral

Parents react negatively, reinforce N-IWM with punishment

Child questions, re-tests with behavior, experiences lack of safety

Parents react negatively, reinforce N-IWM with punishment

Child questions, re-tests with more behavior, experiences lack of safety

Parents react negatively, reinforce N-IWM with punishment

Child questions, re-tests with more severe behavior, is not safe

Downward Spiral Result: Child Is Removed

Upward Spiral Result: Healing Emotional Connections

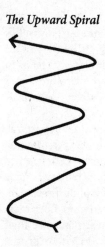

The Upward Spiral

Child experiences safety

Parents match affect, empathize, reframe, natural consequences

Child questions, re-tests with behavior, experiences safety

Parents match affect, empathize, reframe, natural consequences

Child questions, re-tests with behavior, experiences safety

Parents match affect, empathize, reframe, natural consequences

Initial Disruptive Behavior:
Child Lacks Trust, Uses Behaviors to Express Distress

10. We may need respite.

Dear _____,

Respite is when our child stays at another person's home for a short period of time. It is a service offered to families with emotionally-disturbed children. We use this resource for our family's emotional well-being. After a few sleepless nights or major problems with services, coupled with chaotic behaviors, we need a break. With this time, our family is given the opportunity to recover "our therapeutic attitude" and catch up on our sleep.

These stays are not like an overnight party. If they were, our child would not want to return home again. This would become his new home. He has moved from home to home so many times, another one would not matter. The respite provider will encourage our child to miss us. She may not give him all the nice things we have around our house, like dessert or hugs or mommy time. These things only come from the ones who love him. He will have chores and few toys. She is specially trained for this service.

During his stay, the respite provider will constantly remind him that he has a family who loves him. She will direct him back to Mom if he is in need of a hug or nurturing. She may "allow" him to call Mom for encouragement. If she demanded that he make connections with Mom, his defiance may surface.

The goal is for him to go to respite less and less. As he makes progress in therapy, he will be more fun at home. Right now, he has days when he just isn't fun to be around. So, it is really important that we keep "our therapeutic attitude" to convey the healing love that he needs.

When he comes home, we are happy to see him. We do not nag or threaten to send him back to respite if he misbehaves. He knows why he went and, hopefully, does not want to go back. Remember, we are teaching him behavior and consequences. So, if a few trips to respite help guide in the process, we are thankful.

If you would like more information (or would like to be a respite provider), please watch Nancy Thomas's respite video, *Give Me a Break.*

Thanks for being there for us,

_____

EPILOGUE

When co-author John Biever took note of research psychologist Kent Kiehl, PhD's findings regarding a remarkably consistent pattern of structural brain abnormalities in psychopaths, he was struck—though not that surprised—to realize that some of the same brain regions that appear abnormal in persons with psychopathy have been repeatedly referred to in attachment research literature as malfunctioning in children with attachment disorders. In his book, *The Psychopath Whisperer*, Dr. Kiehl shared the results of his extensive brain imaging studies of psychopaths—persons who relate to others with callous disregard for their feelings due to an absence of empathy.[56]

Dr. Kiehl rightly observed that, while virtually all persons with psychopathic personalities had traumatic childhoods, most children with similar traumatic childhoods did not develop a psychopathic personality. Genetic, gestational and other early developmental risk factors no doubt were also at play. Nevertheless, the finding, in ongoing research, of the great similarity in brain structures and life stories between psychopathic personalities and children with attachment disorders seems to mandate that villagers will confront three questions.

First, how do we marshal the resolve of the village to effectively address the problems of neglect and abuse of our most valuable natural resource—our infants and toddlers? All is not lost after the damage is done. However, the village must be prepared for a long and arduous effort in bringing about the healing of a child victim of early trauma.

This is a worthy expenditure of the village's resources. We can't forget the *infectious* nature of attachment disorders, recreating and spreading the initial trauma in a myriad of ways and places throughout the village—family, school, commercial establishments and beyond. Furthermore, we know that another route of infection is parent-to-child. Research confirms that parents with insecure attachment capacities are very likely to have children with attachment disorders.

Even so, we are not inclined to think of attachment-disordered children as a significant threat to the safety of the village. Yet what about those research findings we just noted? By addressing the root causes of attachment disorders, we will simultaneously be substantially reducing the incidence of the psychopathic personality. We all know that psychopaths can hurt people.

Second, now that we've gotten the village's attention and focus, how do we adequately educate all the villagers regarding the risk factors for attachment disorders? As we see it, this begins with stamping out the still prevalent belief that children have no memory of their infancy. We've illustrated the various ways in which memories of infancy emerge in later childhood: strange sensory experiences, distorted perceptions sometimes verging on paranoia, emotional reactions that do not fit the present situation, fundamentally false beliefs regarding the nature of the world and its inhabitants and, of course, disruptive and often destructive behaviors.

Once the "They won't remember it anyway" fallacy is put to rest, villagers can spread the good news that there are identifiable things to avoid and identifiable things to do in caring for our infants, that will foster secure attachments now and healthy relationships for the rest of their lives. We are all in this together.

Finally, are we really convinced that we *need* a village in the first place? More of our time, energy and attention is being devoted to an inherently limited kind of relatedness to others in distant places due to the Internet, while proportionately less of those commodities are devoted to strengthening the interrelatedness and sense of community in our villages.

We are in the midst of a great debate, whether we are conscious of it or not. Do we really *need* to do the difficult work of establishing and maintaining the intimate ties of neighborhood and village, wherein conflicts, frustrations and disappointments cannot be disposed of when we can instead utilize the ease of the click of a computer mouse?

We believe the answer lies in our belief about what it means to be human in this universe. We have devoted our professions to helping people to overcome or cope with their emotional pain. But our greatest satisfaction is not in seeing the pain reduced, but in being witness to the transcendent joy in the hearts of those who have faced and mastered difficult emotional challenges with our help. Is this life not ordained for the pursuit of that joy for all of us by way of our intimate relatedness to family, neighbor and villager?

The three authors of this book really do believe it *does* take a village— for our safety, for our individual development, but most importantly, for our maximum enjoyment of life!

BIBLIOGRAPHY

Brooks, D., J. Allen and R. Barth. 2002. "Adoption services use, helpfulness, and need: A comparison of public and private agency and independent adoptive families." *Children and Youth Services Review*, 24, no. 4: 213–238.

Clinton, H. 1996. *It Takes A Village: And Other Lessons Children Teach Us.* New York: Simon & Schuster.

Keck, Gregory C. and Regina Kupecky. 1995. *Adopting the Hurt Child: Hope for Families with Special-needs Kids: A Guide for Parents and Professionals.* Colorado Springs, CO: Piñon Press.

TRAUMA LENS PARADIGM SHIFT

Resources to Use to Develop More Understanding:

Fraiberg, Selma. 1996. *The Magic Years: Understanding and Handling the Problems of Early Childhood.* New York: Simon & Schuster.

Greenspan, Stanley I. and Beryl Benderly Lieff. 1998. *The Growth of the Mind: And the Endangered Origins of Intelligence.* Reading, MA: Perseus.

Hatkoff, Amy. 2007. *You Are My World: How a Parent's Love Shapes a Baby's Mind.* New York: Stewart, Tabori & Chang.

Hughes, Daniel A. 2012. *Principles of Attachment-focused Parenting: Effective Strategies to Care for Children.* New York: W.W. Norton.

Hughes, Daniel and Jonathan Baylin. 2009. *Brain-Based Parenting: The Neuroscience of Caregiving for Healthy Attachment.* S.l.: WW Norton.

Keck, Gregory C. and Regina Kupecky. 1995. *Adopting the Hurt Child: Hope for Families with Special-needs Kids: A Guide for Parents and Professionals.* Colorado Springs, CO: Piñon Press.

Keck, Gregory C., Regina Kupecky and Lynda Mansfield Gianforte. (2002). *Parenting the Hurt Child: Helping Adoptive Families Heal and Grow.* Colorado Springs, CO: Piñon Press.

Mahler, Margaret S., Fred Pine and Anni Bergman. 2000. *The Psychological Birth of the Human Infant: Symbiosis and Individuation.* New York, NY: Basic.

Sears, William and Martha Sears. 1995. *The Discipline Book: Everything You Need to Know to Have a Better-behaved Child—from Birth to Age Ten.* Boston: Little, Brown.

Siegel, Daniel and Mary Hartzell. 2005. *Parenting from inside out.* London: Thorsons.

Siegel, Daniel J. 2007. *The Mindful Brain: Reflection and Attunement in the Cultivation of Well-being.* New York: W.W. Norton.

Strohm, Kate. 2005. *Being the Other One: Growing up with a Brother or Sister Who Has Special Needs.* Boston: Shambhala.

Verrier, Nancy Newton. 1993. *The Primal Wound: Understanding the Adopted Child.* Baltimore: Gateway.

REFERENCE

Walters, Everette, Judith Crowell, Melanie Elliott, David Corcoran, and Dominique Treboux. 2002. "Bowlby's Secure Base Theory and the Social/ Personality Psychology of Attachment Styles: Work(s) in Progress A Commentary on Shaver & Mikulincer's Attachment-related Psychodynamics." *Attachment and Human Development* 4: 230–242.

Cook, A., J. Spinazzola, J. Ford, C. Lanktree, M. Blaustein, M. Cloitre, R. DeRosa, R. Hubbard, R. Kagan, J. Liautaud, K. Mallah, E. Olafson, and Bessel Van der Kolk. 2005. "Complex trauma in children and adolescents." *Psychiatric Annals* 35, no. 5: 390–398.

Cox, N. 1997. "Treating parents and children together: a feminist look at exclusionary practices in family therapy and in child psychotherapy." *Women and Therapy* 20, no. 2: 89–101.

Gottman, John. 1997. *Raising an Emotionally Intelligent Child.* Simon and Schuster: New York.

Kramer, L. and D. Houston. 1998. "Supporting families as they adopt children with special needs." *Family Relations* 47, no. 4: 423–432.

Pickover, S. 2002. "Breaking the cycle: A clinical example of disrupting an insecure attachment system." *Journal of Mental Health Counseling* 24, no. 4: 358–367.

Power, T. 2003. "Promoting children's mental health: reform through interdisciplinary and community partnerships." *School Psychology Review* 32, no. 1: 3.

Rosenthal, J., V. Groze and J. Morgan. 1996. "Services for families adopting children via public child welfare agencies: use, helpfulness, and need." *Children and Youth Services Review* 18, no. 1/2: 163–182.

Ryan, E. 2002. "Assessing sibling attachment in the face of placement issues." *Clinical Social Work Journal* 30, no. 1: 77–93.

Scheel, M. and T. Rieckman. 1998. "An empirically derived description of self-efficacy and empowerment for parents of children identified as psychologically disordered." *The American Journal of Family Therapy* 26, no. 1: 15–28.

Schofield, G. and M. Beek. 2005. "Providing a secure base: Parenting children in long-term foster family care." *Attachment & Human Development* 7, no. 1: 3—25.

Siegel, Daniel J. 1999. *The Developing Mind: How Relationships and the Brain Interact to Shape Who We Are.* New York: Guilford.

Sheperis, Carl J., Anthony R. Doggett, Nicolas E. Hoda, Tracy Blanchard, Edina Renfro-Michel, Sacky H. Holdiness, and Robyn Schlagheck. 2003. "The development of an assessment protocol for Reactive Attachment Disorder." *Journal of Mental Health* 25, no. 4: 291.

Tuber, Steven. 2008. *Attachment, Play and Authenticity: A Winnicott Primer.* Lanham, MD: Jason Aronson.

Wallin, D. 2007. Attachment in Psychotherapy. Guilford, New York, NY.

Whitman, W. 1926. *Leaves of Grass.* Garden City, NJ: Doubleday & Co.

PARENTING SKILLS

Resources That Will Help Gain These Skills:

Hughes, Daniel. 2006. *Building the Bonds of Attachment.* Lanham, Maryland: Jason Aronson.

Hughes, Daniel and Jonathan Baylin. 2012. *Brain Based Parenting.* New York: W. W. Norton.

James, Beverly. 1989. *Treating Traumatized Children: New Insights and Creative Interventions.* Lexington, MA: Lexington.

Karen, Robert. 1998. *Becoming Attached: First Relationships and How They Shape Our Capacity to Love.* New York: Oxford UP.

Keck, Gregory C. and Regina Kupecky. 1995. *Adopting the Hurt Child: Hope for Families with Special-needs Kids: A Guide for Parents and Professionals.* Colorado Springs, CO: Piñon Press.

Keck, Gregory C., Regina Kupecky and Lynda Mansfield Gianforte. 2002. *Parenting the Hurt Child: Helping Adoptive Families Heal and Grow.* Colorado Springs, CO: Piñon Press.

McCurry, Christopher. 2009. *Parenting Your Anxious Child with Mindfulness and Acceptance: A Powerful New Approach to Overcoming Fear, Panic, and Worry Using Acceptance and Commitment Therapy.* Oakland, CA: New Harbinger Publications.

Siegel, Daniel and Mary Hartzell. 2005. *Parenting from inside out*. London: Thorsons.

Siegel, Daniel J. 2007. *The Mindful Brain: Reflection and Attunement in the Cultivation of Well-being*. New York: W.W. Norton.

REFERENCES:

Powell, Bert, Glen Cooper, Kent Hoffman and Bob Marvin. 2014. *The Circle of Security Intervention*. New York: Guilford.

Van der Kolk, Bessel. 2014. *The Body Keeps the Score*. New York, New York: Penguin Group.

Tuber, Steven. 2008. *Attachment, Play and Authenticity: A Winnicott Primer*. Lanham, MD: Jason Aronson.

Team Resources

TOPIC	AUTHOR
Attachment and trauma	Daniel Siegel
	Daniel Hughes
	Bessel Van der Kolk
	Deborah Gray
Negative Working Model	John Bowby
Developmental Delays	Stanley Greenspan, MD
	Terry Brazelton, MD
	William Sears, MD
Ages and Stages	
Emotional Response	Bessel Van der Kolk
	Bruce Perry, MD
	Daniel Siegel
Object Relationships	Caroline Archer and Christine Gordon
	Holly Van Gulden
Self-regulation	Daniel Siegel
Sensory Dysfunction	The Out of Sync Child and activity book
(Consult with a specialist in Sensory Integration)	

REFERENCES:

Cox, N. 1997. "Treating parents and children together: a feminist look at exclusionary practices in family therapy and in child psychotherapy." *Women and Therapy* 20, no. 2: 89–101.

Erich, S. and P. Leung. 2002. "The impact of previous type of abuse and sibling adoption upon adoptive families." *Child Abuse and Neglect* 26, no. 10: 1045–1058.

Hughes, Daniel and Jonathan Baylin. 2012. *Brain Based Parenting.* New York: W. W. Norton.

Scheel, M. and T. Rieckman. 1998. "An empirically derived description of self-efficacy and empowerment for parents of children identified as psychologically disordered." *The American Journal of Family Therapy* 26, no. 1: 15–28.

COMMUNITY RESOURCES

Cox, N. 1997. "Treating parents and children together: a feminist look at exclusionary practices in family therapy and in child psychotherapy." *Women and Therapy* 20, no. 2: 89–101.

Hughes, Daniel and Jonathan Baylin. 2012. *Brain Based Parenting.* New York: W. W. Norton.

Peters, Laurence. 1977. *The Peter Plan: A Proposal for Survival.* New York: Bantam Books.

Scheel, M. T. Rieckman. 1998. "An empirically derived description of self-efficacy and empowerment for parents of children identified as psychologically disordered." *The American Journal of Family Therapy* 26, no. 1: 15–28.

Sousa, David A. 2001. *How the Brain Learns: A Classroom Teacher's Guide.* Thousand Oaks, CA: Corwin.

ENVIRONMENT RESOURCES:

Circle of Security: http://circleofsecurity.net/

McCurry, Christopher. 2009. *Parenting Your Anxious Child with Mindfulness and Acceptance: A Powerful New Approach to Overcoming Fear, Panic, and Worry Using Acceptance and Commitment Therapy.* Oakland, CA: New Harbinger Publications.

Fay, Jim and Charles Fay. 2000. *Love and Logic Magic for Early Childhood: Practical Parenting from Birth to Six Years*. Golden, CO: Love and Logic.

Fraiberg, Selma. 1996. *The Magic Years: Understanding and Handling the Problems of Early Childhood*. New York: Simon & Schuster.

Greenspan, Stanley I., Serena Wieder and Robin Simons. 1998. *The Child with Special Needs: Encouraging Intellectual and Emotional Growth*. Reading, MA: Addison-Wesley.

Gulden, Holly Van, and Lisa Bartels-Rabb. 1993. *Real Parents, Real Children: Parenting the Adopted Child*. New York: Crossroad.

REFERENCES:

Walters, Everette, Judith Crowell, Melanie Elliott, David Corcoran and Dominique Treboux. 2002. "Bowlby's Secure Base Theory and the Social/Personality Psychology of Attachment Styles: Work(s) in Progress A Commentary on Shaver & Mikulincer's Attachment-related Psychodynamics." *Attachment and Human Development* 4: 230–242.

Goodyear-Brown, Paris. 2010. *Play Therapy with Traumatized Children*. New Jersey: Wiley.

Hughes, Daniel and Jonathan Baylin. 2012. *Brain Based Parenting*. New York: Norton.

Kinniburgh, K., Blaustein, M. and Spinazzola, J. 2005. "Attachment, self-regulation, and competency." *Psychiatric Annals*, 35(5): 424–430.

Love and Logic Press. http://www.loveandlogic.com/

Towley, Megan. Sept 3 2013. http://www.reuters.com/investigates/adoption/#article/part1

TRAUMA-DISRUPTED COMPETENCIES:
Negative Internal Working Model

Resources to help increase these skills:

Ballard, Robert L. 2009. *Pieces of Me: Who Do I Want to Be?: Voices for and by Adopted Teens*. Warren, NJ: EMK.

Hatkoff, Amy. 2007. *You Are My World: How a Parent's Love Shapes a Baby's Mind*. New York: Stewart, Tabori & Chang.

James, Beverly. 1989. *Treating Traumatized Children: New Insights and Creative Interventions*. Lexington, MA: Lexington.

Karen, Robert. 1998. *Becoming Attached: First Relationships and How They Shape Our Capacity to Love*. New York: Oxford UP.

Karr-Morse, Robin and Meredith S. Wiley. 1997. *Ghosts from the Nursery: Tracing the Roots of Violence*. New York: Atlantic Monthly.

Keck, Gregory C. and Regina Kupecky. 1995. *Adopting the Hurt Child: Hope for Families with Special-needs Kids: A Guide for Parents and Professionals*. Colorado Springs, CO: Piñon Press.

Siegel, Daniel J. 1999. *The Developing Mind: How Relationships and the Brain Interact to Shape Who We Are*. New York: Guilford.

Siegel, Daniel J. 2007. *The Mindful Brain: Reflection and Attunement in the Cultivation of Well-being*. New York: W.W. Norton.

Solomon, Marion Fried and Daniel J. Siegel. 2003. *Healing Trauma: Attachment, Mind, Body, and Brain*. New York: W.W. Norton.

Stern, Daniel N. 2000. *The Interpersonal World of the Infant: A View from Psychoanalysis and Developmental Psychology*. New York: Basic.

Verrier, Nancy Newton. 1993. *The Primal Wound: Understanding the Adopted Child*. Baltimore: Gateway.

REFERENCES:

Cook, A., J. Spinazzola, J. Ford, C. Lanktree, M. Blaustein, M. Cloitre, R. DeRosa, R. Hubbard, R. Kagan, J. Liautaud, K. Mallah, E. Olafson and Bessel Van der Kolk. 2005. "Complex trauma in children and adolescents." *Psychiatric Annals* 35, no. 5: 390–398.

Covey, Steven. http://www.stephencovey.com/blog/?tag=emotional-bank -account

Van der Kolk, Bessel. 2014. *The Body Keeps the Score*. New York, New York: Penguin Group

Pickover, S. 2002. "Breaking the cycle: A clinical example of disrupting an insecure attachment system." *Journal of Mental Health Counseling* 24, no. 4: 358–367.

Wallin, D. 2007. Attachment in Psychotherapy: New York, NY: Guilford.

TRAUMA-DISRUPTED COMPETENCIES:
Emotional Response

Resources to use to increase understanding:

Hatkoff, Amy. 2007. *You Are My World: How a Parent's Love Shapes a Baby's Mind.* New York: Stewart, Tabori & Chang.

James, Beverly. 1989. *Treating Traumatized Children: New Insights and Creative Interventions.* Lexington, MA: Lexington.

Karen, Robert. 1998. *Becoming Attached: First Relationships and How They Shape Our Capacity to Love.* New York: Oxford UP.

Karr-Morse, Robin and Meredith S. Wiley. 1997. *Ghosts from the Nursery: Tracing the Roots of Violence.* New York: Atlantic Monthly.

Keck, Gregory C. and Regina Kupecky. 1995. *Adopting the Hurt Child: Hope for Families with Special-needs Kids: A Guide for Parents and Professionals.* Colorado Springs, CO: Piñon Press.

Siegel, Daniel J. 1999. *The Developing Mind: How Relationships and the Brain Interact to Shape Who We Are.* New York: Guilford.

Siegel, Daniel J. 2007. *The Mindful Brain: Reflection and Attunement in the Cultivation of Well-being.* New York: W.W. Norton.

Solomon, Marion Fried and Daniel Siegel J. 2003. *Healing Trauma: Attachment, Mind, Body, and Brain.* New York: W.W. Norton.

Stern, Daniel N. 2000. *The Interpersonal World of the Infant: A View from Psychoanalysis and Developmental Psychology.* New York: Basic.

Verrier, Nancy Newton. 1993. *The Primal Wound: Understanding the Adopted Child.* Baltimore: Gateway.

TRAUMA-DISRUPTED COMPETENCIES:
Developmental Delay

Resources:

Developmental maturation may begin with infant or toddler play before attempting mature activities such as board games or organized sports. A traumatized child's development may become arrested with holes or gaps from missing simple and healthy parent/child interactions, lack of exposure to age appropriate activities and the inability to manage the emotions evoked from the trauma.

The following resources provide ideas for learning through the senses such as with finger painting, modeling clay, playing on the playground and in a sandbox, sharing picture books, working alongside a parent, nature walks, building block towers, playing catch, making and playing with crafts, etc.

Books:

1.	*I Love You Rituals*	Becky Bailey
2.	*365 Days of Baby Love*	Shelia Ellison & Susan Ferdinandi
3.	*The Preschooler's Busy Book*	Trish Kuffner
4.	*The Children's Busy Book*	Trish Kuffner
5.	*Sharing Family Time*	Aid Association for Lutherans
6.	*Baby Games*	Elaine Martin
7.	*Games to Play with Babies*	Jackie Silberg
8.	*101 Ways to Tell Your Child I Love You*	Vicki Lansky
9.	*10 Minute Activities*	Priddy Bicknell
10.	*Focus on the Family Clubhouse Family Activity Book*	Marianne Kering
11.	*Preschool Play & Learn*	Penny Warner
12.	*The Happy Family Game*	Karin Phillips Tate
13.	*The Family Hand-Me-Down Book*	Debbie O'Neal
14.	*The Special Needs Child*	Stanley Greenspan
15.	*Touchpoints*	T. Berry Brazelton
16.	Discovery Toy Company offers multiple options	

REFERENCES:

Kinniburgh, K., M. Blaustein and J. Spinazzola. 2005. "Attachment, self-regulation, and competency." *Psychiatric Annals* 35, no. 5: 424–430.

Solomon, Marion Fried and Daniel J. Siegel. 2003. *Healing Trauma: Attachment, Mind, Body, and Brain.* New York: W.W. Norton.

TRAUMA-DISRUPTED COMPETENCIES:
Object Relations

Resources:

Adler, Bill and Peggy Robin. 2001. *Outwitting Toddlers.* New York: Kensington.

Allen, K. Eileen and Lynn R. Marotz. 1999. *Developmental Profiles: Pre-birth through Eight.* Albany: Delmar.

Brazelton, T. Berry and B. A. King. 1984. *To Listen to a Child: Understanding the Normal Problems of Growing up.* Reading, MA: Perseus,

Clinton, Timothy E. and Gary Sibcy. 2006. *Loving Your Child Too Much: How to Keep a Close Relationship with Your Child without Overindulging, Overprotecting, or Overcontrolling.* Nashville, TN: Integrity.

Fay, Jim and Charles Fay. 2000. *Love and Logic Magic for Early Childhood: Practical Parenting from Birth to Six Years.* Golden, CO: Love and Logic.

Greenspan, Stanley I. and Nancy Lewis Breslau. 2000. *Building Healthy Minds: The Six Experiences That Create Intelligence and Emotional Growth in Babies and Young Children.* Cambridge, MA: Perseus Publication.

Kopp, Claire B. 1993. *Baby Steps.* Washington: Freeman.

Hanly, Sheila. 1998. *Peek-a-boo!: 101 Ways to Make Baby Smile.* New York: DK Publications.

Hennessy, B. G. and Anthony Carnabuci. 1992. *Sleep Tight.* New York, NY: Viking.

Huddleston, R., W. Madgwick and T. Linsell. 1996. *Time for Bed.* Brookfield, CT: Copper Beech.

LeComer, L. 2006. *A Parent's Guide to Developmental Delays: Recognizing and Coping with Missed Milestones in Speech, Movement, Learning, and Other Areas.* New York: Perigee.

Martin, E. 1988. *Baby Games: For Every New Parent.* Toronto, Canada: Stoddart Publishing.

Masi, Wendy and Roni Leiderman. 2001. *Baby Play.* San Francisco, CA: Creative Pub. International.

Ripley, R. and Marie J. Ripley. 1997. *Your Child's Ages & Stages.* Carefree, AZ, USA: Carefrez.

Rosemond, John. 1993. *Making the "Terrible" Twos Terrific!* Kansas City: Andrews and McMeel.

Silberg, J. 1993.*Games to Play with Toddlers.* Mt. Rainier, MD: Gryphon House.

Weston, D. and M. Weston. 1993. S. *Playful Parenting: Turning the Dilemma of Discipline into Fun and Games.* Los Angeles: Tarcher/Putnam.

Warnick, E. 1998. *Bedtime.* San Diego, CA: Browndeer.

REFERENCES:

Erikson, Erik. http://psychology.about.com/od/psychosocialtheories/a/trust-versus-mistrust.htm

Mahler, Margaret S., Fred Pine and Anni Bergman. 2000. *The Psychological Birth of the Human Infant: Symbiosis and Individuation.* New York, NY: Basic.

Maslow, Abraham. 2012. *A Theory of Human Motivation.* E-book edition: Start Publication

Piaget, Jean. http://piaget.weebly.com/stages-of-cognitive-development.html

TRAUMA-DISRUPTED COMPETENCIES:
Self-Regulation

Resources:

- Webinar: "Food for Thought: The Impact of Poor Nutrition in Early Development": http://www.adoptionlearningpartners.org/nutrition_webinar.cfm
- Adoptive Families Magazine article about nutrition: http://www.adoptivefamilies.com/articles.php?aid=2116
- The Feeding Doctor: http://thefeedingdoctor.com
- TrulyFood-classes including the Your Vibrant Child
- Webinar: Nutrition and Institutionalized Children, Zeina Makhoul, PhD, RD.
- Webinar: Introduction to Nutrition and Feeding for Internationally Adopted Children, Presenters: Dr. Zeina Makhoul, Kate Ward, Spoon Foundation.
- Webinar: Feeding the First Year Home: Transitioning through feeding stages and to a new diet, Presenter: Kate Nelson Ward, MPH, CHES, SPOON Foundation.
- Ellyn Satter, Child of Mine; Feeding with Love and Good Sense
- Dr. Katja Rowell, Love Me, Feed Me: The Adoptive Parent's Guide to Ending the Worry About Weight, Picky Eating, Power Struggles, and More
- *SPOON Foundation-nutrition for orphaned fostered, and adopted children one spoonful at a time. http://adoptionnutrition.org

BOOKS:

Berg, F. M. 1997. *Afraid to Eat: Children and Teens in Weight Crisis.* Healthy Weight Publishing Network.

Piran, N., M. Levine and C. Steiner-Adair. 1999. *Preventing Eating Disorders: A Handbook for Interventions and Special Challenges.* Taylor & Francis.

Siegel, M., J. Brisman and M. Weinshel. 1997. *Surviving an Eating Disorder: Strategies for Family and Friends.* Harper Perennial.

Levenkron, S. 1982. *Treating and Overcoming Anorexia Nervosa: Classic Guide with a New Introduction.* Warner Books, Inc.

Nelson, T. 2008. *What's Eating You? A Workbook for Teens with Anorexia, Bulimia & Other Eating Disorders.* Instant Help Books.

Natenshon, A. 1999. *When Your Child Has an Eating Disorder: A Step-by-Step Workbook for Caregivers.* Jossey-Bass Publishers.

DVD:

Eating Disorders Foster Parent College, Northwest Media, Inc. 2003.

VIDEOS:

1. Anorexia and Bulimia Video Set Video set includes Tape 1 & 2. Educational Video Network, 1999.
2. Thea's Mirror: A Parent's Guide to Helping Teens with Eating Disorders The Bureau for At-Risk Youth, 1995.

REFERENCES:

Greenspan, Stanley. 1992. *Infancy and Early Childhood: the Practice of Clinical Assessment and Intervention with Emotional and Developmental Challenges*. International Universities Press, Inc: Madison, Conn.

Van der Kolk, Bessel. 2014. *The Body Keeps the Score*. Penguin Group: New York, New York.

Smolen, A. 2001. Connecting with Sara: facilitating attachment. *Smith College Studies in Social Work*, 72(1), 53–77.

Wallin, D. 2007. Attachment in Psychotherapy: Guilford, New York, NY.

TRAUMA-DISRUPTED COMPETENCIES:
Sensory Processing

Resources:

In Sync Activity Cards Simple, Fun Activity Cards to Help Every Child Develop, Learn, and Grow! 2012. Future Horizons.

Kranowitz, C. and J. Newman. 2010. *Growing an In-sync Child: Simple, Fun Activities to Help Every Child Develop, Learn, and Grow*. New York: Perigee.

Kranowitz, C. 2005. *The Out-of-sync Child: Recognizing and Coping with Sensory Processing Disorder*. New York: Skylight Book/A Perigee Book.

Kranowitz, C. 2003. *The Out-of-sync Child Has Fun: Activities for Kids with Sensory Processing Disorder*. New York, NY: Perigee Book.

McClure, Vimala Schneider. 2000. *Infant Massage: A Handbook for Loving Parents*. New York: Bantam.

Miller, L. and D. Fuller. 2007. *Sensational Kids: Hope and Help for Children with Sensory Processing Disorder (SPD).* New York: Perigee.

Promislow, S. 1999. *Making the Brain/body Connection: A Playful Guide to Releasing Mental, Physical & Emotional Blocks to Success.* West Vancouver, B.C., Canada: Kinetic Pub.

Tuber, Steven. 2008. *Attachment, Play and Authenticity: A Winnicott Primer.* Lanham, MD: Jason Aronson.

REFERENCES:

Sheperis, C., E. Renfron-Michel and R. Doggett. 2003. "In-home treatment of reactive attachment disorder in a therapeutic foster care system: a case example." *Journal of Mental Health Counseling* 25, no. 1: 79–89.

Zero to Three. http://www.zerotothree.org/child-development/early-child hood-mental-health/dc-0-3-revisions.html

ENDNOTES

1. Alexandra Cook, Joseph Spinazzola, Julian Ford, Cheryl Lanktree, Margaret Blaustein, Caryll Sprague, Marylene Cloitre, Ruth DeRosa, Rebecca Hubbard, Richard Kagan, Joan Liautaud, Karen Mallah, Erna Olafson and Bessel van der Kolk, "Complex trauma in children and adolescents." *Psychiatric Annals, 35*(5), 2005, 390–398.
2. Thomas J. Power, "Promoting children's mental health: reform through interdisciplinary and community partnerships," *School Psychology Review*, 32 (1), 2003, 3–16.
3. Alexandra Cook et al, "Complex trauma in children and adolescents." *Psychiatric Annals*, 390–398.
4. Court Appointed Special Advocates 2007 Statistics, http://www.casalasvegas.org/about/about-clark-county-casa/statistics/.
5. Ellen Ryan, "Assessing sibling attachment in the face of placement issues." *Clinical Social Work Journal*, 30(1), 2002, 77–93.
6. David J. Wallin, *Attachment in Psychotherapy* (New York: Guilford, 2007).
7. N. Cox, "Treating parents and children together: a feminist look at exclusionary practices in family therapy and in child psychotherapy." *Women and Therapy*, 20(2), 1997, 89–101.
8. Michael J. Scheel and Traci Rieckmann, "An empirically derived description of self-efficacy and empowerment for parents of children identified as psychologically disordered." *The American Journal of Family Therapy*, 26(1), 1998, 15–28.
9. Laurie Kramer and Doris Houston, "Supporting families as they adopt children with special needs." *Family Relations*, 47(4), 1998, 423–432.
10. Carl J. Sheperis, Anthony R. Doggett, Nicholas E. Hoda, Tracy Blanchard, Edina L. Renfro-Michel, Sacky H. Holdiness and Robyn Schlagheck, "The development of an assessment protocol for Reactive Attachment Disorder." *Journal of Mental Health*, 25(4), 2003, 291.
11. Steven B. Tuber, *Attachment, Play, and Authenticity: A Winnicott Primer.* (Lanham, MD: Jason Aronson, 2008).
12. Alexandra Cook et al, "Complex trauma in children and adolescents." *Psychiatric Annals*, 390–398.
13. Ibid., 392.

14. Everette Walters, Judith Crowell, Melanie Elliott, David Corcoran, and Dominique Treboux, "Bowlby's Secure Base Theory and the Social/ Personality Psychology of Attachment Styles: Work(s) in Progress A Commentary on Shaver & Mikulincer's Attachment-related Psychodynamics." *Attachment and Human Development* 4: 2002, 230–242.

15. Gillian Schofield and Mary Beek, "Providing a secure base: Parenting children in long-term foster family care." *Attachment & Human Development,* 7(1), 2005, 3—25.

16. Sheri Pickover, "Breaking the cycle: A clinical example of disrupting an insecure attachment system." *Journal of Mental Health Counseling,* 24(4), 2002, 358–367.

17. Bessel Van der Kolk, *The Body Keeps the Score.* (New York: Penquin Group, 2014), 161.

18. Ibid., 112.

19. Ibid.

20. Marion Fried Solomon and Daniel J. Siegel, *Healing Trauma: Attachment, Mind, Body, and Brain.* (New York: W.W. Norton, 2003), 115.

21. Ibid., 116–117.

22. Ibid., 78–79.

23. Daniel Hughes and Jonathan Baylin, *Brain Based Parenting.* (New York: W. W. Norton, 2012).

24. Stephen Erich and Patrick Leung, "The impact of previous type of abuse and sibling adoption upon adoptive families." *Child Abuse and Neglect,* 26(10), 2002, 1045–1058.

25. Nicole Cox, "Treating parents and children together: a feminist look at exclusionary practices in family therapy and in child psychotherapy."

26. Michael J. Scheel and Traci Rieckmann, "An empirically derived description of self-efficacy and empowerment for parents of children identified as psychologically disordered."

27. Nicole Cox, "Treating parents and children together: a feminist look at exclusionary practices in family therapy and in child psychotherapy."

28. Ibid., 3.

29. "Adoption Disruption and Dissolution Statistics," *Adoption.com,* accessed March 18, 2015, http://statistics.adoption.com/information/statistics-disruption -dissolution.html.

30. Megan Twohey. "Americans use the Internet to abandon children adopted from overseas." Sept 9, 2013. http://www.reuters.com/investigates/adoption/#article/ part1.

31. Nicole Cox, "Treating parents and children together: a feminist look at exclusionary practices in family therapy and in child psychotherapy."

32. Everette Walters, Judith Crowell, Melanie Elliott, David Corcoran and Dominique Treboux, "Bowlby's Secure Base Theory and the Social/Personality Psychology of Attachment Styles: Work(s) in Progress A Commentary on Shaver & Mikulincer's Attachment-related Psychodynamics." *Attachment and Human Development* 4: 2002, 230–242.

33. Kristine Kinniburgh, Margaret Blaustein and Joseph Spinazzola, "Attachment, self-regulation, and competency." *Psychiatric Annals,* 35(5), 2005, 424–430.

34. Paris Goodyear-Brown, *Play Therapy with Traumatized Children* (New Jersey: Wiley, 2010), 135.
35. Ibid., 143.
36. Ellen Ryan, "Assessing sibling attachment in the face of placement issues," 82.
37. Bessel Van der Kolk, *The Body Keeps the Score*, 129.
38. Ibid.
39. Sheri Pickover, "Breaking the cycle: A clinical example of disrupting an insecure attachment system," 365.
40. Alexandra Cook et al, "Complex trauma in children and adolescents," 395.
41. David J. Wallin, *Attachment in Psychotherapy*.
42. Kristine Kinniburgh, Margaret Blaustein and Joseph Spinazzola, "Attachment, self-regulation, and competency," 429.
43. Marion Fried Solomon and Daniel J. Siegel, *Healing Trauma: Attachment, Mind, Body, and Brain*.
44. Erik H. Erikson, *Childhood and Society*. (New York: W. W. Norton & Company, 1950), 247.
45. Andrew Maslow, "A Theory of Human Motivation," *Psychological Review*, Vol 50(4), Jul 1943, 370-396.
46. Kendra Cherry, "Piaget's Stages of Cognitive Development: Background and Key Concepts of Piaget's Theory." *Psychology.com*, http://psychology.about.com/od/piagetstheory/a/keyconcepts.htm.
47. M.S. Mahler, R. Pine and A. Bergman, *The psychological birth of the human infant: Symbiosis and individuation*. (New York: Basic Books, 1975), 54.
48. Bessel Van der Kolk, *The Body Keeps the Score*, 161
49. Stanley Greenspan, *Infancy and Early Childhood: the Practice of Clinical Assessment and Intervention with Emotional and Developmental Challenges*. (International Universities Press, Inc: Madison, Conn., 1992), 601.
50. Daniel J. Siegel, *The Developing Mind: How Relationships and the Brain Interact to Shape Who We Are*. (New York: Guilford, 1999), 32.
51. Bessel Van der Kolk, *The Body Keeps the Score*, 61.
52. Carl J. Sheperis et al, "The development of an assessment protocol for Reactive Attachment Disorder," 5.
53. *Diagnostic Classification of Mental Health and Developmental Disorders of Infancy and Early Childhood (DC: 0-3R)*, National Center for Clinical Infant Programs, Revised edition (May 1, 2005).
54. M.S. Mahler, R. Pine and A. Bergman, *The psychological birth of the human infant: Symbiosis and individuation*, 54.
55. David J. Wallin, *Attachment in Psychotherapy*, 82.
56. Kent Kiehl, PhD, *The Psychopath Whisperer*. (New York: Crown Publishers. 2014).